Landmarks in Rhetoric and Public Address

Landmarks in Rhetoric and Public Address

David Potter, *General Editor*

PURITAN RHETORIC

The Issue of Emotion in Religion

BY

Eugene E. White

Foreword by

David Potter

SOUTHERN ILLINOIS UNIVERSITY PRESS
Carbondale and Edwardsville

Feffer & Simons, Inc.
London and Amsterdam

Printed in the United States of America
Designed by Gary Gore
International Standard Book Number 0–8093–0563–1
Library of Congress Catalog Card Number 76–181987

*To Roberta
and E. R. L.*

Contents

Foreword *by David Potter*   ix
Preface   xi

PART ONE: *The Developing Exigence*
The Inheritance   6
Transition and Culmination   23
The Great Awakening   48

PART TWO: *Readings*
The Future Punishment of the Wicked Unavoidable and
   Intolerable   *Jonathan Edwards*   67
Distinguishing Marks   *Jonathan Edwards*   81
Enthusiasm Described and Caution'd Against
                                   Charles Chauncy   103
Concerning the Nature of the Affections, and Their
   Importance in Religion   *Jonathan Edwards*   119
Natural Religion   *Ebenezer Gay*   158

PART THREE: *Inquiry*
Strategies of Argument   175
Strategies of Style and Composition   191
Strategies of Disposition   193

Notes to Part One   197
Bibliography   213

Foreword

By David Potter

There have been occasions during the past ten years when my equilibrium and sleep have been disturbed by the capering of a chorus straight from Gilbert and Sullivan: "An editor's life is not a happy one." Bleak thoughts have been engendered. Consider: one offends old friends by rejecting new proposals, distresses the director of his press by seeming ignorance of the economic realities of publishing, and infuriates the community of academic critics by saving money at the expense of adequate indices and footnotes. And all the while one worries—about his lack of specific knowledge in an area, about the maintenance of standards, about possible rejection of a volume (and the series) by the scholarly public.

Happily, no nightmares accompanied the manuscript of Eugene E. White's *Puritan Rhetoric: The Issue of Emotion in Religion*. I sought the volume when friend White announced its availability. Director Sternberg gladly agreed to extensive footnoting. The subject matter was familiar and dear to me. Indeed, Gordon L. Thomas and I were deeply disappointed that publishing costs and consequent restrictions on the length of our volume allowed us to include only one of the sermons, the Chauncy item, in our *Colonial Idiom*. Finally, the reputation of Dr. White, buttressed by his Winans Award-winning "Master Holdsworth and 'A Knowledge Very Useful and Necessary,'" the Speech Communication Association's Golden Anniversary Award for "Puritan Preaching and the Authority of God," and his impressive bibliography of articles and reviews should more than satisfy the questioning attitude of most scholars whether in rhetoric, history, or theology.

In short, I believe that this slim volume should add tremendously by virtue of its contents and methodology to the understanding of a germinal period in our history.

Preface

In preparing this volume I have wished to interest a broader spectrum of readers than those concerned with Puritans or with rhetoric—even than those who seek keys in the past to unlock the inner secrets of the present. What is discussed in these pages is so identifiable with the present confrontations between reason and emotion that—with suitable interpolations —one may read here a living dialogue between the forces of quasi-static rationalism and revolutionary anti-intellectualism. My hope is that the general reader may be encouraged to seek here for insights concerning man's continuing problems of adjusting his nature and his needs to the perplexities of his environment.

One of the tasks of Part One is to introduce the Puritan as a surprisingly contemporary figure and to translate "the issue of emotion in religion" in some of its broader implications. Other tasks are equally important: to explain how society worked itself into such a position that a resisting conservatism was inevitably assaulted by an aggressive counterforce; to interpret how the precarious balance which the founding Puritans maintained between reason and emotion—as manifested in their rhetoric, theology, and psychology—came to be disrupted by the Great Awakening, the most important social movement in the Colonies prior to the Revolution; to unfold how in New England the confrontation between the rationalists and the revivalists split the society, sending shock waves through the centuries. In addressing these tasks, I have attempted to apply something of a new approach and, in addition to meeting the requirements of the non-specialists, to contribute some new conceptualizations which may yield at least a fragmental increment to existing scholarly knowledge.

The second part of the volume consists of five speeches with headnote introductions and interrogative notes. The speeches—most of which are here given their first readily accessible modern printing—illuminate the stages of the Awakening and the confrontations among the protagonists.

The first reading is a revival sermon of Jonathan Edwards, "Future Punishment," possibly the finest example of terror preaching in our literature. At the time this speech was delivered, April 1741, the revivalists were in dominion, the revolution against conservative rationalism in religion was approaching its peak in intensity, and the opposition was muted.

The next two speeches represent an oblique apposition between the chief protagonists of the revival. In one of these—"Distinguishing Marks," delivered in the fall of 1741 during the Yale commencement observances—Edwards defended the dominant role of emotion in religion and launched a confident attack upon the yet silent opponents of the revival. By the following year, emotional excesses had brought the Great Awakening into disrepute among the conservatives. During the Harvard commencement proceedings of 1742, Charles Chauncy delivered "Enthusiasm Described and Caution'd Against," in which he defended the traditional, controlled balance between reason and emotion, delivered the first major blast at the new emphasis upon emotion, and, implicitly, gave forewarnings of the polarization of positions yet to come.

In the last brace of speeches, Edwards "confronts" his foremost opponent of the post-Awakening period, Ebenezer Gay. Chastened by the excesses of the revival and by the rising tide of opposition, Edwards was quietly persuasive in his lecture, "The Nature of the Affections." In this sermon, he argued that emotion is the substance of religion and that man cannot respond to God through the agency of a dispassionate objective intellect. The entire man must become involved—spontaneously and completely. In striking contrast to Edwards, and in antipodal opposition to revivalists who went well beyond Edwards in decrying reason and exalting emotion, Gay's lecture, "Natural Religion, as Distinguished from Revealed," represented the ultimate position of the Congregational antirevivalists: both re-

vealed and natural religion are rational in character, the emotions having no substantive role in religion.

Thus our speeches illustrate that the traditional balance between reason and emotion was upset and that New England society was divided into two camps: the revivalists who endorsed the emotional involvement of the entire man in religious matters and the antirevivalists who denegrated emotion, exalted reason, and viewed the intellect as an objective, distant regulator which —like a sluice gate—interposed its impersonal control between man and the flow of spontaneous response.

To provide levers for opening up the speeches, I have supplied interrogative notes, which are suffixed to each selection and which are conceptually cued to running citations in the text. They are designed to show you what to look for in terms of the methodologies of the speaker and the requirements of his case. I intend them to guide your reading, not to interfere with it. If they have been properly formulated, they will be provocative and implicative, rather than didactic and prescriptive. Hopefully, some may tease you, leaving you frustrated with the insightful recognition that in rhetorical assessment there are no "easy" or "unassailably correct" answers.

Part Three of our volume is the Inquiry, which contains a mixture of critical analysis and suggestive appraisals. Its function is to help you to exploit the interpretations contained in Part One, the approaches of the various speakers, and the lines of inquiry introduced in the interrogative notes. As throughout the earlier portions of the book, the goal is to encourage you to consider the rhetorical situation confronted by the speakers, the options available to them, the choices they make, and the wisdom and effect of their choices.

Finally, I should mention my appreciation for the assistance of others. For stipends which made possible my sojourns at the great British repositories as well as those in this country, I am indebted to The Institute for the Arts and Humanistic Studies of the Pennsylvania State University and to The American Philosophical Society. Although it is impossible to mention all of the staff members and directors of libraries who gave cordial, efficient help, I should like to express thanks to Mr. James

Claydon, then Director of the Anderson Room, Cambridge University Library, whose remarkable kindness and good spirits brought warmth and cheer to the dank English weather. I am appreciative to Professor Don J. Geiger of the University of California, who originally suggested that I write this volume. I am grateful for the cogent advice given by my son, Eugene Robert White, who read the entire manuscript, and for the suggestions offered by various of my graduate students who read portions of the study. As always in such matters, I am especially grateful to my wife, Roberta F. White, for her continued understanding and good humor.

                                                            EUGENE E. WHITE

University Park, Pennsylvania
April 23, 1971

PART ONE

The Developing Exigence

Until recently, the popular view has considered the founding Puritan to be a singularly unattractive ancestral relic, better forgotten than remembered. Especially in the last two or three decades, however, much careful research has gradually removed enough of the encrusted fictions and distortions to expose a more realistic—and somewhat more likeable—image of the Puritan. Instead of the utterly drab, stony, and inhibited figure of myth, the "restored" Puritan upon occasion could laugh, wear "bright" clothes, resort to alcoholic as well as divine spirits, and enjoy marital sex. Instead of being stolid and unimaginative, the "restored" Puritan was nervously sensitive and at least as cerebral in his approach to life as today's American. Although inevitably bound by his inherited conceptions of the authority of God and the nature of man and of the social order, the "restored" Puritan was far from being anti-intellectual. He was sensitively aware of the problems of his emerging society and he struggled with considerable inventiveness to solve them.

Most importantly, recent research has demonstrated that our own self-interest will not permit the "restored" Puritan to be consigned to the esoteric limbo of the Colonial specialist. The value judgments, the decisions, and the successful—as well as the abortive—attempts of the Puritans to solve their personal and societal problems exerted an immense influence upon the flow of history. Our society today is different because of the Puritans. More than this, some of the basic problems with which we now grapple are refractions of the predicaments which confronted the Puritans and which, having been modified by the Puritan personality and character, were passed along unsolved to succeeding generations.

3

One of the problems of our contemporary society is the conflict between the emotions and the intellect, between the intellectual—who seeks satisfaction as well as practical answers in the exercise of the mind, and the anti-intellectual—who sanctifies intuitive wisdom or emotive empathy, minimizes the usefulness of knowledge, and suspects as potentially dangerous the unrestricted operation of the rational intellect. If space permitted, the antagonism between mind and feeling could be traced backward—from recent episodes such as the campus protests of anti-intellectual students who consider social ends rather than advancement of learning to be the objective of a university and the rejection of reason by many youths who seek liberation of the nonrational aspects of their nature by means of drugs, mysticism, and aberrant dress and behavior—through the McCarthy era, Progressivism, Populism, the Darwinian controversy, Southern parochialism, transcendentalism, the Jacksonian period, the Jeffersonian triumph of 1800, and the Revolutionary War—to the Great Awakening.

Beginning roughly in 1739 and continuing in the 1740s, a revival called the Great Awakening swept over the Colonies. Only distantly related to evangelical developments in England and on the continent, the Awakening arose primarily from stresses within the American society. The most important social movement in the Colonies prior to the Revolution, in New England it probably attained high tide by the middle of 1742, when the excesses of some of the "awakened" caused increasing numbers of persons to question the divine motivation of the turmoil. In the ensuing protracted and acrimonious debate over the proper balance between piety and reason in religion, the ministry and the people split into two groups. The supporters of the revival were called New Lights in New England and New Sides in the Middle Colonies. Forsaking the Puritan scholasticism of previous years, which had assigned emotions to the keeping of the intellect, the revivalists emphasized the primacy of emotions in the religious experience. The opponents of the revival were called Old Lights or Old Sides. In substantial measure, they, too, abandoned Puritan scholasticism, by magnifying to an unprecedented degree the role of rationalism and by minimizing that of emotion.

The issue of emotion in religion which caused the bifurcation of Colonial society is one of the most pervasive and significant controversies of pre-Revolutionary America. In its essential features, the Colonies-wide confrontation is perhaps best exemplified in the New England experience. The examination of this division of the Puritan commonwealth offers unique rewards to those who seek to understand the present by discovering prototypal patterns in the lights and shadows of the past.

In bringing into focus the debate over reason vs. emotion in New England, it is imperative that the highlight cast upon the basic issue should not thrust into obscuring shadows the background understanding which alone can provide the substance of reality. The function of our Developing Exigence, Readings, and Inquiry is not to enable one to see the issue superimposed upon an historical backstop, but to see and to sense the involvement of the issue in the dynamism of the times—thus to become creatively aware of the rhetorical problems inherent in the communicative situation, the options open to the speakers, the choices they make, and the sagacity and consequences of their choices.

The Great Awakening and the attendant divisions over the role of emotion in religion were not unexplainable vagaries of chance. They occurred because over a period of many years a complex of interacting forces had moved the Colonial mind ineluctably toward such a confrontation. Analogously, the meaning of a gigantic geological fault does not exist in the surface manifestations. What the eye sees is the result. The meaning of the fault must be sought in the causes, the great pressures which once lay hidden deep beneath the earth's crust. So, too, the issue of emotion in religion was the product of pressures buried deep within the Puritan psyche.

Of the underlying forces involved, one of the most significant was the contrasting theology of the revivalists and the antirevivalists. Conceived primarily as a means of accommodating Reformation religion to the needs of English society, the Puritan theology was applied with considerable success during the first generation in New England. Its workability soon proved to be imperfect, however, and it gradually underwent profound changes, some of which proved to be critically divisive. A second

major force was the contrasting rhetorical theory of the protagonists. Possibly our issue of emotion in religion presented a more immediate nexus between social action and oral communication than has been exemplified in any other major crisis in our history. It can be argued that no other issue has exhibited so strikingly a polarization into camps which were identified by, or more accurately—were caused by, divergent conceptions concerning the application of rhetoric to man's nature. An intrinsic part of the Puritans' theologic expression, their rhetorical theories were transplanted from England. During the first years of the Colonial experiment they served effectively, but changing societal conditions almost imperceptibly forced corresponding evolvements in the theory and practice of preaching.[1]

In the following discussion we shall first consider the Puritan inheritance, especially as it relates to the compartmentalization of the mind and the controlled balance between the intellect and the emotions. Next, we shall trace the evolvement of Puritan thought, a principal strain of which culminated in Jonathan Edwards's approachment to a unification of man and the pervasion of the emotions. Finally, we shall look at the triumph of emotion over reason which occurred during the Great Awakening; the confrontation between the adherents of reason and those of emotion which, during the Epitasis and Catastrophe of the Awakening, divided society into two camps; and the continuing consequences of the issue of emotion in religion.

The Inheritance: Compartmentalization of the Mind and the Precarious Balance Between Intellect and Emotions

Theology of the Covenants. In their efforts to return Christianity to the unsullied nature of the teachings of Paul and the Gospels, both Martin Luther and John Calvin had found inspiration in the works of St. Augustine.[2] The greatest of the early Fathers, St. Augustine believed that depraved man was completely dependent upon God for salvation. From the standpoint of the great reformers, it was tragically sinful that over the centuries the Roman Catholic Church had lost sight of

primitive Christianity and had embraced those "presumptuous" views of man which St. Aquinas was to enunciate. "True," the Thomists would argue from their Aristotelian base, "all things ultimately depend upon God; but man has been endowed by his creator with capabilities which he can employ to assist his salvation." In refutation, the Protestant reformers would argue that the great systematizer had fundamentally erred in permitting man to be an "efficient" cause; God was both the "efficient" and "final" cause of every detail concerning salvation. Reformation of Catholicism was necessary—and this was the point on which the great humanist Erasmus broke with his friends Melanchton and Luther—not primarily because of excesses and immoralities within the Church, but because the Church itself was based upon false premises concerning the merit of man, the diminishment of God, and the relationship between the two.

The principal intellectual defense of the Reformation, Calvin's *Institutes of the Christian Religion*,[3] emphasized the polarity taught by St. Augustine and St. Paul: totally sovereign God and utterly impotent and debased man. Since at times the French reformer tended to write in broad sweeps, the premises of his theological edifice were sometimes spun together with filaments of faith rather than interlocked with the syllogistic development of reason and fact—as oak, iron, and stone are conjoined in a great cathedral meant to withstand the ages.[4] As a result of his failure to reinforce sufficiently the details of his theology, the Reformed scholastic theology, which grew out of his teachings, particularized his doctrines and, in the process, intensified the severity of Calvinism.[5]

Such absolutism produced at least two grave theological and psychological problems. First, the Reformed God was terrifyingly total: completely powerful, utterly inscrutable, implacably unforgiving, perfectly merciful. Inasmuch as man's understanding grows out of his awareness and inasmuch as little, if anything, exists in his experience to prepare him for the allness of an absolutely sovereign God, man could not easily understand or serve such a deity. Because he could not personalize such a God, he could not easily identify with Him. Hence,

only the devout or the credulous could bring themselves to love Him. Second, according to Reformed theology, man was absolutely without power either to promote or to impede his salvation. Because of Adam's fall from grace, God had consigned all succeeding generations of men to hell except for the few persons whom, from the beginnings of time, He had capriciously selected for salvation. Fallen man was utterly sinful and completely unable to improve his spiritual state through his own efforts. Salvation was totally a free, unmerited gift, and God would not hear the pleas nor value the efforts of the unelected. In addition to its psychological consequences, man's terrifying helplessness had grave social implications. If man could not in any way influence his chances for salvation, religion could no longer fulfill its traditional function of coercing him to behave morally and soberly, as needful by a stable society.

Partly in the effort to resolve these theological and psychological problems, during the reign of Henry VIII various innovators, apparently borrowing heavily from the Rhineland reformers, began to evolve a labyrinthine system based principally upon a series of covenants or compacts. (Without permitting our narrative to be diverted into an excursion over the brier fields of early Puritanism, it is necessary to recognize that the covenant doctrine probably evolved from disparate sources. As a result of the discovery of the reformers that the concept of covenantal relationships was a basic thrust of the Scriptures, covenant theology was perhaps another instance of the "Protestant recovery of biblical teaching." Probably the innovators were influenced by the conceptual traditions of natural law and social contract and by the basic assumptions of Protestant thought: individualism, election, and the antithetical natures of God and man. Finally, if it was not a theology indigenous to England, covenant theology may have been in part the outgrowth of the efforts of the homecoming Marian exiles to systematize Calvin's teachings, such as the following: the elected person can contribute to his preparation for salvation; "the commencement of faith is knowledge; the completion of it is a firm and steady conviction"; conversion involves the gradual transformation of man's faculties of Understanding, Will, and

Affections; covenantal relationships provide the "key" to the "God-man relationship.") [6] Brought substantially to maturity during the latter part of the sixteenth and the early years of the seventeenth century, covenant theology taught that God had voluntarily limited the exercise of His power, binding himself into partnership with man.

For our purposes we can conceive of Puritan covenants as consisting essentially of two "external" and one "internal" compacts between God and man. The church covenant and the social covenant were "external" agreements which God initiated with men as members of the visible church and of a Godly state. In return for man's walking as faithfully as he could in divine paths, God would bless both the church and the land itself. Inasmuch as election must remain a manifestation of God's secret will, saints could not be distinguished with certainty from sinners. Inevitably the state and the earthly church would include both tares and wheat. Therefore, neither the church covenant nor the social covenant provided for individual salvation. That was offered in the "internal" covenant of grace. According to this doctrine, in the beginning God had engaged with Adam in a covenant of good works, by which Adam was guaranteed salvation in return for obedience. By his sin, however, Adam had voided the saving quality of this agreement and had earned damnation for himself and all of his descendants. Despite the rightfulness of universal condemnation, out of the perfection of His mercy God had introduced the covenant of redemption, by which He accepted the sacrifices of Christ as redeeming mankind, and the corollary covenant of grace, by which He extended salvation through Christ to Christ's followers. To share in the covenant of grace as a disciple of Christ, man was required to satisfy only one condition: to believe Him.[7]

In its ultimate values, the covenant of grace did not mitigate the terrors of Calvinism. Man, himself, could not achieve his half of the equation: conditional promise by God and matching requirement of faith by man. Only the Deity, through His predestined election, could provide man with saving faith. Thus, only the elected could covenant with God.

Nevertheless, the analogy of the covenants provided the

means of acquiring a better apprehension of God's nature, and the rationale of the covenants seemed to furnish some protection from the unpredictable power of a total God. The ambiguities which interlaced the system of the covenants helped preserve the spark of encouragement that man needed to prevent his dispair and to harness his sinful nature to the cause of morality. In their preaching of the covenants, the most prominent English theologians, like William Perkins, John Preston, and Richard Sibbes, emphasized the conditional promises to such an extent that the absolute values sometimes receded out of the focus of primary attention.[8] Of perhaps greatest significance, by the early years of the seventeenth century, various English divines had rationalized the conditional and the absolutist aspects of the covenant of grace into a morphology of conversion which energized the Puritan to vigorous, continuous striving for salvation.

The Morphology of Conversion and the Psychology of Man. To the Puritan, God designed the universe as the manifestation of His idea, and every blade of grass—every hawking of a sea gull—every postulate of the arts and sciences—was an expression of divine intent.[9] As in all other matters, God followed His system of universal laws in the process by which He awakened the first stirrings of hope in the mind of the elected person, guided him through a preparation stage, and eventually disclosed to him that he possessed saving faith. To discover this pattern, the Puritans studied the observable behavior of the earnest seeker in his progress from doubt to assurance and correlated such findings with their understanding of the psychological nature of man.

Inasmuch as God adhered to the laws of nature in bringing about conversion, He necessarily operated through the natural faculties of man. Out of the voluminous mélange of writing on faculty psychology by medieval and renaissance writers—like Thomas Aquinas, Albertus Magnus, John Huarte, and Phillippe de Mornay—and by ancient authors—like Seneca, Augustine, Cicero, and, especially, Aristotle—the Puritan systematizers drew firm conclusions concerning the psychological nature of man, both in relation to his fall from grace and in relation to his rebirth under the covenant of grace.[10]

According to the standard Puritan configuration, God originally designed man's effector mechanism as a reflex arc that perfectly interpreted and responded to the divine will. Although in its effect the circuit functioned unitively, it was composed of separate faculties, each of which possessed its assigned location and function. Thus, a sense impression was carried to the Common Sense faculty in the mind, where it was identified; it was then given imagery by the Imagination, stored in the Memory, judged by the Understanding, and embraced or rejected by the Will—located in the heart—which then directed the Affections. Because of Adam's misuse of his faculties, God had withdrawn His blessing from the arc, causing—on all spiritual matters—the total paralysis of the faculties and the disruption of the automatically unidirectional flow along the stages of the arc. As a result of the malfunctioning of his faculties, man could no longer understand, nor believe, nor accept, the perfection of God's will. Man was totally fallen. In order for him to be restored to grace, his entire series of faculties had to be freed from their paralysis. Fallen man could, of course, achieve "historic" faith by means of his faculties; but this possessed no spiritual merit. Saving faith could be secured only when all of his faculties responded fully to God's wisdom, a condition which occurred in the act of conversion when the person realized that he had been chosen for salvation.

Inasmuch as the divine design was the perfection of reason, inasmuch as God always treated man as a reasoning and reasonable being, and inasmuch as God had originally given man the power of reason so that he could understand and accept the divine will, the Understanding was the king of the faculties. Unless the Understanding were restored, the judgment which was passed along to the Will would necessarily be corrupt. All saving grace had to pass through the Understanding, for it was in the Understanding that the mind perceived and became convinced of the rightness of God's plan.

Once the Understanding had made its decision concerning the truth or falsity of a spiritual matter, the Will—as the Queen of the faculties—should automatically embrace the true and reject the false. The corrupted Will, however, could not choose

correctly. Because of its sinful nature, it must inevitably mis-
choose sin. Only through God's intervention could the Will be
restored to its former capacity for correct choice.[11]

It is important to note, however, that in bringing the elect
to the recognition of his salvation God dispensed to the Understanding a divine knowledge or light which differed from the
rational process, or ratiocination, of which man himself was
capable.[12] Not until the mind of the elected person had thus
understood and accepted the divine will would God flood his
being with the raptures of saving grace. In contradistinction to
Catholic theologians, who minimized, or bypassed, the reasoning faculties in their evocation of the emotional response of
"blind" faith, the Puritans distrusted the emotions.[13] Even though
they highly respected and valued them, the emotions were to
be kept harnessed and under the supervision of the higher
faculties, the Understanding and Will.

Although man's entire nature had to be remade before
conversion could be completed, God employed a sequential
pattern in drawing elected persons to Him.[14] Roughly following
the arc of the faculties, the divine morphology of conversion
consisted of stages by which the earnest seeker could identify
his progress. In the *Cases of Conscience,* William Perkins dis-
cerned ten steps in the "working and effecting of man's salvation."[15] Most preachers applied a less detailed process, however, as did William Ames in his *Conscience with the Power
and Cases Thereof:* (1) Man should "seriously look into the
Law of God, and make an examination of his life and state according to" the Law. (2) There must "follow a conviction of
Conscience" by which the seeker recognizes that he is "a being
without excuse" and "under sin." (3) "After this conviction of
Conscience, there must follow a despair of salvation, both in
respect of all strength of our own and of any help which is to
be had from the creatures." (4) "After all these, there must
follow a true humiliation of heart, which consists in grief and
fear because of sin, and doth bring forth confession." Only after
man had passed through these four stages would God provide
"the first entrance into the state of saving grace." Man should
then "employ his greatest care, labor and industry about this
business" of ensuring and improving his holy state.[16]

Although the details of the various treatments of conversion differed somewhat, a remarkable agreement existed concerning the route itself. Knowledge and understanding of Biblical truths always preceded the sequent steps: conviction, "legal fear," humiliation, and, finally, the awareness of the possible presence of faith. The smallest "spark of faith" which God "kindled in the heart" was a sufficient conversion to provide the elect with the "will and desire to believe," thereby ensuring his salvation. Once he received faith, man could not lose it—regardless of his behavior. Nevertheless, man could never be absolutely sure that his faith was genuine. Therefore, as soon as he received faith, or thought that he had been converted, his being was disturbed by "combat" between, on the one hand, "doubting, dispair, and distrust," and, on the other hand, faith which manifested itself by "fervent, constant, and earnest invocation for pardon." Destined to be always an unrequited seeker for perfect assurance, man could achieve relative tranquility only after much inward struggle.

Puritan Homiletics and the Striving for Grace. Without a matching theory of preaching, the Puritan system of the covenants would have lacked the genius necessary to impel spiritually passive man to strive for grace and, once he thought he had received it, to struggle endlessly for comforting assurance. Puritans believed that, as a part of the divine pattern, God provided the means by which the elect would progress along the various steps of the morphology of conversion: attending to the preaching of the word, studying the Bible, praying, sharing in the sacraments of baptism and the Lord's Supper, and striving constantly to follow Christ's example. During the course of their efforts, the elect eventually would be admitted to the covenant of grace. Natural man, of course, could never achieve everlasting life, no matter how persistently he might try. Nevertheless, since no one could tell in advance whether or not he was elected, and since God had appointed the route and the means, all who wished salvation must energize themselves to continued effort.

Of the types of striving, the "chief ordinary means to beget faith" was the analytical listening to sermons. Central in Puritan

theology was the concept that the sermon provided the means by which the function of the church would be realized: to foster saving grace through enlightened understanding. It is natural, therefore, that the Puritans would develop a homiletic theory which would coalesce their concepts concerning the covenants, the psychological nature of man, and the morphology of conversion.

In estimating Puritan homiletic theory, fortunately one is not limited to the printed sermons, which, by the way, exist in abundance. Many of the major Puritan theologians demonstrated their abiding concern with oral communication by writing widely on homiletics. Since all of these men served assignments as college tutors, deans, or masters, they were able to influence directly the rhetorical concepts of young men who went into the ministry. This was especially true at Emmanuel College of Cambridge University, which was founded by the ardent Puritan Sir Walter Mildmay for the express purpose of training "fit instruments" for the pulpit. Among Emmanuel's distinguished masters who were renowned preachers and who wrote on rhetoric were John Preston and Richard Holdsworth. In his "Directions for a Student in the University," Holdsworth prescribed for the entire undergraduate program the textbooks to be studied, including those in rhetoric, logic, and psychology, as well as the kinds and amounts of exercises, and so on.[17] In addition to such printed and manuscript materials, much data exists concerning the extent to which the official statutory regulations were followed in the university programs and in the programs of the colleges at Cambridge and Oxford. Education at the English universities was prescribed by statutes to center in the teaching of rhetoric and logic and in the oral exercises of disputations and declamations.[18] In addition, largely untapped until most recently, are the many thousands of manuscript pages of student workbooks, manuals, letters, journals, college records, shelf lists, and the like.[19]

Out of this almost overwhelming volume of closely and distantly related materials, there emerges a Puritan rhetorical theory which was brilliantly adapted to its needs. Although a unique codification, Puritan sermonology stemmed primarily from

classical rhetorical theory, with modifications in tone and cast being drawn from various neoclassicists and from the French reformer Peter Ramus.[20] The core of this theory can be presented quickly. Before this is done, however, the reader should be cautioned to accept this distillation for what it is and nothing more. It represents what in the author's view is the pith of the Puritans' general sermonic tendencies and practices—especially those who followed the great William Ames. Puritan theology was not monolithic, nor was Puritan rhetoric. Nevertheless, a long-term and meticulous examination of the available primary evidence suggests that the logical and rhetorical inheritance, which the Puritans brought with them to New England and which they practiced widely in early New England pulpits, can be epitomized in the following manner.[21]

(1) *The ends of the sermon and the duties of the preacher: an incipient conflict.* The basic thrust of Puritan rhetoric was dichotomized into a devotion to logic and a recognition of the tremendous influence of the emotions.[22] Nevertheless, a distinguishing theme of prototypal Puritan rhetoric echoed that of Aristotle's *Rhetoric:* [23] the listener is a reasonable, reasoning man—a judge; his initial end in listening is to render a rational judgment; for him to arrive at a rational acceptance he must follow an orderly, systematic pattern of reasoning; since "truth and justice are by their nature more powerful than their opposites," by logical explication and argument, especially by use of the enthymeme, the listener can be brought to a correct apperception of the truth. Enthymemic reasoning presupposes the understanding and acceptance by the listener of the values inherent in the basic premises, as well as the willingness and ability to follow the push of the argument to its conclusion— plus the intellectual and emotional readiness to accept the conclusion once its validity is established by logical processes. Thus, both the Aristotelian and the Puritan listeners were expected to be judicious and informed. According to this Aristotelian-Puritan view, the sermon must provide the systematic thought development which would enable the listener to make a rational discernment. Logic should be the initial means to persuasion. Emotional values were, most assuredly, extremely important;

but, by their nature they were antagonistic to the reasoning process and should be restricted essentially to a reinforcing function. Furthermore, in themselves, they carried no power to convince. Properly, they served to intensify previously established conviction. Thus, the power of emotions to influence should be released only after the listener had been persuaded through rational means.[24]

It was largely the Puritans' acceptance of this equilibrium, this bifurcation, of logic and emotion—along with their acceptance of the primacy of logic as the "Queen" of discourse and the other arts,[25] teaching as the principal function of the minister, reasoned argument as the *modus operandi* of the sermon, "a close, naked, natural way of speaking" as the proper sermon style, clarity as the basic determinant of speech development, and edification leading to conversion as the end of preaching—that attracted many of them to the theory of Peter Ramus. To Ramus, speaking and teaching were synonymous. The speaker was a teacher. The listeners were learners who would believe and act upon what they were taught because, when Ramerian methods were employed, the truth would become self-evident. By following commonsense logic in a progressive movement from universal thoughts through definitions and bifurcated divisions to particular extrusions, the Ramist speaker could guide the thinking of his listeners to manifest and infallibly correct conclusions. Thus Ramus's absolutist logic matched perfectly the absolutist theology of the Puritans. Believing that reason was more important in persuasion than the emotions, Ramus attempted a fairly rigid separation of the two, restricting the emotions to a supportive role. Believing that logic was amenable to apodictic proof, or certitude, Ramus discarded the classical paraphenalia of establishing the absolute proof of Aristotle's scientific demonstration, the probable truth of Aristotle's dialectic, which was directed to educated and discerning audiences, and the possible truth of Aristotle's rhetoric, which was directed to audiences of "ordinary intelligence" who "cannot grasp many points in a single view, or follow a long chain of reasoning." [26] From the art of rhetoric, Ramus disjoined the process of finding and organizing arguments and assigned

them to logic, leaving to rhetoric only the functions of committing the speech to memory, style—which included the evocation of the emotions, and delivery. As will be seen shortly, Ramus's concepts were especially influential in the construction and composition of the Puritan sermon.

Despite the attractiveness of Ramus's teaching, the Puritans were not the thoroughgoing Ramists that Perry Miller[27] and Wilbur Howell[28] have contended. In their academic training in rhetoric and logic, the English Puritans studied principally from texts in the neoclassical tradition. Therefore, they were exposed to an integrated and functional system of training in oral communication. The structure and development of the speech, as well as the communicative act itself, were recognized as integrative processes. Puritans might theorize that the first end of speaking was to evoke rational judgment and that the primary means to this end was logical argument. Nevertheless, at Emmanuel and at other Cambridge colleges the Puritan students learned from classical sources[29] and from neo-Ciceronian sources, such as Gerard Vossius's *Rhetorices Contractae*, that the purpose of the orator is to persuade and that in order to speak appropriately to persuasion, the duties of the orator are "*docere, conciliare, & permovere.*"[30] According to this neo-Ciceronian view, for practical results the orator must do more than to instruct (*docere*) his listeners; he must also win their acceptance (*conciliare*), and excite their feelings (*permovere*).

The recognition of the psychological needs of man, in combination with their devotion to logic, caused the Puritans to build into their concept of the ends and means of the sermon an incipient conflict between teaching and persuasion that was to have increasingly severe consequences.[31] One part of the dichotomy was the conviction that the initial end of preaching was to facilitate the making of a rational decision for Christ; the emotions were distrusted and were to be employed in reinforcement of the judgments previously made by the Understanding. The second half of the dichotomy was the realization that the entire man is involved in the decision-making process; man cannot be sufficiently energized by appeals to his Understanding; he must also be stirred by appeals to his Affections and Will. At the time

was especially well suited to Puritan sermonology. To Cicero, amplification meant "to win credence" by arousing the emotions; the emotions were to be evoked through the use of "powerfully illuminating" language (this conformed to Ramus's concept that "style" provided the means of exciting the feelings), as in an "enlargement" on "love," "affection," and "moral considerations." In the Puritan schema, the arousing of emotions was a legitimate function of the *Application,* theoretically the one place in the entire sermon in which the preacher could directly address the Affections.

(3) *The composition of the sermon.* The compartmentalization of the Puritan mind and its disjoining of logic and emotions is nowhere better illustrated than in the composition of the sermon. The first three parts of the sermon were directed to the reasoning or judging faculty: the Understanding. In "laying open" the text, the speaker attempted to extract the grammatical, logical, and figurative meaning. In his division, explication, and proofs of the doctrine, he taught universal, absolute truths. Such truths, to the extent that man could discover them, had already been set down in the Bible. By drawing each proposition from the sense of Scriptural evidence and by connecting it to supportive Biblical passages, the preacher could demonstrate to the authoritarian and legalistic minds of his listeners that his argument led inescapably to a particular rational judgment. Therefore, his arguments were theoretically those of absolute demonstration—not the probable truths of Aristotle's dialectics nor the likely truths of Aristotle's rhetoric. When such apodictic proofs were explained in a "plaine" and "painful" style, those listeners who possessed restored Understandings—the elect—would recognize and believe the truth.

A key to much that follows in this book is provided by an understanding of the composition of the fourth part of the sermon, the *Application.* It was only in the *Application* that the preacher was theoretically permitted to consider the entire sequence of the faculties. In the notes on preaching which were taken as a student at Cambridge by Henry Dunster, who later became the first president of Harvard College, this advice appears: "In handling the doctrine be as plain as may be, only

look [at] what concerns the understanding of the doctrine. Look especially at the logic. The rhetorical passages are only profitable in the Uses when you come to the Affections. . . . From the Doctrine come to Application to the soul wherein consists the life of preaching. You shall first apply it to the Understanding, secondly to the Will & Affections for therein consists the labor; & as to reach & inform the Understanding, so to stir up the people's hearts to the things taught." [37]

Notice that on the one hand Dunster's notes emphasized the sequential primacy of the intellect and the compartmentalization of the mind. In those parts of the sermon preceding the *Application*, the speaker's duty was to "reach and inform the Understanding," with emotional evocation being avoided. Even in the *Application*, appeals to the emotions and to the Will were to be made only after the speaker had applied the doctrine to the Understanding. Furthermore, clearly underscoring the supplementary nature of the Affections, the function of stirring "up the people's hearts" was to reinforce "the things taught." Notice on the other hand, however, that the ultimately crucial significance of the Will and Affections was recognized: in the *Application* "wherein consists the life of preaching," the address to the Will and the Affections "consists the labor." Thus, it was in the *Application* that the preacher was expected to fulfill the second and third duties of Cicero's orator: to win over the listener and to excite his emotions.

Up to the *Application* segment of the sermon, relatively little concession had been made to natural man. The function of earlier divisions basically had been to enable the listener's Understanding to recognize rationally the truth of the Scriptural doctrine. In the *Application*, however, the Puritan sermon called for the listener to be up and about the task of seeking or reaffirming his conversion. As though natural man could improve his spiritual state, as though the preceding parts of the sermon had indeed enlightened his Understanding, the listener was then entreated to apply the spiritual truths to his own life for his spiritual and moral uplifting. It was primarily the *Application* that provided the Puritan preacher the means to energize his congregation to a continued seeking of saving grace.[38]

1. *Paradigm suggesting roughly the compartmentalization of the Puritan system during earliest years in New England.*

PARTS OF SERMON	DUTIES OF PREACHER	ENDS OF LISTENER	FACUL-TIES OF MAN	MOR-PHOLOGY OF CON-VERSION
Laying open the text Doctrine Reasons [41]	To teach, or to advise, by means of informa-tion and logical anal-ysis	To render, and accept, a rational judgment	Understand-ing (the faculty of judging) [Will] [40] (the fac-ulty of embracing or rejecting)	Knowl-edge [39] Conviction
Application	By the ap-plication of the spiritual truths now logically es-tablished, to teach, to win over the listener, and to ex-cite his emotions	To strive for saving grace or for reas-surance of grace	Under-standing Will Affections	Knowledge Conviction Legal fear Humiliation Ecstasy of faith

Perhaps a suitable means of summarizing the Puritan in-heritance is to present the paradigm (figure 1) which suggests the compartmentalization of the Puritan mind and the balance maintained between the intellect and the emotions. Inasmuch as the paradigm provides an important summarizing focus, its purpose should be made quite clear. *It is designed to suggest the pattern of implicit interrelationships which constituted the core of the Puritan rhetorical system. It is not intended to imply that the Puritan system was rigid or monolithic, or even that the chief architects were consistent within their own writings.*[42] *The various components of the schema represent general tendencies*

rather than hermetic units. Too, not all Puritans adhered to the commonly accepted views concerning the nature of man, the morphology of conversion, or the principles of sermonology. One nonconformist, for example, was John Cotton, who did not endorse the morphology of conversion or the concept of preparation itself. Another was Thomas Hooker, who strongly disagreed with the primacy assigned by many Puritans to the faculty of the Understanding. In his *A Survey of the Summe of Church Discipline,* Hooker anticipated the later revivalists by asserting that "the scope of" the minister's "office is to work upon the Will and the Affections. . . . Not that the pastor may not interpret the text, and lay open the meaning so far as he may make way for the truth to work more kindly, and prevail more effectually with the Affections, but that is not his . . . main work. . . . His labour is to lay open the lothsome nature of sin, and to let in the terror of the Lord upon the conscience." [43]

Transition and Culmination: Unification of Man and the Pervasion of the Emotions

As a consequent of their recurrent emphasis upon the conditional promise of the covenant of grace, most English Puritan ministers tended to preach an optimistic religion. At times, in their stressing the rationality of true religion and the necessity for an intellectual acceptance of Christian doctrine, they seemed almost to teach that man could reason himself to salvation. At times, in their accentuation of sin, the need for reformation, and the reforming influence of saving faith upon man's behavior, they very nearly seemed to teach that piety indicated justification and that man might "will" himself to grace. [44]

In comparison to the preaching of English Puritans like John Preston and Richard Sibbes, during the first generation of the New England experience, the generality of the ministers probably preached a somewhat less optimistic theology, with a somewhat greater emphasis upon the absolute values of the covenants. A reason for this difference in stress may be partly that many of the settlers believed themselves to be the spiritual seed of Abraham. God had selected them to establish the promised

land and had bound them to Him in a church and a social covenant. As a chosen people they were predestined to a privileged status and, therefore, were possibly more receptive to the preachments of a totally sovereign God and of the terrors of the Law. It is perhaps indicative that in New England John Cotton appears to have emphasized to a significantly greater extent the absolute aspects of the covenants than he had previously in Old England.[45]

Generally speaking, during the first generation the New England ministers applied the sermon format soberly and intently to the faculties of their hearers. The basic tone of the sermon was that of reasoned argument. The style was "plaine" and "painful." The thrust of the sermon appears to have been directed principally to church members and their children— the consequential element in the congregation and in society— rather than to the unconverted nonmembers who were compelled to attend services. Although exceptions existed, as in the exhortations of Thomas Hooker and Thomas Shepard, instead of serving a strongly evangelistic function, the sermon basically sought to guide the elect to the realization of their predestined saving faith and to reaffirm the rational convictions and strengthen the piety of those who already believed they possessed saving grace, or fervently hoped that they did.[46]

During the first years in the American wilderness, the Puritan system served effectively the needs of society. Virtually from the very start, however, emergent problems forced modifications in pulpit practice. Because of space limitations, these envolvements can be treated in only the most general sort of way. Perhaps the reader should be cautioned, therefore, that such compression tends to produce a historical time-lapse photographic effect, converting what was complex into the overly simple, what were general tendencies into sharply etched processes, and what were incrementally produced changes into escalated transformations.[47]

Early Changes. Never monolithic in character, the New England society almost immediately began to fragment, and the social covenant began its attenuated course to extinction.[48] For

the social covenant to work, society had to be "knit together as one man" in furthering the design of God. If zeal were lacking or if sin were untrammeled, God would punish the land and, if the offenses were sufficiently great, He would void the covenant. Thus, the entire population had to be continuously vigilant in the effort to identify and to extirpate sin. Unfortunately for the Puritan cause, however, her theologians tended to equate "sin" with any deviation from the concepts of the New England founders. To a significant degree "spiritual virtue" was, thereby, identified with the impossible state of suspended animation, and "sin" with the inevitable condition of change.

Within a few years, the waves of immigration began to dilute the original religious zeal; the needs of an expanding society increasingly directed the energies of the people into channels of trade and commerce; and, eventually, the currents of liberalizing thought reached the New England shores, weakening the hold of old values. Instead of accepting societal changes as being the concomitants of a developing culture, the clergy considered them to be violations of the covenant. Every Indian attack, every smallpox scourge, every sinking of a fishing vessel, every new restriction imposed by the British government, was identified as an evidence of God's growing displeasure. Because of the sins of the people, God was punishing the land and was threatening to send even greater calamities.

According to the absolute values of the social covenant, God would withdraw the inflicted punishments after man abandoned the sin which had offended Him, *provided* this entire sequence conformed to the divine pattern. The will of God would not be altered, of course. It was not God who had changed; it was man—and man's change necessarily adhered to God's plan. In their continuous attacks upon sin, however, the ministers increasingly developed the practice of exhorting the listeners to forsake sin. At first only ambiguously, later more openly, many of them taught what amounted to a *quid pro quo* equation: if man would forsake his sin and repent, he might assume that God would forgive and would bless the land.

Under this continued emphasis upon the conditional aspects of the social covenant, without their recognition of the ongoing

change, the perceptual world of the ministers and the people gradually became accustomed to an expanded view of the capacity of man. It became easier to assume the efficacy of pious behavior to influence God or, even, to compel Him to modify His will. Instead of a purely temporal sequence, adhering to predestination, the sequence of repentance-reformation-forgiveness-prosperity tended seemingly to become a series of causally related stages.[49] This intrinsic implication of the capacity of man's actions to influence God's reactions was not limited to pulpit importunities. It became ingrained in the Puritan orientation to reality as the ecclesiastic and civic leaders called for reformation in an endless series of lamenting and denunciatory complaints or jeremiads, fast day ceremonies, and proclamations.[50] Despite all such efforts, however, the New England society became increasingly worldly.[51] Long before the Massachusetts Bay charter was revoked in 1684, it was apparent that the land was no longer in special covenant with the Lord.

Parallel to the social covenant, beginning with the first years of settlement, the application of the church covenant brought to the Puritan system increasing stresses, which weakened the viability of the church covenant and which forced modifications in the preaching of the covenant of grace. Partially because the almost overwhelming number of immigrants included many who obviously were not visible saints, during the first decade the fathers attempted to preserve the spiritual purity of the church by adopting a much more restrictive church policy than that followed by the English Puritans. To be accepted into the church, a candidate had to convince the members that, according to the most searching human judgment, he did indeed possess saving grace.[52] By limiting membership to visible saints, the founders insured the highest degree of purity which was humanly possible. The admission standards were so exacting, however, that their application posed immediate, unsolvable problems.[53]

Although the fathers were perhaps not surprised that few of the unchurched applied for membership, they soon became dismayed that their admission policies excluded increasing numbers of their own children. The sacrament of baptism had been automatically extended to the children of church members

in the assumption that as they grew to maturity they would come under the influence of the spirit and would apply for membership. Great numbers of children, however, either did not experience conversion or they were unwilling to defend before the church their claim to saving faith.[54] By 1662 the decline in the relative numerical strength of the church membership had become so perilous that the strategem of a "half-way covenant" was adopted.[55] The intent of the "half-way covenant" was to reconcile the policy of exclusionary membership with the extraordinary birthrate and the policy of infant baptism, thereby securing both the vigor of an enlarged church congregation and the protection of the inner church. According to this arrangement, the baptized but unconverted children of church members would be considered partial members with the right to claim baptism and a similar limited church membership for their own offspring. Until they could make a satisfactory public claim to grace, however, they could not vote in church matters or be admitted to the Lord's Supper.[56]

Despite the tempest which immediately arose over the "half-way covenant," the ministers soon gradually began to extend the practice, accepting into partial membership not only the descendants of the visible saints but also those persons who had no family history of church membership but who possessed "historic" faith, lived upright lives, and had attained satisfactory knowledge concerning the Scriptures. Before the end of the seventeenth century, this practice had become widely established and the typical church consisted of a relatively small center of full members, a larger congregation of partial members, and a perimeter of nonmembers, who were compelled to contribute to the support of the church and to attend services.[57]

Although the "half-way covenant" did not prevent the continued decline in the relative number of full members, it recognized the changing nature of the church auditory and, eventually, it encouraged the shaping of the Puritan sermon. Inasmuch as the half-way members possessed only "historic faith," they were presumed to be damned. Nevertheless, their having been admitted to the sacrament of baptism gave them an indeterminate spiritual status. They belonged to the church and were subjected to its discipline. Unlike the unchurched, the partial

members perhaps were not utterly impotent, but possessed some incremental power to prepare themselves for grace. Acting upon this possibility, the ministers demanded from them a more active striving for grace and for pious deportment and threatened them with a greater intensity of eternal punishment.[58] As a part of the continuous pressure upon the partial members, during the latter years of the seventeeth century, the practice developed of owning the covenant. On the appointed day, the minister would deliver a jeremiad, lamenting the declension of the land and the deficiencies of the congregation and calling for reformation. Then, all of the half-way members were required in unison to renew their profession of faith and obedience. Possibly reflecting a growing tendency of the time, various ministers supplemented their exhortations with imprecations of fire and brimstone.[59]

Later Transitions. As the New England experience moved into the eighteenth century, it provided increasingly clear evidence that the transformation of the wilderness into a thriving civilization had evoked correspondingly pervasive changes in the Puritan system. The social covenant had disintegrated. The composition of the church had altered to such an extent that its claim to covenantal relationship with God was in jeopardy; articulate critics were contending that the concept was outmoded and unscriptural; some churches, especially those in the Connecticut valley, had abandoned the church covenant and had accepted into full church membership all pious persons who professed "historic" faith. Even the covenant of grace had undergone significant alteration. The twin thrusts of the modern age— individualism and the elevation of man—had emphasized the capacity of man's individual initiative to affect his environment and his adaptability to his environment. Against these inexorable pressures, Calvinist New England struggled to prevent the fragmenting of the "great universal" of innate sin into individual sins warranting individual punishment and of the "great universal" of election into individual claims to salvation based upon individual merit. Nevertheless, despite the language of absolutism which still embellished the preaching of the covenant of grace, the substance of the typical sermon portrayed a partially

humanized deity, one who—because of His acceptance of covenantal restrictions on the exercise of His power—was somewhat less than totally sovereign, inscrutable, or implacable. The average New Englander continued to be intensely concerned about his soul. Unlike the devoted followers of John Cotton, however, he probably did not fully accept his own spiritual passivity but hoped that somehow he might assist himself along the route to salvation by moral living, zealous striving, and pious deeds.

Although New England remained doctrinally committed to Calvinism, to a considerable extent, by the early years of the eighteenth century the pith of the homiletic principles had gradually shriveled, leaving the husk of form and language. The verbalism of faculty psychology had been maintained, the divisions of the sermon retained, and the primacy of reason repeatedly reasserted. Nevertheless, the arts which gave to Puritan sermonology its substance—that is, the arts of scholastic logic, rhetoric, and psychology—had lost much of their viability. Presaged in part, at least, in tutor Michael Wigglesworth's 1653 lectures on eloquence at Harvard College,[60] the changes in sermonology represented a highly significant shift away from the compartmentalization of man and the primacy of the intellect and toward a unification of man and the pervasion of the emotions.

These general tendencies can be quickly identified. The "ends" of the listener became less the rendering of a rational judgment and more the striving actively for grace. The "duties" of the preacher became centered less in teaching, or in proving a rationale for reasonable decision-making, and more in persuading in the Ciceronian sense, that is, in combining—or blending—the functions of teaching, winning over the listeners, and exciting the emotions. Thus, the doctrinal parts of the sermon lost some of their significance to the *Application*. Also, the "duties" of winning over the listener and of arousing his feelings intruded into the *Doctrine* and *Reasons*, which, as the reader will recall, were the parts of the sermon formerly devoted to teaching and argumentative analysis.

(1) *Cotton Mather.* Of exceptional importance in the evolvement toward the unification of man and the pervasion of emotions was the pietist Cotton Mather (1663-1728), minister

of Boston's Second Church.[61] Realizing that the cosmology of the past was unrenewable, in his autumnal years Mather attempted to establish a new theological accommodation to the times.[62] By persuading New Englanders to engage in a pervasive pattern of daily spiritualizing and pious deeds, he hoped to reassert ministerial control over the lives of the people and to substitute the unifying motives of serving God and mankind for the divisive motive of profit seeking. In his *Manuductio ad Ministerium*,[63] a widely read manual for ministerial students,[64] the aging Mather provided a detailed account of his simplified piety and sermonology.[65]

In the *Manuductio*, Mather minimized systematic theology. Instead, he urged ministers to center their pastoral efforts around the "glorious" and "everlasting" maxims of piety: to believe in God and the universal applicability of the Scriptures, to accept Christ as a means of "reconciliation to GOD," to love one's neighbor and "forever do unto *other men*, as I must own it reasonable for them to do unto *myself*," to "maintain a *brotherly fellowship* with all good men," and to provide an "encouragement in the church for all that observe the grand MAXIMS of PIETY, accompanied with a free *indulgence* of *civil rights* in the *state*."

Although in his own preaching he had retained the church and social covenants, Mather overlooked them in the *Manuductio*. In his treatment of the covenant of grace, he ignored absolutist values, as well as the horrors and inevitability of hell. "Let the spirit of that *covenant* animate and regulate all your performances," he urged the ministerial student, by showing "the people of GOD how to take the comfort of their *eternal election*, and *special redemption*, and *ensured perseverance*; and at the same time fetch mighty incentives to *holiness*, from those *hopes*, which will forever cause those that have them to *purify themselves*."

In discussing the morphology of conversion, Mather went beyond the English Puritans in reaching out toward a universal calling, in minimizing the trauma and the difficulty of conversion, and in stressing the radiant finding of salvation. Genuflecting toward Geneva, Mather admitted, "you will not come to" the true service of God "until the glorious GOD . . . give you a

new heart, and cause a *regenerating work* of His grace to pass upon you." Nevertheless, in discussing the prospects of salvation, he was ravished with joyous optimism: "Now that you may arrive to all the blessedness of . . . a *soul saved from death,* I will briefly describe to you that *process of repentance* which you must go through." In the ensuing four pages, he presented a nonintellective formula for acquiring conversion, which omitted the traditional steps of "knowledge" and "conviction"— perhaps because he was addressing ministerial candidates who presumably already possessed "historic" faith and Scriptural knowledge. "First," he advised, *"humbly* and indeed, *lying in the dust,* own your self *unable,* to do any thing effectually of your self in *changing* of your heart. . . . Say, *O glorious* GOD, I justly perish. . . . Under such an humiliation, go on, and lay before your self a *catalogue* of . . . the *innumerable evils . . . encompassing* of you. . . . Own upon it: *O great GOD . . . I deserve to be thrown into the place of dragons. . . ."* Although Mather's description of "humiliation" followed the form employed by William Perkins and William Ames in their treatments of the morphology of conversion, it did not involve the poignant abasement envisioned by the English covenanters. Also, Mather did not dwell long upon "humiliation," but turned quickly to the affirmation: "Now, behold the SON of GOD . . . undergoing the punishment which was due to you. . . . Admire the *free grace* of the glorious GOD, which allows you to make this plea, for your *justification."* Then, all but denying the implacability and inscrutability of John Calvin's God, he exhorted, *"Plead* it, that you may be *justified.* Plead it, with a *comfortable persuasion* of your finding a *kind reception* with your SAVIOUR. Don't think that you *honor,* but that you *reproach* your SAVIOUR, if you doubt your *kind reception* with HIM."

In discussing the "grand aim" of preaching, Mather made no mention of providing the listener with a rationale for making a reasoned decision for Christ and, although he urged that ministers should "entertain the people of GOD with none but *well-studied sermons,"* he did not mention the duty of the preacher to be a teacher. His preoccupation with the duties of "winning over the listener" and "exciting his feelings" is evidenced by his

definition of the purpose of the sermon: to "save them that hear you" by preaching the "PIETY of the *everlasting Gospel*" which "may *animate* them, or *accomplish* them, for *living* unto GOD."

As might be expected, Mather did not share the suspicion of the emotions which had caused most of the first-generation Puritan theologians to tend to subordinate the affections to the intellect and to prescribe that the feelings should be approached only through the Understanding. Instead of considering man to be compartmentalized into separate faculties, with the Understanding being the "King" of the faculties, Mather seemed to envisage man as an integrated being in whom reason and emotion were conjoined. Instead of advocating that the affections be evoked only in the *Application*—and then only after prior appeal to the Understanding, Mather ignored the traditional compartmentalization of the sermon. Instead, he endorsed a "rational emotionalism" which throughout the sermon should exert a combined appeal to reason and emotion. "I would have you usually try, as much as with *good judgment* you can, to set the *truths on fire*, before you part with any head that you are upon; and let them come *flaming* out of your hand with excitations to some *devotion* and *affection* of Godliness, into the *hearts* of those whom they are addressed unto." "Exhibit the *terms of salvation*, and the proposals of the Gospel," as well as "the *desires* of PIETY, in such a manner, that they must have their *hearts burn within* them."

An exceedingly significant index of the changing attitudes toward emotion-reason in religion was Mather's ridicule of scholastic logic. As the reader will recall, traditional Puritan theology was a derivative of Calvinism cast in a series of concatenated covenants. During the early years in New England, the function of the sermon was to foster the elected person's recognition or reassurance of his salvation by explaining to his Understanding the reasonable truths of some Scriptural doctrine and by applying those truths to his Understanding, Will, and Affections. Except in the *Application*, the sermon content was supposed to consist principally of logical argument and explanation, which were based upon apodictic proofs drawn from the Bible and from God's creation. For such preaching, the ministry

had to be highly skilled in dialectics and the congregation had
to be willing and able to follow the enthymemic unraveling of
the thought. Furthermore, and this point is *central* to our entire
discussion, during the first decades in New England the Puritan
sermon—upon which was based Puritan theology—was in its
turn based upon scholastic logic. Because in the traditional sermon the presentation of reasoned proofs followed a basically
consistent pattern of syntactical relationships and linguistic
values, the mechanical operations of Aristotelian-Ramerian logic
provided a suitable and necessary apparatus for both speaker
and listener.

Puritan theology and sermonology had been moving incrementally away from the reasoned argumentation of John Cotton,
however. From the extreme excursion of the pendulum, in the
Manuductio Mather recommended a simplified piety, which constituted a joyous outpouring of the spirit unbridled by the ratio-
cinations of formal logic. Instead of labored intellection, his
sermonology was directed toward the spontaneity of intuitive
reason and emotion. To some extent portending the later position of the revivalists, Mather recognized that the apparatus of
formal logic was irrelevant to preaching which was hortatory in
its linguistic development and which was frequently inductive in
its logical undergirding.[66] Formal logic, he asserted, was a "pomp-
ous form of an *art*" teaching "what every one does by meer
nature and *custom*." "The very termination" of logic is *"the
doctrine of syllogisms,"* the sole value of which is "to confirm you
in a *truth* which you are already the owner of." Instead of concerning oneself with the "meer *morology*" of logic, the earnest
seeker and preacher should accept the "reasons of the heart"
and the "voice of God."

(2) *Solomon Stoddard.* In the evolvement toward the unification of man and the pervasion of the emotions, a figure
perhaps even more important than Cotton Mather was the
autocratic Solomon Stoddard (1643–1729),[67] minister at
Northampton and a long-term foe of both Cotton and his father
Increase.[68] To promote increased religious devotion—under control of the church, early in his ministry Stoddard initiated
important changes in admission policies, liturgy, and church

organization.[69] Discarding the church covenant, Stoddard attempted to sweep the entire town into the church. He sought to admit all "non-scandalous" persons into full church membership, thereby coercing them to incur maximum spiritual obligations by accepting the sacrament of the Lord's Supper. To establish greater control over individual churches and, consequently, over the individual person, Stoddard established the Hampshire Association, which served as a model for other quasi-Presbyterian church organizations in the Valley and for the official ecclesiastic structure adopted in 1708 by the Connecticut General Court.[70]

Of somewhat greater significance to the issue of emotion in religion, Stoddard's condemnation of erudite preaching, his challenging of scholasticism, and his emphasis upon education by experience tended both to liberate rhetorical style and to deemphasize the academism of ministerial training. Of even greater significance, Stoddard was the first teacher of revivalism.[71] In his extensive and influential writings, he presented a profoundly searching examination of the psychological aspects of conversion, which not only added new dimensions to sermonology and to the understanding of the religious experience but which also found later refractions in the tracts of Jonathan Edwards. Of perhaps greatest importance, Stoddard was New England's foremost exponent of convulsionary conversion and its first major revivalist. Well before the exhortations of Theodore Frelinghuysen stirred awakenings in New Jersey, Stoddard had employed an integrated pattern of persuasion to initiate revivalism in New England. In his freshlets of 1679, 1683, 1696, 1712, and 1718, Stoddard introduced a *modus operandi* which was exploited with even greater success by Jonathan Edwards in the Northampton revival of 1734-35 and in the Great Awakening.[72]

Although to the critical student, Stoddard's writings present a specious patchwork of ambiguities and contradictions, in the perspective of his times, his theories assume a seeming consistency with themselves and with Puritan theology. He made revivalism possible by applying to the conditional promises and the absolutist premises of Puritan theology new emphases

and techniques, such as radical expansion of the means of grace, rationalized exploitation of the irrational nature of man, astute manipulation of psychological inducements to climatic conversion, and the most powerful—up to that time—preaching of the stark terror of inscrutable judgment and of hell's torments.

Stoddard's concept of the deity approached—or, perhaps, even exceeded—that of John Calvin: an implacable God of hatred and fury, albeit a loving and "just God," who "delighted in sending the unelected to hell." Because men were "despicable," "dead fish," and "vermin," God hated them with a "divine vengence" until they were converted. It was impossible for men to *make their own hearts better*, however, because "God has put a spirit of self-love into men, and binds them to love themselves." Such self-love was the "cause of all evil." It was the "depraved instinct" which led man always to misuse his "great freedom of choice," to *chuse the ways of sin*, and to "hate God." Although "grace and nothing but grace takes away the government of self-love," God was completely a "free agent" in the dispensing of grace: "there is nothing in God's nature that does compel him to shew mercy to any man" and "there is nothing in any man to sway the will of God in any way." Furthermore, "the *only reason* why God sets his love on one man and not upon another is, *because he pleases*." Thus, in order "to glorify His vindictive justice," God employed this irrational paradox: He decreed "that men shall sin," that He shall "then punish them for their sin," and that, as a manifestation of His mercy, He shall select—purely "by caprice"—a few for salvation.

Stoddard obviated the spiritual passivity and the inate depravity of man, however, by teaching that "men must not wait for a willing spirit as a *ground of encouragement* to come to Christ." Because "before God converts men, it is His manner to prepare them for it by a common work of His spirit, which is called *preparatory*," he reasoned that it is therefore "the *duty of the sinner* to do those things wherein preparation doth consist." Furthermore, the act of striving provided man's only hope: "If God designs to bring men to salvation, He will make them to seek after it."

In his discussions of the morphology of conversion, Stod-

dard made extremely significant contributions to the issue of emotion in religion. Emphasizing "the great consequences for awakened sinners to be guided aright under this work," he simplified the conventional interpretation of preparation into two stages, "conviction" and "humiliation," which were followed by the "assurance of faith." The thrust of his theory went critically further, however, virtually telescoping the two stages into one and negating the effectiveness of human knowledge or reason to promote even "the outward call" of "conviction" and "humiliation."

Maintaining an apparent consistency with orthodox preparation, he defined faith as a "rational understanding action." Understanding must precede faith, and knowledge must precede understanding. Redundantly he intoned that "man's natural reason makes them understand the *sense* of the proposition" and that God gives men "an Understanding and free-Will" in order for them to "understandingly praise Him." Instead of dealing with men "as sticks and stones by mere force," God "deals with them as reasonable creatures. He convinces them" and, thereby, "prevails upon their hearts in a way suitable to their nature." The heart, or the Will, "always follows the last dictates of the Understanding," he explained in the language of conventional faculty psychology. Inasmuch as "the Understanding is the guide of the Will" and inasmuch as "the Will always follows its direction," "men would offer violence to their nature, if they should do otherwise" than to embrace what their Understanding directs. Conversely, however, the real substance of his thought stridently underscored the merciless and irrational character of God's justice and the inadequacy of human knowledge or reason to accomplish the "outward call."

In discussing the ministerial guidance necessary to direct a sinner through the stages of preparation, Stoddard prepared the way for the later vituperative assaults upon "reasonable" ministers. Moral and learned preachers who possess "only the common work of the spirit" are "very unfit to judge the state of other men" and cannot "speak exactly and experimentally to such things as souls want instruction in." "If the blind lead the blind," he argued, "both shall fall into the ditch." Despite the

Puritan tradition of great respect for education and despite the learned Increase Mather's pronouncement that broad knowledge, especially of literature, was essential to a minister, Stoddard ridiculed the capacity of ministerial erudition, and of learning in general, to promote preparation.

Although not explicitly stated, the essence of Stoddard's description of "conviction" and "humiliation" as stages of preparation was that in reality the two were indistinguishable, with "conviction" ultimately being dependent upon the emotional values of "humiliation." Natural reason may be useful, he admitted, to "work some conviction of this truth, and discover so much of it that a man may come to look upon it [as] very rational and probable." Nevertheless, "this perswasion is not sufficient to encourage a soul to venture himself on Jesus Christ." "Before they will be convinced of the preciousness of Christ," he explained, "men must be led into the understanding of the badness of their hearts . . . till driven out of themselves. Men must feel themselves dead in sin, in order to their believing. . . . Men must see themselves poor & miserable, wretched & blind & naked, before they receive that counsel of buying of Christ gold tried in the fire and white raiment." Usually man passes slowly through preparatory "conviction"-"humiliation" and is not ready for conversion until he lies helpless at the feet of Christ, "accepts his fitness to be damned," and acquieses in God's sending him to hell for "His own glory" if He should so please.

Of his numerous tracts, possibly the one which was most influential in preparing the way for the rhetoric of emotion was his *A Guide to Christ*, a manual containing explicit "DIRECTIONS HOW TO GUIDE SOULS THROUGH THE WORK OF CONVERSION." In this volume he effectually inverted the traditional tenets of Puritan sermonology, his divorcement from reasoned argumentation being epitomized by this cardinal principle: "God leads men through the whole work of preparation partly by *fear,* and partly by *hope.*" In *A Guide to Christ*, there is no echo of the Puritan-Aristotelian concepts that the listener is a reasonable, reasoning man—a judge—and that emotions, being antagonistic to the reasoning process, should be restricted to a subsidiary function. *The hub of the entire dis-*

cussion of the issue of emotion in religion may be this implicit inversion of Stoddard's: in place of the judgments of Aristotle that in themselves the emotions carried no power to convince and that properly they served only to intensify previously established conviction, Stoddard substituted the primacy of emotions both in initiating the process of persuasion and in compelling ideational acceptance.[73]

Because of the weaknesses and propensities of natural man, so Stoddard believed, man's intellection had to be approached through his emotions. "Fear and dread of hell," he insisted, "make men do what they do in religion." Although at times he expressed skepticism of the value, or the propriety, of appealing to fear, his standard theme was that "there is that principle in every man by nature that carries him out necessarily to seek his own happiness" and "fear of damnation" directs him "unto this way as the safest." "Men cannot exercise faith till the heart be prepared by a *sense of danger.*" The initial propulsion "that sets them going is *terror;* fear makes them reform and pray; they are scared into religion." "God's way is to bless suitable means," he pointed out. "He don't bless healing plaisters to eat away proud flesh," or "rhetorical strains of speech" which "may tickle the fancies of men and scratch itching ears." To become "sensible of their danger . . . men need to be terrified and have the arrows of the Almighty in them." Therefore, "ministers should be sons of thunder" and should *"preach in such a manner as is most proper to take with the conscience."* In his own preaching, Stoddard's appeals to fear fell short of the dramatic horrification employed later by Gilbert Tennent, James Davenport, and, upon occasion, by Edwards. Nevertheless, in their stridency his evocations exceeded anything preached in New England prior to his death in 1729.

Despite his tenet that if men "be but thorowly scared, they will be brought to an universal reformation," Stoddard advised ministers to maintain a balance between fear and hope in guiding seekers through the stage of preparation: "If they run into either extream, to have fear without hope, or hope without fear, they are like a ship that goes beside the channel, and is in danger to be broken to pieces; a mixture of fear and hope makes

men diligent." Once the seeker became thoroughly frightened concerning his state of salvation, encouragement should be extended. Of tremendous significance to later evangelic preaching and in apparent contradiction to the absolutist elements of his theology, Stoddard opened wide the door to conversion: as a "universal offer without an exception," God invites all sinners "to eternal life on condition of one act of believing." Inasmuch as "we are *invited* to come to Him for help . . . it is not to be thought that God would lovingly and with a great deal of tenderness perswade men to set their feet in slippery places and build their hopes upon a sandy foundation." "It must needs be a safe thing to trust in Christ." "Besides, there is an absolute connexion between faith & salvation," he asserted, "if you believe in Christ that will be a sure sign of election. . . . [You] will not be rejected if you come." By accepting Christ, so Stoddard assuaged, the seeker would achieve safety from hell, freedom from fear, and the peaceful happiness of joining "the glorious company in heaven."

Stoddard's description of the act of conversion itself, which for elected persons followed the stage of preparation, was important to the emotional preaching of the later revivalists, in at least four ways. First, conversion was sudden. Although "men are generally a long time . . . labouring to get an interest in Christ," conversion is "wrought in the twinkling of an eye" when "God breaks out of the clouds, and makes a discovery of His own glory to the soul." Since "the least degree of faith makes a man a convert," the "inward call" might occur unexpectedly at any moment, by "the hearing of one passage in a sermon, by the remembering of one Scripture."

Second, although upon occasion Stoddard set forth various observable signs of election, his basic concept was that "grace is known only by intuition," by a state of feeling or spiritual tonus.

Third, conversion produced an "exceedingly remarkable," "wonderfully sharp" change in the individual. Admittedly, at times Stoddard stated conversely that "the inward call is no distinct call": its function "is only to *clear up* the outward call" which "gives men their *warrant* to believe." Nevertheless, his standard theme was much more evocative, suggesting the emo-

tional preachments of Whitefield, Edwards, and Tennent: "Conversion is the greatest change that man undergoes in this world." It is that ecstatic "supernatural" change "from darkness to light, from death to life, from the borders of despair to a spirit of faith in Christ," which "makes men to aim at the glory of God, and to hate everything in the world in comparison of God and Christ."

Fourth, the act of conversion was overwhelming and irresistible. Because "it is for want of conviction and understanding that men do reject Christ," and because the Will is a "blind faculty," "God gains the Will by convincing the mind." When God communicates to the individual that he is chosen, He illuminates his Understanding with "such a supernatural light" that man "is under constraints to come to Christ" and "all the wit in hell can't perswade him to stay away." Upon receiving the "saving light," the convertee is "delivered from the kingdom of darkness" and for the first time is able "to discern the glory of Christ" and "the mysteries of the Gospel." *Of incalculable significance to the unification of man and the pervasion of the emotions,* Stoddard effectually reduced all faculties to a common denominator: "the Understanding and Will in man being faculties of the same soul & really one and the same thing, the same act of God upon the soul that puts light into the Understanding does also suitably incline the Will . . . we believe and love, believe and repent, believe and fear, believe and submit, believe and so venture on Christ."

The Culmination: Jonathan Edwards. In 1726 the Reverend Solomon Stoddard invited his grandson Jonathan Edwards (1703–58), then a Tutor at Yale College, to serve as his associate and eventual successor.[74] Although Northampton was noted for its history of revivals, to Edwards the community was afflicted by an "extraordinary *dulness* in religion" and by a *"licentiousness"* which "greatly prevailed among the *youth* of the town." [75] After Stoddard's death, Edwards exploited the prestige and the pulpit of his grandfather to stir his grandfather's people to emotional outpourings in 1734–35. Greater than any of Stoddard's freshlets, Edwards's revival became a significant social force, partly because of the extensive publicity afforded by his ac-

count of the affair, published in Boston in 1737; *A Faithful Narrative of the Surprising Work of God in the Conversion of Many Hundred Souls in Northampton and the Neighboring Towns and Villages.* Receiving almost instantaneous success, the *Narrative*, in its several editions and numerous printings, introduced much of New England, as well as substantial numbers of readers in England, Scotland, and Europe, to the hysterical obsessions of Abigail Hutchinson and little Phoebe Bartlett, four years old. By popularizing emotionalism as an appropriate response to divine inspiration, the *Narrative* helped prepare the way for the Great Awakening and encouraged the mode of sensationalism which still remains a characteristic of revivals. The excitement of the Northampton revival mounted until the suicide of Edwards's obsessed uncle Joseph Hawley in May 1735 damped the ecstasies and brought a rapid return to convention. Edwards's efforts during the next five years to rekindle the spirit were of major consequence in agitating into being the wildfire of the Great Awakening. In this effort and throughout the Awakening and its aftermath, the evocative thrust of his sermons and lectures represented oblique extensions of his private thoughts concerning the unity of man and the pervasion of the emotions.[76]

In addition to being Colonial America's foremost philosopher and theologian, Edwards was the first to apply the principles of modern psychology and science to homiletics. Out of his preaching and writings emerge an approachment to man as a unitary being in whom the emotions are primary and pervasive.[77] To a large extent his thinking grew out of external constraints, such as the backlash of resistance to the rationalism of the enlightenment, the Puritan inheritance, the new scientific method, and the wide-ranging innovations of thought and practice initiated by transitional figures like Cotton Mather and Solomon Stoddard. Nevertheless, Edwards was a uniquely creative and constructive thinker. In his private notebooks and obliquely in his preaching, Edwards transformed the system of metaphysics, theology, and rhetoric which had given coherence to the New England experiment. *Perhaps the essence of the Edwardian thought and the key to the difference between*

Edwards—along with the evangelical Calvinists who followed him—and the traditional Puritan thought is that Edwards changed the focus from divine truth to divine beauty. Because of this the emergent evangelical Calvinism became committed to a new strain of emotional religion and, thereby, the stream of history was altered. As the pivotal figure in the issue of emotion in religion, Edwards merits close attention.

First, despite the hazards which attend the distillation of a complex system of thought, perhaps it can be said that Edwards's theories concerning the role of emotion in religion stem from his adaptations of Calvinism, as represented in the following summary. Because God viewed all men—living, dead, and yet-to-be-born—as a single, sustained entity, He imputed Adam's sin to the entire family of man. Thus the "supernatural" identification and affinity with God, which Adam had originally possessed, had been abrogated for him and all of his descendants, with the exception of a chosen few. Certain persons, including individuals yet unborn, had been selected by God to retain the capacity for Adam's original insightful response to His beauty and His love and to the rightness and magnificence of His design—without regard for their own self-interest. In essence, this "supernatural" spiritual quality was an irresistible "inclination" or "predisposition" which compelled the elected to respond in harmony with the divine disposition. Because God operated within His fixed system of stimulus-response, cause-effect, propulsion-resistance, and because God Himself was the efficient cause of all spiritual effects, the elect were brought to the actualization of their divine "predisposition" by means of a kind of spiritual evolution or training, utilizing sense experiences. Since all impressions came to man through his senses, it was by means of sense experiences that the elected person's Will became conditioned and habituated to respond in affinity with the divine Will. The awareness that one possessed this affinity—in other words, the experiencing of conversion—came suddenly to the chosen as a flash of insight, producing a joyous psychic shock. Thus, regeneration involved both the "idea" which the elected person possessed of the divine loveliness and the "delight" which flooded his being upon his apprehension of

that "idea." Those, of course, who did not possess the divinely given capacity for affinity could acquire only a spurious, speculative understandings—never the inspired, insightful relationship.

Second, Edwards necessarily accompanied his adaptations of Calvin's theology with radical revisions concerning Calvin's scholastic conceptions of the nature of man and concerning the traditional Puritan emphasis upon the intellect. Despite the considerable ambiguity which exists in his writings, his ultimate intent seems apparent. Instead of the compartmentalization of man and the primacy of the intellect, Edwards based his homiletic theories upon an approachment to the unification of man and the pervasion of the emotions. Thus, he rejected the concept of the mind as a unitive circuit, composed of separate faculties which operated sequentially in the performance of their assigned functions. In Edwards's view, man approached being a unified organism which responded instantly to spiritual stimulus, in accordance with its predetermined "inclination." Although he accepted Calvin's conception that the Understanding and the Will constituted the two basic faculties of the mind, the effect of his physics was to telescope the two into a single faculty, the "inclination." Calling this "inclination" the Will, Edwards considered it to be a response of movement toward the spiritual stimulus.

Because the "inclination" was the whole man responding or "choosing," and because the "inclination" was a habituated response developed as a result of experience acquired through the senses, no clearly independent role existed for the scholastic faculty of the Understanding. Like Calvin, Edwards wrote—sometimes at least—of the Understanding as being the "perceiving" faculty and of the Will as being the "choosing" faculty.[78] Unlike Calvin's conception, however, in Edwards's thought the Understanding did not effectually interpose a temporal and judicial barrier between stimulus and choice. Inasmuch as faith was the process of man choosing—choosing instantly and automatically because of his basic predisposition—the Understanding was minimized as a control station passing suspensive judgment on the truth and righteousness of a matter. This does not

mean, of course, that Edwards ignored intellection but that the ultimate effect of his thinking was to fuse the Understanding in a supportive relationship with the Will. This "union" he was sometimes inclined to call the "heart." In his *Religious Affections,* he defined "the nature of spiritual understanding, as consisting most essentially in a divine supernatural sense and relish of the heart." Such a "relish," he insisted, did not arise from "a train of reasoning." Although logic enables one to recognize truth, it cannot provide one with the apperception of beauty and excellence.[79]

Retaining essentially the scholastic concept of the Will as the act of choosing, Edwards made this action the basic function of the mind. In his thinking, the Will did not pass directives to the emotions, impounding them or freeing them to act under the continued supervision of the higher faculties. Although he was not completely consistent on this point, the main thrust of Edwards's system was to regard the Affections as an intrinsic part of the Will. Man's Will was his motion to respond, his choosing of response to stimulus, his predisposed reaction or conditioned consent to external reality. Thus, the reception of a "new simple idea" was accompanied by "a sense of the heart" whose unique emotional apperception of the divine beauty necessarily resulted in a harmonious response to the "idea." Thus, "the spirit of God is given to the true saints to dwell in them . . . as being there so united to the faculties of the soul, that"— so Edwards expressed it in his *Religious Affections*—it influences "their hearts, as a principle of new nature, or as a divine supernatural spring of life and action." [80] In spiritual matters, such a movement of response was primarily an emotional involvement, utterly unachievable through the agency of reason alone. Therefore, the Affections could not be turned on, or turned off, or closely regulated as to the intensity or volume of flow—like wine from a spigot. Since man was more feeling than intellection, since the Will was man willing or choosing according to his "predisposition," and since the act of willing was man responding to the radiant beauty, righteousness, and love communicated by God, the nature of elected man and the nature of faith compelled him to respond affectionately to religious stimuli.

Third, Edwards's concepts of the nature of man caused him to reject the morphology of conversion which has been evolved by the framers of the covenant of grace and which had been applied by Thomas Hooker and Thomas Shepard and the generality of their descendants. Edwards's theories concerning the process of preparation represented the culmination of the transitional teachings of innovators such as Cotton Mather and, especially, Solomon Stoddard. As noted earlier in this discussion, Stoddard suggested that in spiritual matters the Understanding and the Will were "really one and the same thing" and that "the same act of God upon the soul that puts light into the Understanding, doth also suitably incline the Will." A concomitant of Stoddard's tendency to unify the nature of man was his reduction of the steps in preparation to two, "conviction" and "humiliation," and his further inclination to merge the two, making "conviction" ultimately dependent upon the emotional properties of "humiliation." Thus, in effect Stoddard accepted the primacy of the Affections in spiritual persuasion. In addition, Stoddard appears to have sponsored the role of the emotions in initiating and in determining the ideational conviction of the Understanding. Even more than this, Stoddard considered that preparation for conversion customarily required a considerable period of earnest striving which, when successful, resulted in a sudden, emotionally overwhelming "supernatural light." Although undoubtedly influenced by such teachings of his grandfather, Edwards was genuinely creative in unifying the process of conversion according to the laws of stimulus-response. In Edwards's system, preparation was not a route divided into sequential stages of development, corresponding roughly to the sequence of the faculties. It was a process of continued sense experiences by which God enabled the Will of the elect to become more responsive to the emanations of the divine Will. When true atunement to God's disposition was achieved, the recognition of this spiritual conversion would come as an instantaneous flash of joyous insight.

Fourth, Edwards exceeded both Cotton Mather and Stoddard in diminishing the importance of rational judgment as an end of the seeker in his listening to sermons and religious

lectures. Throughout his ministry, Stoddard had maintained the semblance of orthodoxy by giving redundant, if ambiguous, lip service to the concept of faith as a "rational understanding action." Both Stoddard and Mather, however, had considered "rational understanding action" to be the intuitive judgment of the ordinary man arrived at automatically and instaneously. Both Stoddard and Mather believed that the unconscious application of common sense provided a more accurate spiritual wisdom than did the ratiocination of the scholar schooled in formal logic. Edwards carried this line of thinking to its ultimate conclusion, identifying the ends of the listener with the pervasion of the emotions. The chief purpose in attending to sermons, according to Edwards, was to attain saving faith, that is, to develop the basically emotional "predisposition" of the Will which would enable the elect to respond harmoniously to the beautiful, lovely, and righteous disposition of God.

Fifth, more than Cotton Mather, more even than Stoddard, Edwards negated the Ciceronian duties of the speaker which, in effect, had been generally followed as sequential steps in the sermons of the founders: to teach, to win over the listeners, and to excite the emotions. Instead of consisting of separate duties, Edwards's sermonic persuasion tended toward being unitary in its rhetorical functions and its exhortative effect. Successful spiritual evocation was comprised of sensible stimuli which would help to condition the Will toward a more affectionate responsiveness to God's Will. In order to facilitate the habituation of the Will, the sermon not only had to evoke emotional response but also had to "win over the listener" by the reasonableness of the communication. By this process of conditioning the Will, the speaker was also simultaneously accomplishing the duty of teaching.

Sixth, Edwards's theory and practice of homiletics brought a new vitality to the Puritan sermon. On the one hand, he customarily employed the traditional format: he applied the orthodox skeletal structure, with the parts (Text, Doctrine, Reasons, Application) being subject to an endless series of divisions and subdivisions, each fragment being identified as to its position and relevance; he spoke deliberately with quiet intensity and

2. *Paradigm suggesting roughly Edwards's theories concerning rhetoric, the unity of man, and the pervasion of the emotions.*

PARTS OF SERMON	DUTIES OF PREACHER	ENDS OF LISTENER	FACULTIES OF MAN	MORPHOLOGY OF CONVERSION
The traditional skeletal structure of the sermon was retained, with the function of the parts tending to be modified toward unitary exhortation.	To provide sense experiences which would assist in properly conditioning the Will of the elect.	To habituate one's Will in accordance with the emanation of God's Will. Instead of seeking a rational acceptance of, and obedience to, divine truth, one should be primarily concerned with seeking atunement to God's beauty, loveliness, and excellence.	The two chief faculties, Will and Understanding, seem to be coalesced into one: the Will. Supplemented by the Understanding and virtually equated with the Affections, the Will was man himself responding in accordance with his spiritual predisposition.	The accretion of sensible experiences conditions and habituates the Will of the elect to respond according to the divine Will, resulting in a sudden, joyously insightful awareness of conversion.

impeccable, inexorable logic. On the other hand, he infused the traditional format with the thrusting power of a new rhetoric. Rather than a compartmentalized address to the seriate faculties, Edwards's sermons tended toward being unitary evocations. Applying the language of sensational psychology, Edwards brought into marvelously effective focus the unity, spontaneity, and emotional pervasiveness which he thought characterized

the ends of the listener, the nature of man, and the nature of the conversion process.

The Great Awakening
Emotions in Crisis and Conflict

The Protasis of the Great Awakening. For thirty-four years (1736–70), the Anglican evangelist George Whitefield sought converts in England, Scotland, Wales, Gibraltar, Bermuda, and in Colonial America, which he visited seven times.[81] The out-of-doors was often his chapel; and a mound, tree stump, hogshead, or horse's back served frequently as his pulpit. In the course of his itinerant wanderings, by his own estimate he delivered about eighteen thousand sermons to more than ten million auditors. For a generation, according to Clinton Rossiter, he was "the best known man in Colonial America."[82]

Early in 1739 stories began to appear with increasing frequency in the New England papers concerning the size of Whitefield's English audiences, the amount of his collections, and the innovation of his preaching in the streets and fields on weekdays. So numerous and so acclamatory were the reports that, as stated in the *Boston Evening-Post*, the minds of the people became "greatly prepossessed" in his favor as a *"wonder of piety, a man of God, so as no one was like him."*[83] On September 14, 1740, when he stepped ashore at Newport, he was received as *"an angel of God . . . as the apostle St. Paul was received by the churches in Galatia,"* so the Reverend Benjamin Colman later recorded.[84] During his seven-week tour of New England, the immediate and continuing stir created by his two sermons daily and his almost constant exhortations in the streets and private homes agitated into motion and shaped the expression of previously prepared forces of revivalism.

After three triumphal days in Newport, Whitefield whirled through a ten-day stay in Boston.[85] As described by the hostile Timothy Cutler, "When Mr. Whitefield first arrived here, the whole town was alarm'd . . . immediately the bells rung, and all hands went to lecture, and this show kept on all the whole

time he was here. The town was ever alarm'd, the streets filled with people, with coaches & chaises, all for the benefit of that holy man." [86] So great became the popular approbation of the young minister that, as reported by the *Boston Evening-Post*, to speak critically of him was considered to be almost synonymous with committing a *"sin against the Holy Ghost."* [87] Interrupting his preaching to the crowded auditories of Boston, for a week Whitefield itinerated along the coast, preaching sixteen times at places like Marblehead, Salem, Maulden, Ipswich, Newbury, Hampton, Portsmouth, and York. Returning to Boston, Whitefield found that the crowds that followed him from meetinghouse to meetinghouse seemed even larger than before. So intense grew the excitement that on Sunday, October 12, the final day in Boston, ferryboats began plying the Charles early in the morning, and unprecedented numbers of persons afoot, on horseback, and in wagons, crossed over the neck from the mainland. By late afternoon a vast audience of perhaps twenty thousand persons had gathered on the Commons to await his benediction. [88] The next morning, accompanied by a party of admirers, Whitefield began his journey toward the west.

After preaching at small towns along the way, on Friday afternoon he arrived in Northampton. Three years later, Jonathan Edwards recalled that the congregation had been "extraordinarily melted" by each of the Englishman's four sermons, "almost the whole assembly being in tears for a great part of sermon time." [89] Late Sunday evening Whitefield set out southward and, after electrifying a succession of audiences from Westfield to Stamford, on the afternoon of October 29th he crossed from Connecticut into the colony of New York. [90]

By his perigrination, Whitefield had brought the Protasis of the Awakening to thousands of New Englanders who would not otherwise have been reached. His spectacular method of moving about constantly from place to place, frequently in the company of numerous horsemen, had provided exciting pageantry and a valuable analogy to Christ and his prophets. With criers and newspaper bulletins preceding him, he attracted crowds of almost unbelievable size whenever he reined in his

lished the archtype of emotionalism and of ministerial practice which shaped the Epitasis and made inevitable the Catastrophe of the Great Awakening.

The Epitasis and Catastrophe of the Great Awakening. Following the departure of Whitefield, the revival was pushed to even greater heights of emotionalism by Gilbert Tennent, Jonathan Edwards, James Davenport, and other evangelists. At the invitation of revivalists in New England, the strident Tennent, a dominant member of the famed family which had helped agitate the Awakening in the Middle Colonies, arrived in Boston in mid-December, 1740. For three months he preached to increasingly distraught audiences a Calvinism more terrifying than that of Whitefield. According to the thoroughly prejudiced Timothy Cutler, Tennent proved himself to be a "monster! impudent & noisy" who "told them all they were *damn'd, damn'd, damn'd!* This charm'd them! And in the dreadfullest winter that I ever saw, people wallowed in the snow night & day for the benefit of his beastly brayings." [93]

Like many other ministers that winter the dignified Edwards mounted his horse to spend months preaching in pulpits other than his own. In April he delivered "Future Punishment," which he later considered to be his most effective horrific sermon (Reading Number One). Perhaps the high point of the Awakening was reached in his "Sinners in the Hands of an Angry God," which he preached at Enfield, Connecticut, July 8, 1741. [94] Very probably the most famous discourse in American homiletics, this sermon unfortunately has served to stereotype Edwards as a preacher of terror, a role which he assumed only upon occasion—and that rarely after Enfield. It has also served to stereotype revival sermons as terroristic, whereas the most consistent emphasis of such sermons was placed upon the sublime emotions attending conversion. Furthermore, the reputation of the Enfield sermon as the personification of horror exaggerates its original impact.

As measured by the intensity of the emotional response, the preaching of Edwards and Tennent may have been less productive than that of James Davenport. Unfortunately for

the revival, during his New England tour Whitefield had praised highly the ministrations of psychologically unstable Davenport. In 1741 and 1742, Davenport made repeated forays into New England from his pulpit at Southold, Long Island. Caught up in the emotionalism of his own preaching, Davenport apparently vastly exceeded the prototypal emotionalism of Whitefield. He damned individual ministers by name, declaring that drinking rat poison was a safer procedure than listening to the preaching of godless men who were seducing the innocent into hell. Parties of disciples followed him about, singing and chanting passages of Scripture. Brawls sometimes accompanied his field preaching. Not infrequently, according to newspaper reports, at night services in meetinghouses lighted by a few weirdly burning tapers entire congregations succumbed to Davenport's hypnotic spell.[95]

Under Whitefield's preaching only mild tendencies toward uninhibited physical behavior had been evident, but under the less restrained preaching of some of his emulators, the pure waters of pious feeling became increasingly sullied by emotional extravagance. Numerous ministers and lay exhorters moved about the provinces, sometimes invading church services to denounce the minister as unconverted. Some churches were split into revivalistic and conservative wings, and a number of clergymen who failed to preach demonstratively were dismissed.[96] By the middle of 1742, the Awakening had lost much of its momentum as a movement, and it rather quickly disintegrated into abrasive confusion and sporatic localized outbursts of religious fervor.

The downward spiral of the revival can be quickly illustrated. In May of 1742, the General Assembly of Connecticut prohibited ministers from preaching in pastorates other than their own without the consent of the clergyman involved.[97] Earlier the same year, in a contrite letter Gilbert Tennent apologized for his own censorious *"excessive heat of temper"* and condemned "extraordinary things" in Davenport's conduct as being unscriptural and schismatic.[98] More embarrassing to the Awakening than the printing of Tennet's "apology" in the newspapers of Boston and the Middle Colonies, were the trials and

confessions of Davenport himself. In June of 1742, the Connecticut Assembly convicted Davenport of being a public menace and banished him from the colony.[99] Two months later, after Davenport invaded Massachusetts, he was arrested, pronounced insane, and deported to his New York home.[100] Disturbed by Davenport's irrationalism, fourteen ministers in the Boston–Charleston area issued to the newspapers a declaration against him,[101] and the prominent minister of the First Church of Boston, Charles Chauncy (1705–87), preached and published the widely-read *Enthusiasm Described and Caution'd Against. . . . With a Letter to the Reverend Mr. James Davenport* (Reading Number Three).

Early in March, 1743, the separatists of New London, Connecticut, invited Davenport to help them organize their new church. As part of the procedure of gathering the church, Davenport urged the people to collect their idolatrous possessions, such as wigs, gowns, hoods, cloaks, rings, necklaces, and books and sermons written by Increase Mather, Benjamin Colman, Charles Chauncy, and other ministers. On a Sabbath afternoon, he directed the burning of these articles upon the town wharf. As the fire ate into the pile, he led the participants in chanting incantations and singing "Glory to God" and "Hallelujah." [102] In the attempt to control such excesses as well as the schismatic tendencies of the New Lights, the Connecticut Assembly revoked the toleration act of 1708 and prohibited the formation of new churches without the prior approval of the legislature.

Partly as a result of the publicity given to the New London episode, in May of 1743 a convention of Massachusetts ministers published a testimony against the Awakening, attributing its emotional manifestations more to the devil than to God.[103] Two months later, the lines between the New Lights and the Old Lights were clearly drawn when an assembly of revivalistic ministers meeting in Boston issued a counter declaration, defending the Awakening as a *"happy and remarkable revival of religion in many parts of this land, thro' an uncommon divine influence*; after a long time of great decay and deadness." Although it admitted that many disorders were disturbing the

churches of New England, the testimony vindicated both the emotional substance of evangelistic sermons and the emotional response of earnest seekers: "No; we never so much as call'd these bodily seizures, *convictions;* or spake of them as the *immediate* work of the Holy Spirit. Yet we do not think them inconsistent with a work of GOD upon the soul at that very time; but judge that those inward impressions which come from the spirit of GOD, those terrors and consolations of which He is the author, may, according to the natural frame and constitution which some persons are of, occasion such bodily effects.—And therefore that these extraordinary outward symptoms, are not an argument that the work is delusive, or from the influence and agency of the evil spirit." [104] Although the ministers and the people remained sharply divided among themselves concerning the merits of the revival, the cloak of peace gradually settled upon New England. In the comparatively mellow mood of 1744, the Davenport era came to an anticlimactic end when he penned a public letter during the summer, apologizing for his "misguided zeal" and "*false spirit.*" [105]

A critically important aspect of the issue of emotion in religion, which was fissuring the New England society, was the continuing "debate" between Jonathan Edwards and Charles Chauncy. On September 10, 1741, Edwards delivered a lecture at Yale College which he amplified and published later that year as *The Distinguishing Marks of a Work of the Spirit of God* (Reading Number Two). A forceful attempt to maintain the momentum of the Awakening, the work was secondarily a warning to the revivalists and a defense of emotions. Recognizing that some extravagances were accompanying the Awakening, he explained that overpowering physical manifestations were inevitable because the human system was too frail to withstand spiritual shocks. Candidly he warned, however, that emotional behavior might also be caused by overheated imaginations. Also, he urged New Lights to be less censorious and to complain less of persecution "like swine, that are apt to scream aloud when they are touch'd." A detailed refutation of Edwards's work, commonly—though perhaps inaccurately—thought to have been written by Chauncy, was published in 1743: *The Late*

Religious Commotions in New England Considered. Systematically relentless in his attack, the author of *Religious Commotions* went to the extreme of employing his preface to refute the preface by William Cooper which introduced Edwards's *The Distinguishing Marks.*

Appearing too late in 1742 to be noticed by the *Religious Commotions,* Edwards's second publication in the "debate" was his *Some Thoughts Concerning the Present Revival of Religion,* a labored analysis and defense of emotions and a charge to the New Lights to ferret the true from the fraudulent emotions. The next year Chauncy published his *Seasonable Thoughts,* probably the most influential writing of the Awakening. Adroitly adapted to refute point by point Edwards's *Some Thoughts,* Chauncy's extended volume sought to prove that the Awakening was not divinely motivated. His most compelling rhetorical strategy was to relate numerous examples of riotous disorders produced in New England as a concomitant of the revival. He carefully documented these specific instances as being based upon interviews which he had conducted throughout the provinces or upon newspaper accounts. The culmination of this "debate" came well after the demise of the Awakening when Edwards published his *Religious Affections* in 1746. Growing out of a series of sermons preached in the winter of 1742–43, the *Religious Affections* is possibly the most persuasive defense and the most searching and provocative analysis of emotion in religion ever published (the first lecture in this series is reprinted here as Reading Number Four).

Well before the publication of Edwards's *Religious Affections,* however, during the relative quiet of the fall of 1744, George Whitefield returned to New England. Although during his absence of nearly four years he had helped agitate a great revival in England, Wales, and Scotland, and although his preaching once more attracted huge throngs, there was no suggestion of a mass movement. Nevertheless, to the conservatives who feared a return to emotionalism, the evangelist's return was a bugle call to action. As a consequent, the Old Lights hurried to the presses pamphlet after pamphlet designed to destroy Whitefield's influence and the revival impulse. The New

Lights counterattacked, and a Paper War was on. Even some laymen announced positions or condemned the ministers for their contentiousness.[106] Individual ministers as well as associations of ministers published testimonies in which they explained their reasons for offering [107] or refusing to offer [108] their pulpits to Whitefield. Both Harvard [109] and Yale [110] issued lengthy manifestoes against the evangelist. Whitefield and his defenders were so rudely treated by various publications, frequently anonymous, that some New Lights were probably intimidated into remaining silent. Thomas Foxcroft's *An Apology* and William Hobby's *An Inquiry*, two of the most important defenses of the evangelist, brought a series of rebukes. Hobby, in particular, was maligned and insulted. It is difficult to realize how vituperatively irrational were the writings of some of the conservative ministers unless one reads such imprints as *A Twig of Birch for Billy's Breech; A Letter to the Reverend Mr. William Hobby* by Nathanael Henchman; and *Pride Humbled, or Mr. Hobby Chastised* by Richard Pateshall.[111] By the middle of 1745 it became obvious that there would be no rebirth of religious hysteria, and by the spring of 1746 the Paper War gradually wore itself out.

Lengthening Shadows: The Psychic and Social Inheritance of the Great Awakening. Arising from great pressures hidden deep beneath the Puritan psyche, the Awakening sent seismic shock waves throughout New England society, altering the substance and expression of events many years yet in the unfolding.

Among the most important influences of the Great Awakening, in a wide variety of ways it encouraged a development of the democratic sentiment. Although it was not a class manifestation and although its immediate effect seemed to be a reduction in status antagonisms, the revival drew the greater bulk and the more sustained intensity of its support from persons of modest social, economic, and educational attainments. The revival stripped the monopoly of public speaking from the small minority of educated men and gave voice and a ready audience to any one who wished to step out of his previous role of silent acqui-

escence. Leveling implications existed in Tennent's assertions that a direct correlation existed between increased wealth and increased wickedness and in Whitefield's teachings that the rich were as deeply tainted with Adam's sin as the poorest and most illiterate persons, that the wealthy and the distinguished rarely reached heaven, and that the Lord had special affection for the poor. Out of the upsetting of the old decorum there emerged new religious and social patterns, which assigned to the common man a somewhat greater share in the shaping of church affairs and which eventually proved conducive to religious liberty and to the disestablishment of religion. As Alice Baldwin has pointed out in *The New England Clergy and the American Revolution*, the Awakening "had stimulated men to new and lively thinking in religious and civil affairs. It had brought with it much intolerance, yet out of it had grown a passionate conviction in man's right to freedom of conscience and a struggle, partially successful, to obtain it." [112] Especially in Connecticut, the abrasive conflict between New Lights and Old Lights gradually resolved itself in the consciousness that conflicting interests could coexist peacefully in a democratic society. As new pressures for freedom from civil and ecclesiastical restraint arose out of the revival, the American colonists were pushed toward new levels of democracy. Furthermore, as the first mass movement which tended to draw the colonies together in a common bond, the Awakening offered a new emotional identification, a democratic unification, and an inclination toward intercolonial unity transcending sectionalism and denominationalism.

The Awakening accelerated the growth of various evangelical denominations, the multiplicity and diversity of which aided in the development of the democratic spirit. In attending to the needs of the westward moving pioneers, staid, well-educated, conservative ministers could not compete successfully with the unlettered, zealous circuit riders and exhorters. Even before 1741, New Side Presbyterian ministers entered the backcountry of Pennsylvania, Virginia, and North Carolina, which was filling up with Scotch-Irish and German immigrants. Early in 1743, a small revival was agitated into life in Hanover County, Virginia, and, encouraged by New Side evangelists summoned from the Middle Colonies, a genuine awakening gradually

spread to other Virginia counties and to North Carolina. During the ensuing years, New Side Presbyterian ministers accompanied the tide of the Scotch-Irish across the Shennandoah Valley and the Blue Ridge Mountains. Although the Baptists in New England and the Middle Colonies may have received little immediate benefit from the Awakening, during the next generation they profited enormously. The handful of Baptist churches in New England at the time of the revival multiplied so rapidly that before the end of the century there were perhaps three hundred and twenty-five such churches, and, just as important, the dominant Arminian cast of the New England Baptists became reshaped in the model of evangelical Calvinism. In 1755, two Connecticut Baptists, who had been converted previously by Whitefield, settled at Sandy Creek, North Carolina, and soon stimulated a religious movement which spread throughout much of North Carolina and Virginia. By the beginning of the Revolutionary War there were several thousand Baptists in the two colonies. When the pioneers entered the valleys of Kentucky, Tennessee, and Ohio, they were accompanied by Baptist preachers who taught the inward experiencing of Christ in regeneration. With the help of other evangelical denominations, the Baptists were to set in motion successions of revivals in the land west of the Alleghenies. Near the close of the century the Methodists, who followed the evangelistic spirit of Whitefield and the Wesleys, became a powerful factor in the religious, and hence social, life of the frontier.

Thus, from the Awakening a recurrent revival tempo flowed into the mainstream of the emerging American society. The pattern of religious emotionalism established during Jonathan Edwards's Northampton revival, and given definite form by the Great Awakening, furnished the prototype for the successive revivals: a simple, emotional plea for personal salvation forcefully delivered by dynamic preachers. Such revivals, of course, shared directly in shaping the social and intellectual character of the nation. In their encouragement of democratic optimism, the "New School" awakenings of Charles G. Finney, for instance, contributed to the explosive potential of the Jacksonian revolution.

Also, out of the Great Awakening there emerged a greater

sense of empathy for the unfortunates of society. Whitefield's
dislike of slavery, his highly successful solicitation of financial
support for his Bethesda orphanage, as well as the concern of
numerous revivalists for Indian missions, all tended to be re-
flected in a more sensitive humanitarianism.

The consequence of the Awakening which is of central
significance to this volume is the resultant intellectual division
of society. From the earliest days of New England a hairline
fissure had been evident to the discerning eye: the issue of emotion in religion and the subsidiary issue of the nature of man had
always been potentially divisive. During the epitasis and catastrophe of the Awakening the fissure between piety and reason
had deepened and widened until society became basically disjoined into revivalists and antirevivalists, with no really tenable
mid-position remaining for the adherents of the old covenant
theology or for those moderates who wished to mediate or ignore the division.

In the following decades both the revivalists and the antirevivalists sustained their departure from the old logic, physics,
and rhetoric, with the revivalists retaining the rhetoric of the
Affections and the antirevivalists the rhetoric of the Understanding.

The revivalists continued to focus their sermons, and their
response to sermons, upon the emotions. They continued to
view the nature of man as representing an approachment to a
unified being, with reason clearly subordinated to emotion.
They continued to employ the emotions as a primary means to
effect belief, minimizing the contributory role of reason. They
continued to regard "conviction" and "humiliation" as unnecessary preliminaries to the New Birth, which was a joyous, spontaneous response of the creature to the irresistible experiencing
of the Holy Spirit. It was many years before the Edwardian
view of man began to dim, and mistaken disciples distorted it
into rigid, unattractive lines. Just as they were opposed to the
fragmentation of man into parts, or faculties, each of which being designed to perform a specific task, so were the revivalists
opposed to the functional fragmentation of the sermon into the
traditional specialized compartments: Text, Doctrine, Reasons,

and Uses. The sermon, so they thought, should constitute a unified evocation to a unified man.

Following the Awakening, the antirevivalists continued their opposing excursion of the pendulum. To a much greater extent than had been traditional, they stressed the rationality of man and minimized the role of emotions. Accepting scholastic physics, they considered man to be a compartmentalized being, whose effector mechanism followed the sequence of the faculties. In their interpretation of this sequence, however, they increased the emphasis on the cognitive aspects at the expense of spontaneous feeling. In their view, the Understanding should indeed be the dictating sovereign of the faculties, and the passions should be gravely suspect. Being alien to the process of rational decision-making, the emotions not only could not share directly in the process of persuasion but also should be evoked only with the most extreme caution, as a mere supplement to the logical thrust of the sermon. Man was not brought to holiness by instant conversion, but only through careful thought, close study, and persevering application. (For an example of Liberal preaching, see Ebenezer Gay's "Natural Religion," Reading Number Five.)

Thus, the opponents of the revival—the "Liberals" or rationalists, as well as the advocates of the revival—the evangelists or emotionalists, rejected their intellectual-rhetorical inheritance and moved to new postures considerably different from the traditional Puritan value systems discussed earlier in this chapter.

This split between the revivalists and the rationalists, which occurred during the epitasis and catastrophe of the Awakening, was soon codified by opposing theologians, and it remained pervasive throughout the Colonial period. In addition to its continued importance concerning the issue of emotion in religion, the intellectual dichotomy exerted fundamentally significant influences upon society. According to Alan Heimert, in his *Religion and the Colonial Mind,* the character and impact of the Calvinists and of the rationalists have been badly misunderstood. The Liberals were in fact not at all liberal, politically, socially, or intellectually. Instead, Liberalism "was a profoundly elitist

and conservative ideology." Evangelical Calvinism possessed a
revolutionary impulse, on the other hand, which became "the
instrument of a fervent American nationalism" and which constituted a "radical and even democratic challenge to the standing order of Colonial America." While not completely denying
the positive influence of the Liberal ministers upon the Independence movement, Heimert sees the revivalists' emphasis upon
the "New Birth" as the "evangelical version of the pursuit of happiness" and the Revolutionary War as a kind of analogy of the
Great Awakening: "It would appear that the uprising of the
1770's was not so much the result of reasoned thought as an
emotional outburst similar to a religious revival." [113] If filaments of truth exist in Heimert's thesis, which requires nearly
seven hundred pages in the unfolding, a substantial rethink-
ing may be in order concerning the currently accepted interpretation of the Revolution as an intellectual movement,
uniquely cerebral among the Western revolutions. Conceivably
the ideational, ideological aspects of the Revolution may have
been overemphasized at the expense of the emotional, behav-
ioral aspects.

Although at least latently present from the earliest days in
New England, the incipient conflict between emotion and
reason was wrenched into societal consciousness and given fate-
ful impetus by the Post-Awakening and Post-Revolutional
division between evangelical Calvinism and liberal rationalism.
If the Declaration of Independence was an emotional expression of the libertarian spirit, the Articles of Confederation may
also have been an expression of the affections. Debated for more
than a year by unrealistically suspicious states and refused
adopton for three additional years, the Articles provided a "sort
of diplomatic assembly presiding over a league" of jealously
sovereign states.

Fearing the emotionalism and irrationality of unchecked
popular rule which seemed to ensue under the Articles, and at
the same time fearing the administrative weaknesses of the
central government, the rationalists staged a "moderate" counterrevolution. Identified by Professors Carl J. Friedrich and
Robert G. McCloskey as "a sober, serious, property-conscious,

well-informed, even scholarly minority," the rationalists evolved and, over the objections of probably a majority of the people, pushed through to ratification the Constitution of the United States.[114] In their distrust of the emotions of the people, the Fathers of the Constitution sought to prevent the establishment of any policy-making machinery which would afford a direct, unprocessed expression of majority opinion. Although they misjudged in various ways the eventual development of the several branches of government, they succeeded brilliantly in achieving their immediate task of providing for national survival with freedom, as well as their ultimate task of fashioning a design sufficiently flexible to permit gradual adjustments to the developing contours of national life. To the framing Fathers the concept of equilibrium provided the key, both for the establishment of a viable government and for protection of individual freedoms, property rights, and the interests of society. Accordingly, they instituted a pragmatic, pluralistic, checks-and-balances government in which the "separated powers" were intended to be "separated institutions sharing power." Thus the rationalists evolved the true intellectual genius of the American system. The course of American history has largely vindicated the conviction of both Madison and Hamilton that the sharing of power provided the most feasible means of governing and that the equilibrium of power could adjust satisfactorily to changing political-emotional pressures.

Although it is merely an unproved hypothesis that the Constitution represented a "moderate" counterrevolution against emotionalism, there is no doubt that the emotional strain in society soon developed a widespread suspicion of intellectualism and a confirmed resistance to hard or sustained political thinking which became endemic to the party followers of Jefferson and Jackson, the agrarians, the Populists, the social militants, and so on. The breed of pragmatic intellectuals who conceived the Constitution and pushed it through to enactment and who served as the initial party leaders soon gave way to a new breed of nonintellectual, or anti-intellectual, professional politicians whose principal concern was not with issues but with winning elections from a broadly enfranchized electorate. Re-

peatedly, the democratic emotionalism of the Great Awakening would find echoes in movements such as the Second Great Awakening, the "revolutions" of 1800 and 1828, and the abolitionist crusade.

Admittedly the Puritans were Biblicists who centered virtually all arguments in Biblical authority and who, in their attempts to follow the governing rule *Scriptura sola*, placed ultimate reliance upon revelation rather than logic. Nevertheless, never again would the American society place learning and the intellect upon the pinnacle of honor accorded them by the original Puritans. Never again would any group of intellectuals come so close to being a ruling caste or exert such directing influence upon the exercise of state power as did the first generations of Puritan ministers. Never again would the rhetoric of teaching and of intellectual argumentation make such clean appeals to the rational decision-making of popular audiences as did the traditional Puritan sermonology. Puritan rhetoric failed because the Puritan system of the covenants, physics, logic, metaphysics—the entire Puritan intellectual universe—failed. Puritanism failed in part, at least, because it expected both too much and too little of man. Long in the developing, its death struggle was the Great Awakening. Its tragic flaw was the issue of emotion in religion. Its chief legacy may be the continuing conflict between emotion and reason. This conflict is perhaps made more understandable by Professor Heimert's characterization of the New Birth, the central principle of evangelical Calvinism, as "an expression of displeasure with the order of reality that presented itself to the eye of unaided reason, and of a desire to make a happier world in a manner that reason would not allow." [115]

PART TWO

Readings

In this section you will find five speeches of central significance to the issue of emotion in religion, each of which is
accompanied by a headnote introduction and by a set of
running interrogative notes. One of our speeches is a revival
sermon by Jonathan Edwards, and the others are paired
appositions. In one of these, Edwards and Charles Chauncy
discharge cannonades during the respective Yale and Harvard commencement observances. In the other, Edwards
and Ebenezer Gay deliver contrasting lectures on the role
of emotion-reason in religion.

In reading the speeches you should make determined
efforts to visualize each speech as a viable rhetorical act
growing out of complex societal developments and out of
the personal background of the speaker who seeks to influence subsequent events. Although limited by space requirements, Part One of this volume and the headnotes have
been designed to contribute to this orientation. At best, of
course, you can achieve only an imperfect conception of the
rhetorical problems confronted by the speakers and the
options available to them. Nevertheless, if you bring to the

task suitable amounts of interest and imagination, you can realize a sense of involvement which will bring to life the protagonists of this confrontation. If you add to this equation the balance of detached objectivity, you will derive maximum benefits from the interrogative notes. As we mentioned in the Preface, the notes, which are suffixed to each reading and which are conceptually cued to running citations in the text, are intended to serve as levers for opening up the speeches. Your most useful procedure may be to "think through" various lines of response. Possibly you should read uninterruptedly through the text, next survey the notes, and then, as you reread the speech, answer the notes in order. The lines of inquiry suggested by the various sets of interrogative notes will be exploited in the Inquiry section which follows our readings.

The Future Punishment of the Wicked Unavoidable and Intolerable

Jonathan Edwards

Edwards * considered this to be his most powerful horrific sermon. Delivered in April 1741, during the height of the revival, it is in some ways a more artistic effort than the perversely famed (see Part One) "Sinners in the Hands of an Angry God," given three months later at Enfield. Although the record is incomplete, for both of these speeches the congregations apparently were overcome by his emotional assault. Of the many hundreds of printed Puritan sermons, "Future Punishment" † is possibly the finest example of a speaker's drawing upon all the available means of persuasion to evoke an emotional response. In at least two ways the sermon is particularly noteworthy: Edwards's employing vivid imagery as a means of releasing the power of sensory psychology and, thereby, forcing his listeners to move from known and familiar conceptions to the sensory experiencing of otherworldly events; and his using the compulsions of terror to force believers to welcome the joyful liberation of conversionary love.

EZEKIEL 22:14

Can thine heart endure, or can thine hands be strong, in the days that I shall deal with thee? I the Lord have spoken it, and will do it.

In the former part of this chapter, we have a dreadful catalogue of the sins of Jerusalem; as you may see from the first to the thirteenth verse.[1] In the thirteenth, which is the verse preceding the text, God manifests his great displeasure

---

* See Part One: The Developing Exigence.
† The text of this speech comes from *Works*, ed. Sereno E. Dwight, 10 vols. (New York, 1829, 1830), 6:89–105.

and fearful wrath against them for their iniquities. "Behold, I have smitten my hand at thy dishonest gain which thou hast made, and at thy blood which hath been in the midst of thee." The expression of God's smiting his hand, signifies the greatness of his anger, and his preparing himself, as it were, to execute wrath answerable to their heinous crimes. It is an allusion to what we sometimes see in men when they are surprised, by seeing or hearing of some horrid offence, or most intolerable injury, which very much stirs their spirits, and animates them with high resentment; on such an occasion they will rise up in wrath and smite their hands together, as an expression of the heat of their indignation, and full resolution to be avenged on those who have committed the injury; as in chapter 22:17. "I will also smite mine hands together, and I will cause my fury to rest; I the lord have said it." [2] Then, in the text, the punishment of that people is represented.[3]

1. The nature of their punishment is more generally represented in that, God will undertake to *deal* with them. The prophets could do nothing with them. . . . Therefore now God himself undertakes to deal with them.

2. Their punishment is more particularly represented in three things, *viz.* The intolerableness, the remedilessness, and the unavoidableness of it.—The *intolerableness* of it: *can thine heart endure?* Its *remedilessness,* or the impossibility of their doing any thing for their own relief: *can thine hands be strong?* —Its *unavoidableness: I the Lord have spoken it, and will do it.*[4]

Doctrine

Since God hath undertaken to deal with impenitent sinners, they shall neither shun the threatened misery, nor deliver themselves out of it, nor can they bear it.

In handling this doctrine * I shall, 1. Shew what is implied

---

* No separate Reasons section appears in this sermon. As discussed in Part One, frequently Puritan ministers incorporated the Reasons argument into the Doctrine development, in conformity with William Perkins's classic format in his *The Arte of Prophecying.*

in God's undertaking to deal with impenitent sinners. 2. That therefore they cannot avoid punishment. 3. That they cannot in any measure deliver themselves from it; or do any thing for their own relief under it. 4. That they cannot bear it. 5. I shall answer an inquiry; and then proceed to the use.

I. I shall shew what is implied in God's undertaking to deal with impenitent sinners. Others are not able to deal with them. . . . Therefore God undertakes to deal with them. This implies the following things:

1. That God will *reckon* with them, and take of them satisfaction to his justice. In this world God puts forth his authority to command them. . . .[5] But they have no regard to these commands. . . . God threatens, but they despise his threatenings. . . . He offers them mercy, if they will repent and return: but they despise his mercy as well as his wrath. —God calleth, but they refuse. Thus they are continually plunging themselves deeper and deeper in debt, and at the same time imagine they shall escape the payment of the debt, and design entirely to rob God of his due.[6]

But God hath undertaken to right himself. He will reckon with them; he hath undertaken to see that the debts due to him are paid. All their sins are written in his book; not one of them is forgotten, and every one must be paid. If God be wise enough, and strong enough, he will have full satisfaction; he will exact the very utmost farthing. He undertakes it as his part, as what belongs to him, to see himself righted, wherein he hath been wronged. Deut. 32:35. "To me belongeth vengeance." Ibid. 7:10. "He will not be slack to him that hateth him; he will repay him to his face."

2. He hath undertaken to *vindicate* the honour of his majesty. . . . Though they now trample it in the dust, yet that is no sign that it will finally be lost. If God had left it wholly in their hands, it would indeed be lost. But God doth not leave his honour and his glory with his enemies. . . . If the honour of God, upon which sinners trample, finally lie in the dust, it will be because he is not strong enough to vindicate himself.[7] He hath sworn, in Num. 14:21, "As truly as I live, all the earth shall be filled with the glory of the Lord." . . .

3. He hath undertaken to *subdue* impenitent sinners. Their hearts, while in this world, are very unsubdued. They lift up their heads and conduct themselves very proudly and contemptuously, and often sin with a high hand. They set their mouths against the heavens, and their tongues walk through the earth. They practically say, as Pharaoh did, "Who is the Lord? I know not the Lord, neither will I obey his voice." Job 21:41. They say to God, "Depart from us, for we desire not the knowledge of thy ways."

Some, who cover their sin with a specious show, who put on a face of religion, and a demure countenance and behaviour, yet have this spirit secretly reigning in their breasts. Notwithstanding all their fair show, and good external carriage, they despise God in their hearts, and have the weapons of war about them, though they carry their swords under their skirts. . . . Their hearts are full of pride, enmity, stubbornness, and blasphemy, which work in them many ways, while they sit under the preaching of the word, and while the Spirit of God is striving with them: and they always continue to oppose and resist God as long as they live in the world; they never lay down the weapons of their rebellion.

But God hath undertaken to deal with them, and to subdue them. . . . If they will not be willing subjects to the golden sceptre, and will not yield to the attractives of his love, they shall be subject to the force of the iron rod, whether they will or not. . . .

4. God hath undertaken to rectify their *judgments.* Now they will not be convinced of those things which God tells them in his word. . . . Now they are always doubting of the truth of the scriptures, questioning whether they be the word of God, and whether the threatenings of scripture be true.[8] But . . . they will be convinced by dear experience. Now they are always questioning whether there be any such place as hell. They hear much about it, but it always seems to them like a dream. But God will make it seem otherwise than a dream. Now they are often told of the vanity of the world; but we may as well preach to the beasts, to persuade them of the vanity of earthly things.[9] But God will undertake to convince

them of this. . . . There is no sin, not so much as an idle word that they shall speak, but they must give an account of it; Matt. 12:36. And their sins must be fully balanced, and recompensed, and satisfaction obtained. Because judgment against their evil works, is not speedily executed, their hearts are fully set in them to do evil. Yet God is a righteous judge; he will see that judgment is executed in due time.—I come now,

II. To show, that therefore impenitent sinners shall *not avoid* their due punishment. God hath undertaken to inflict it; he hath engaged to do it; he takes it as what properly belongs to him, and we may expect it of him. . . .[10] And that God hath declared that he will punish impenitent sinners, is manifest from many scriptures; as Deut. 32:41. "I will render vengeance to mine enemies, and will reward them that hate me." Deut. 7:10. "He will not be slack to him that hateth him; he will repay him to his face." Exod. 34:7. "That will by no means clear the guilty." Nah. 1:3. "The Lord is slow to anger, and great in power, and will not at all acquit the wicked."

God saith in the text, "I the Lord have spoken it, and will do it"; which leaves no room to doubt of the actual fulfillment of the threatening in its utmost extent. Some have flattered themselves, that although God hath threatened very dreadful things to wicked men for their sins, yet in his heart he never intends to fulfil his threatenings, but only to terrify them, and make them afraid, while they live. But would the infinitely holy God, who is not a man that he should lie, and who speaketh no vain words, utter himself in this manner: *I the Lord have, spoken it and will do it; I have not only threatened, but I will also fulfil my threatenings.* . . .

No; let no impenitent sinner flatter himself so vainly and foolishly. . . . There is no hope that possibly they may steal away to heaven, though they die unconverted. There is no hope that they can deceive God by any false show of repentance and faith, and so be taken to heaven through mistake: for the eyes of God are as a flame of fire; they perfectly see through every man; the inmost closet of the heart is all open to him.

There is no hope of escaping the threatened punishment by sinking into nothing at death, like brute creatures. . . . There is no hope of their escaping without notice, when they leave the body. There is no hope that God, by reason of the multiplicity of affairs which he hath to mind, will happen to overlook them and not take notice of them, when they come to die. . . .

There is no hope that they shall be missed in a crowd at the day of judgment, and that they can have opportunity to hide themselves in some cave or den of the mountains, or in any secret hole of the earth; and that while so doing, they will not be minded, by reason of the many things which will be the objects of attention on that day;—neither is there any hope that they will be able to crowd themselves in among the multitude of the saints at the right hand of the Judge, and so go to heaven undiscovered. Nor is there any hope that God will alter his mind, or that he will repent of what he hath said; for he is not the son of man, that he should repent. Hath he said, and shall he not do it? Hath he spoken, and shall he not make it good? When did God ever undertake to do any thing and fail:—I come now,

III. To show, that as impenitent sinners cannot shun the threatened punishment; so neither can they do any thing to *deliver* themselves from it, or to relieve themselves under it. This is implied in those words of the text, *Can thine hands be strong?* It is with our hands that we make and accomplish things for ourselves. But the wicked in hell will have no strength of hand to accomplish any thing at all for themselves, or to bring to pass any deliverance, or any degree of relief.

1. They will not be able in that conflict to *overcome* their enemy, and so to deliver themselves. God, who will then undertake to deal with them, and will gird himself with might to execute wrath, will be their enemy. . . .

2. They will have no strength in their hands to do any thing to appease God, or in the least to abate the fierceness of his wrath. They will not be able to offer any satisfaction: they will not be able to procure God's pity. . . .

3. They will not be able to find any to *befriend* them, and

intercede with God for them.[11] They had the offer of a mediator often made them in this world; but they will have no such offers in hell. None will befriend them; in hell, all there will be their enemies. They will have no friend in heaven: none of the saints or angels will befriend them. . . . There will be no creature that will have any power to deliver them, nor will any ever pity them.

4. Nor will they ever be able to make their escape. They will find no means to break prison and flee. In hell they will be reserved in chains of darkness for ever and ever. Malefactors have often found means to escape the hand of civil justice. But none ever escaped out of the prison of hell, which is God's prison. It is a strong prison: it is beyond any finite power, or the united strength of all wicked men and devils, to unlock, or break open the door of that prison. Christ hath the key of hell; "he shuts and no man opens."

5. Nor will they ever be able to find any thing to *relieve* them in hell. They will never find any resting place there; any secret corner, which will be cooler than the rest, where they may have a little respite, a small abatement of the extremity of their torment. They never will be able to find any cooling stream or fountain, in any part of that world of torment; no, nor so much as a drop of water to cool their tongues. . . . They will be tormented with fire and brimstone; and will have no rest day nor night for ever and ever. . . .

Having shown that impenitent sinners will hereafter be able, neither to avoid the punishment threatened, nor to deliver themselves from it, nor to find any relief under it; I come now,

IV. To show, that neither will they be able to *bear* it.— Neither will their hands be strong to deliver them from it, nor will their hearts be able to endure it. It is common with men, when they meet with calamities in this world, in the first place to endeavour to shun them. But if they find, that they cannot shun them; then after they are come, they endeavour to deliver themselves from them as soon as they can; or at least, to deliver themselves in some degree. But if they find that they can by no means deliver themselves, and see that

they must bear them; then they fortify their spirits, and take up a resolution, that they will support themselves under them as well as they can.

But it will be utterly in vain for impenitent sinners to think to do thus with respect to the torments of hell. . . . What will it signify for a worm, which is about to be pressed under the weight of some great rock, to be let fall with its whole weight upon it, to collect its strength, to set itself to bear up the weight of the rock, and to preserve itself from being crushed by it?—Much more vain will it be for a poor damned soul, to endeavour to support itself under the weight of the wrath of Almighty God. What is the strength of man, who is but a worm, to support himself against the power of Jehovah, and against the fierceness of his wrath? What is man's strength, when set to bear up against the exertions of infinite power? Matt. 21:44. "Whosoever shall fall on this stone shall be broken; but on whomsoever it shall fall, it will grind him to powder."

When sinners hear of hell-torments, they sometimes think with themselves: Well, if it shall come to that, that I must go to hell, I will bear it as well as I can. . . . However they shall have prepared themselves, and collected their strength; yet as soon as they shall begin to feel that wrath, their hearts will melt and be as water. However they may seem to harden their hearts, in order to prepare themselves to bear, yet the first moment they feel it, their hearts will become like wax before the furnace.—Their courage and resolution will be all gone in an instant; it will vanish away like a shadow in the twinkling of an eye. The stoutest and most sturdy will have no more courage than the feeblest infant: let a man be an infant, or a giant, it will be all one. They will not be able to keep alive any courage, any strength, any comfort, any hope at all.—I come now as was proposed,

V. To answer an inquiry which may naturally be raised concerning these things.

INQ.: Some may be ready to say, if this be the case, if impenitent sinners can neither shun future punishment, nor deliver themselves from it, nor bear it; then what will become of them?

ANS.: They will wholly sink down into eternal death.—
There will be that sinking of heart, of which we now cannot
conceive. We see how it is with the body when in extreme
pain. The nature of the body will support itself for a considerable time under very great pain, so as to keep from wholly
sinking. There will be great struggles, lamentable groans and
pantings, and it may be convulsions. These are the strugglings
of nature to support itself under the extremity of the pain.—
There is, as it were, a great lothness in nature to yield to it;
it cannot bear wholly to sink.

But yet sometimes pain of body is so very exquisite, that
the nature of the body cannot support itself under it; however
loth it may be to sink, yet it cannot bear the pain; there are a
few struggles, and throes, and pantings, and it may be a shriek
or two, and then nature yields to the violence of the torments,
sinks down, and the body dies. This is the death of the body.
So it will be with the soul in hell. . . .[12]

We can conceive but little of the matter; but to help
your conception, imagine yourself to be cast into a fiery oven,
or a great furnace, where your pain would be as much greater
than that occasioned by accidentally touching a coal of fire,
as the heat is greater. Imagine also that your body were to lie
there for a quarter of an hour, full of fire, and all the while
full of quick sense; what horror would you feel at the entrance
of such a furnace! and how long would that quarter of an hour
seem to you! And after you had endured it for one minute,
how overbearing would it be to you to think that you had to
endure it the other fourteen!

But what would be the effect on your soul, if you knew
you must lie there enduring that torment to the full for twenty-
four hours! And how much greater would be the effect, if you
knew you must endure it for a whole year; and how vastly
greater still, if you knew you must endure it for a thousand
years!—O then, how would your hearts sink, if you knew,
that you must bear it for ever and ever! that there would be
no end! that after millions of millions of ages, your torment
would be no nearer to an end, and that you never, never should
be delivered!

But your torment in hell will be immensely greater than
this illustration represents. . . . This is the death threatened
in the law. This is dying in the highest sense of the word.
This is to die sensibly; to die and know it; to be sensible of
the gloom of death. . . .

Application

This subject may be applied in an use of awakening to
impenitent sinners.[13]—What hath been said under this doctrine is for thee, O impenitent sinner, O poor wretch, who
art in the same miserable state in which thou camest into the
world, excepting that thou art loaded with vastly greater guilt
by thine actual sins. These dreadful things which thou hast
heard are for thee, who art yet unconverted, and still remainest
an alien and stranger, without Christ and without God in the
world. They are for thee, who to this day remainest an enemy
to God, and a child of the devil, even in this remarkable
season, when others both here and elsewhere, far and near,
are flocking to Christ; for thee who hearest the fame of these
things, but knowest nothing of the power of godliness in thine
own heart.[14]

Whoever thou art, whether young or old, little or great,
if thou art in a Christless unconverted state, this is the wrath,
this is the death to which thou art condemned. This is the
wrath that abideth on thee; this is the hell over which thou
hangest and into which thou art ready to drop every day and
every night. . . . If thou wilt not be convinced by the word
preached to thee by men in the name of God, God himself
will undertake to convince thee. Ezek. 14:4, 7, 8. . . . Think it
not strange, that God should deal so severely with thee, or
that the wrath which thou shalt suffer should be so great.
For, as great as it is, it is no greater than that love of God
which thou has despised. The love of God, and his grace,
condescension, and pity to sinners, in sending his Son into the
world to die for them, is every whit as great and wonderful
as this inexpressible wrath. . . . Now why shouldst not thou
have wrath, as great as that love and mercy which thou de-

spisest and rejectest? Doth it seem incredible to thee that God
should so harden his heart against a poor sinner, as to destroy
him, and to bear him down with infinite power and merciless
wrath? and is this a greater thing than it is for thee to harden
thy heart, as thou hast done, against infinite mercy, and against
the dying love of God? . . .

What art thou in the hands of the great God, who made
heaven and earth by speaking a word? What art thou, when
dealt with by that strength, which manages all this vast universe, holds the globe of the earth, directs all the motions of
the heavenly bodies from age to age, and, when the fixed
time shall come, will shake all to pieces? . . . The great mountains, the firm rocks, cannot stand before the power of God.
He can tear the earth in pieces in a moment; yea, he can
shatter the whole universe, and dash it to pieces at one blow.
How then will thine hands be strong, or thine heart endure!

Thou canst not stand before a lion of the forest; an angry
wild beast, if stirred up, will easily tear such an one as thou
art in pieces. Yea not only so, but thou art crushed before the
moth. A little thing, a little worm or spider, or some such
insect, is able to kill thee. What then canst thou do in the
hands of God! it is vain to set the briars and thorns in battle-
array against glowing flames; the points of thorns, though sharp,
do nothing to withstand the fire.

Some of you have seen buildings on fire; imagine therefore with yourselves, what a poor hand you would make at
fighting with the flames, if you were in the midst of so great
and fierce a fire. You have often seen a spider, or some other
noisome insect, when thrown into the midst of a fierce fire,
and have observed how immediately it yields to the force of
the flames. There is no long struggle, no fighting against the
fire, no strength exerted to oppose the heat, or to fly from it;
but it immediately stretches forth itself and yields; and the
fire takes posession of it, and at once it becomes full of fire.
Here is a little image of what you will be in hell, except you
repent and fly to Christ.[15] To encourage yourselves, that you
will set yourselves to bear hell-torments as well as you can,
is just as if a worm, that is about to be thrown into a glowing

furnace, should swell and fortify itself, and prepare itself to
fight the flames.

What can you do with lightnings? What doth it signify to
fight with them? What an absurd figure would a poor weak
man make, who in a thunder storm should expect a flash of
lightning on his head or his breast, and should go forth sword
in hand to oppose it; when a flash would in an instant drink
up all his spirits and his life, and melt his sword!

Consider these things, all you enemies of God, and re-
jecters of Christ, whether you be old men and women, Christless heads of families, or young people and wicked children. . . . I suppose some of you have heard all that I have
said with ease and quietness: It appears to you as great sounding words, but doth not reach your hearts. You have heard
such things many times: You have been too much used to the
roaring of heaven's cannon to be frightened at it. It will therefore probably be in vain for me to say any thing further to
you; I will only put you in mind that ere long God will deal
with you. . . .

It is his manner commonly first to let men try their utmost
strength; particularly to let ministers try, that thus he may
show ministers their own weakness and impotency; and when
they have done what they can, and all fails, then God takes
the matter into his own hands. . . .

It will not be long before you will be wonderfully changed.
You who now hear of hell and the wrath of the great God,
and sit here so easy and quiet, and go away so careless; by
and by will shake, and tremble, and cry out, and shriek, and
gnash your teeth, and will be thoroughly convinced of the vast
weight and importance of these things which you now despise.[16]

INTERROGATIVE NOTES

1. In the first sentence notice how Edwards begins to set the mood and
   tempo. Does the mood develop slowly and the pace gradually quicken?
   Or, does the speech move swiftly into high gear?
2. In this passage, as a supportive item Edwards uses a Biblical quota-
   tion, indicates the relevance and significance of the citation to the

thrust of his idea, interprets the citation in terms of God's behavior and of man's behavior, and caps the passage with a related verse of Scripture. Keeping in mind, of course, the nature of the speaking situation, do you believe that Edwards's ideas seem to unfold easily and spontaneously? Or, do you believe that the listeners would sense in this tightly structured composition the hand of the craftsman?

3. Here, and throughout the speech, Edwards attempts to blend the parts together with transitional statements and internal summaries. Does he overdo the transitional aspects, according to what his listeners were accustomed to expect? According to the modern listener?

4. Do you agree that Edwards's "opening of the text" has clarified for his listeners the direction of the sermon? Do you also agree that his clarification step constitutes an appeal to their emotions as well as to their intellects? Why does he begin the Doctrine section by stating the thrust of the sermon and by relisting the immediately preceding divisions? From these passages would you agree that Edwards's style is "endlessly" repetitious? In terms of his rhetorical needs, do you believe that this degree of repetition is helpful or hurtful?

5. Edwards has been called a "word artist." Attune your eyes and ears to his style. In this passage, for instance, notice the short, punchy sentences and the use of antithesis. What effect is Edwards here trying to achieve? When Edwards moves to the next point, does his style change in accordance with the meaning of the content and the effect he is attempting to achieve?

6. Some rhetoricians consider that the figurative analogy and the hypothetical illustration provide weak logical support. In this paragraph, do you think that the allusion adds to the intellectual dimension of the Doctrine? As you move along in your reading, estimate the logical and emotional quality of his numerous figurative allusions.

7. Edwards is appealing to vivid concreteness by his use of such language as, "trample it in the dust," "left it wholly in their hands," and "lies in the dust." Would this language evoke richer imagery in the minds of Edwards's listeners than of modern listeners? Within a few lines there appears this phrase, "their tongues walk through the earth." Is this phrase eloquent, or merely a mixed figure? What constitutes eloquence?

8. Here Edwards again uses contrast, this time in a series of "now . . . but" constructions. What psychological effect is he attempting to achieve?

9. As you read along, notice the number of times, and the manner in which, Edwards slashes at auditors who have resisted revivalistic preaching. Does he here, or elsewhere in the sermon, attempt to conciliate those who disagree with him? To establish rapport with them? Does he assault them without quarter? If you had to assign a label to this kind of rhetoric, what would you call it? Does Edwards seem to place himself and his fellow revivalists on pedestals? For this kind

of rhetoric to be lastingly successful, what conditions must be
present and remain constant?

10. In this sentence, in the remainder of the paragraph, and throughout
the sermon, note that Edwards develops a tremendous thrust by his
multiple reiterations of the same idea. Some rhetoricians suggest that
the presentation of successive items may have a cumulative effect
which greatly exceeds the logical or psychological value of the data,
considered as single entities. By his returning repeatedly to the same
point and by his developing each of the main heads of the Doctrine
as a very similar extension of the purpose statement, is Edwards
deliberately using redundancy as a means of intensifying the emotional values of his content?

11. Edwards begins and closes this paragraph with universal assertions,
and he places particularized assertions between the absolutes. What
logical or psychological purposes do you think that Edwards had in
mind in using this procedure?

12. By extrapolating from the known and familiar to the future and the
unknown, Edwards seeks to force his listeners into a sensory experience of the unknown. How well do you think he succeeds? What
device does he use to make suffering seem excruciatingly eternal?

13. In their appeal to logic and to emotion, do you find any substantial
difference between the Doctrine and the Application? Does Edwards
address separately the emotions and the reasoning of his listeners?
Or, does he conjoin his appeal?

14. How impelling is this use of the bandwagon technique?

15. Does Edwards here, and elsewhere in the sermon, seem to be offering
salvation to all who will seek it?

16. Now that you have read the speech, go back in your thinking to see
if you can recall any substantive logical proof that Edwards has advanced besides the Bible. If his listeners accepted Biblical testimony
as absolute proof, what critical problem of persuasion still confronted Edwards in his use of Scripture? How well do you think he
met this rhetorical need?

In reviewing the speech, does it seem to have a climax? More
than one? Are there peaks and troughs of attention-compelling materials? Or, is there a constant level of exhortation? If different levels
of intensity have been built into the sermon, why—and how—has
Edwards effected this?

Distinguishing Marks

Jonathan Edwards

Some five months after his "Future Punishment," Edwards preached the "Distinguishing Marks" * during the Yale commencement observances. Although some "extravagances" were already beginning to sully the pure expressions of piety, the address was an aggressive, confident assault upon the yet silent and intimidated enemies of the revival. An attempt to demonstrate that the revival was a work of God, it was also an encouragement to the uncommitted to join actively in the awakening. In reworking the sermon for the press,† Edwards may have toned down the Application segment and directed it, not toward the enemies, but toward the overly zealous supporters of the revival. During the bulk of the printed speech, however, he was on the attack, coalescing a defense of emotion into a strident affirmation.

1 JOHN 4:1

Beloved, believe not every Spirit, but try the Spirits whether they are of God; because many false Prophets are gone out into the World.

The apostolical Age, or the Age in which the Apostles lived and preached the Gospel, was an Age of the greatest outpouring of the Spirit of God that ever was; and that both as to the extraordinary Influences and Gifts of the Spirit, in Inspiration and Miracles, and also as to his ordinary Operations,

---

* The text of this speech has been taken from his *The Distinguishing Marks of a Work of the Spirit of God* (Boston, 1741). For additional orientation to the sermon, see Part One: The Developing Exigence.
† Shortly after its delivery it was published in Boston, Philadelphia, London, Edinburgh, and Glasgow. Because the printed version runs considerably longer than the original speech, this text has been pruned more extensively than the others.

in convincing, converting, enlightening and Sanctifying the Souls of Men. But as the Influences of the true Spirit abounded, so Counterfeits did also then abound: The Devil was abundant in mimicking, both the ordinary and extraordinary Influences of the Spirit of God, as is manifest by innumerable Passages of the Apostles Writings. This made it very necessary that the Church of Christ should be furnished with some certain Rules, and distinguishing and clear Marks by which she might proceed safely in judging of Spirits, and distinguish the true from the false, without Danger of being imposed upon. The giving such Rules is the plain Design of this Chapter, where we have this Matter more expresly and fully treated of than any where else in the Bible. . . .

My Design therefore at this Time is to shew what are the true, certain, and distinguishing Evidences of a Work of the Spirit of God, by which we may proceed safely in judging of any Operation we find in ourselves, or see in others. . . .

But before I proceed particularly to speak to these, I would prepare my Way by first observing negatively, in some Instances, What are not Signs that we are to judge of a Work by, whether it be the Work of the Spirit of God or no; and especially, what are no Evidences that a Work that is wrought amongst a People, is not the Work of the Spirit of God.[1]

1. Nothing can certainly be concluded from this, *That the Work that appears is carried on in a Way very unusual and extraordinary.* 'Tis no Sign that a Work is not the Work of the Spirit of God, that it is carried on in such a Way as the same Spirit of God heretofore has not been wont to carry on his Work, provided the Variety or Difference be such, as may still be comprehended within the Limits of those Rules which the Scriptures have given to distinguish a Work of the Spirit of God by. What we have been used to, or what the Church of God has been used to, is not a Rule by which we are to judge whether a Work be the Work of God, because there may be new and extraordinary Works of God. . . .

Therefore 'tis not reasonable to determine that a Work is not the Work of God's Spirit, because of the extraordinary Degree in which the Minds of Persons are influenced and

wrought upon. If they seem to have an extraordinary Conviction of the dreadful nature of Sin, and a very uncommon Sense of the Misery of a Christless Condition, or seem to have extraordinary Views of the certainty and glory of divine Things; and consequent on these Apprehensions, are proportionably moved with very extraordinary Affections of Fear and Sorrow, Desire, Love or Joy: Or if the Change that seems to be made in Persons, the Alteration in their Affections and Frames, be very sudden, and the Work that is wrought on People's Minds seems to be carried on with very unusual Swiftness, and the Persons that are thus strangely affected are very many, and many of them are very young; and also be very unusual in many other Circumstances, not infringing upon Scripture Marks of a Work of the Spirit; these Things are no Argument that the Work is not a Work of the Spirit of God. . . .

There is a great Aptness in Persons to doubt of Things that are Strange; especially it is difficult for elderly Persons, those that have lived a great while in the World, to think that to be right which they have never used to in their Day, and have not heard of in the Days of their Fathers.[2] But if it be a good Argument that a Work is not from the Spirit of God, that 'tis very unusual, then it always was so, and was so in the Apostles Days. The Work of the Spirit of God that was wrought then, was carried on in a Manner that, in very many Respects, was altogether new: There were such Things then that the Jews, then living, nor their Fathers, had never seen nor heard, yea such as never had been since the World stood: The Work was then carried on with more visible and remarkable Power than ever had been before; never were there seen before such mighty and wonderful Effects of the Spirit of God, in such sudden Changes, and such great Engagedness and Zeal in such Multitudes; such a great and sudden Alteration in Towns, Cities and Countries; such a swift Progress, and vast Extent of the Work; and many other extraordinary Circumstances might be mentioned. The great Unusualness of the Work surprized the Jews; they knew not what to make of it, but could not believe it to be the Work of God; many looked upon the Persons that were the Subjects of it as bereft of

Reason; as you may see in *Acts* 2:13. & 26:24. & 1 *Cor.* 4:10.

And we have Reason from Scripture Prophecy to suppose,
That at the Commencement of that last and greatest Out-
pouring of the Spirit of God, that is to be in the latter Ages of
the World, the Manner of the Work will be very extraordinary,
and such as never has yet been seen. . . .[3]

2. A Work is not to be judged of by any *Effects on the
Bodies of Men;* such as Tears, Trembling, Groans, loud Outcries, Agonies of Body, or the failing of bodily Strength. The
Influence the Minds of Persons are under, is not to be judged
of one Way or the other, whether it be from the Spirit of God
or no, by such Effects on the Body; and the Reason is, Because
the Scripture no where gives us any such Rule. We can't conclude that Persons are under the Influence of the true Spirit,
because we see such Effects upon their Bodies, because this
is not given as a Mark of the true Spirit; nor on the other
Hand, have we any Reason to conclude, from any such outward
Appearances, that Persons are not under the Influence of the
Spirit of God, because there is no Rule of Scripture given us
to judge of Spirits by, that does, either expresly or indirectly,
exclude such Effects on the Body; nor does Reason exclude
them. 'Tis easily accounted for from the Consideration of the
Nature of divine and eternal Things, and the Nature of Man,[4]
and the Laws of the Union between Soul and Body, how a
right Influence, a true and proper Sense of Things, should have
such Effects on the Body, even those that are of the most
extraordinary Kind; such as taking away the bodily Strength,
or throwing the Body into great Agonies, and extorting loud
Outcries. . . . We see the Nature of Man to be such, that
when he is in Danger of some Calamity that is very terrible
to him, and that he looks upon himself greatly exposed to,
he is ready upon every Occasion to think that *now* it is coming:[5]
As when Persons Hearts are full of Fear, in Time of War,
looking upon themselves eminently exposed, they are ready
to tremble at the shaking of a Leaf, and to expect the Enemy
every Minute, and to say within themselves, *now* I shall be
slain. If we should suppose that a Person saw himself hanging
over a great Pit, full of fierce and glowing Flames, by a Thread

that he knew to be very weak, and not sufficient long to bear his Weight, and knew that Multitudes had been in such Circumstances before, and that most of them had fallen and perish'd; and saw nothing within Reach, that he could take hold of to save him; What Distress would he be in? How ready to think that *now* the Thread was breaking, *now this Minute* he should be swallowed up in these dreadful Flames? And would not he be ready to cry out in such Circumstances? How much more those that see themselves in this Manner hanging over an infinitely more dreadful Pit, or hold over it in the Hand of God, who at the same Time they see to be exceedingly provoked? No wonder they are ready to expect every Moment when this angry God will let them drop; and no Wonder they cry out of their Misery; and no Wonder that the Wrath of God when manifested but a little to the Soul, over-bears human Strength. . . .

Some object against such extraordinary Appearances, that we have no Instances of 'em recorded in the New Testament, in the Time of the extraordinary Effusions of the Spirit that were then. If this should be allowed, I can see no Force in the Objection, if neither Reason, nor any Rule of Scripture excludes such Things; especially considering what was observed under the foregoing Particular. I don't know that we have any express mention in the New Testament of any Person's weeping or groaning, or sighing, thro' Fear of Hell, or a Sense of God's Anger; but is there any Body so foolish as from hence to argue, that in whomsoever these Things appear, their Convictions are not from the Spirit of God? And the Reason why we don't argue thus is, Because these are easily accounted for, from what we know of the Nature of Man, and from what the Scriptures do inform us in general concerning the Nature of eternal Things, and the Nature of the Convictions of God's Spirit. . . .[6]

The Root & Cause of Things is to be looked at, and the Nature of the Operations & Affections that Persons *Minds* are under, are what are to be inquired into, and examined by the Rule of God's Word, and not the Motions of the Blood and animal Spirits.

3. 'Tis no Argument that an Operation that appears on
the Minds of a People, is not the Work of the Spirit of God,
*That it occasions a great Ado, and a great deal of Noise about
Religion.* For tho' true Religion be of a contrary Nature to that
of the *Pharisees,* that was ostentatious, and delighted to set it
self forth to the View of Men, for their Applause; yet such is
human Nature, that 'tis morally impossible that there should
be a great Concern, and strong Affection, and Engagedness
of Mind amongst a People, that should be general, and what
most of them agree in, and yet there be but little said or done
that should be publickly observable, or that it should not cause
a notable, visible, and open Commotion and Alteration amongst
that People. . . .

4. 'Tis no Argument that an Operation that appears on the
Minds of a People, is not the Work of the Spirit of God, *That
many that are the Subjects of it, have great Impressions on
their imaginations.* That Persons have many Impressions on
their Imaginations, don't prove that they have nothing else.
It is easy to be accounted for, that there should be much of
this Nature amongst a People, where a great Multitude of all
Kinds of Constitutions, have their Minds engaged with intense
Thought and strong Affection about those Things that are invisible; yea, it would be Strange if there should not. Such is
our Nature that we can't think of Things invisible, without a
Degree of Imagination. I dare appeal to any Man, of the greatest Powers of Mind, Whether or no he is able to fix his Thoughts
on God or Christ, or the Things of another World, without
imaginary ideas attending his Meditations? And the more engaged the Mind is, and the more intense the Contemplation
and Affection, still the more lively and strong will the imaginary Idea ordinarily be; especially when the Contemplation
and Affection of the Mind is attended with any Thing of
Surprize; as when the View a Person has is very new, and takes
strong hold of the Passions, either Fear or Joy; and when the
Change of the State and Views of the Mind is sudden, from
a contrary Extreme, as from that which was extreamly dreadful, to that which is extremely ravishing and delightful: [7] And
it is no Wonder that many Persons don't well distinguish be-

tween that which is imaginary, and that which is intellectual and spiritual; and that they are apt to lay too much Weight on the imaginary Part, and are most ready to speak of *that* in the Account they give of their Experiences, especially Persons of less Understanding and Capacity of Distinction. . . .

5. 'Tis no Sign that a Work that appears, and is wrought on the Minds of People, is not from the Spirit of God, *That Example is made use of as a great Means of it.*[8] 'Tis surely no Argument that an Effect is not from God, that Means are made use of in producing it; for we know that 'tis God's Manner to make use of Means in carrying on his Work in the World: and 'tis no more an Argument against the Divinity of an Effect, that this Means is made use of, than if it was by any other Means. 'Tis agreable to Scripture that Persons should be influenced by one anothers good Example: The Scripture directs us to set good Examples to that End, *Math.* 5:16. 1 *Pet.* 3:1. 1 *Tim.* 4:12. *Tit.* 2:7. and also directs us to be influenced by the good Examples that others set, and to follow them, 2 *Cor.* 8:1–7. *Heb.* 6:12. *Phil.* 3:17. 1 *Cor.* 4:16. & *Chap.* 11:1. 2 *Thes.* 3:9. 1 *Thes.* 1:7. By which it appears that Example is one of God's Means; and certainly 'tis no Argument that a Work is not the Work of God, that God's own Means are made Use of to effect it.

And as 'tis a *scriptural* Way of carrying on God's Work, to carry it on by Example, so 'tis a *reasonable* Way. 'Tis no Argument that Men are not influenced by Reason, that they are influenced by Example. This Way of Persons holding forth Truth to one another, has a Tendency to enlighten the Mind, and to convince Reason. None will deny but that for Persons to signify Things one to another by *Words*, may rationally be supposed to tend to inlighten each others Minds; but the same Things may be signified *by Actions*, and signified much more fully and effectually. Words are of no Use any otherwise than as they convey our own ideas to others; but Actions, in some Cases, may do it much more fully. There is a Language in Actions; and in some Cases, much more clear and convincing than in Words.

'Tis therefore no Argument against the Goodness of the

Effect, that one affects and stirs up another; or that Persons are greatly affected by seeing others so; yea, tho' the Impression that is made upon them should be only by seeing the Tokens of great and extraordinary Affection in others in their Behaviour, taking for granted what they are affected with, without hearing them say one Word. . . . If a Person should see another under some extreme bodily Torment, he might receive much clearer ideas, and more convincing Evidence what he suffered by his Actions in his Misery, than he could do only by the Words of an unaffected indifferent Relator. In like Manner he might receive a greater Idea of any Thing that is excellent and very delightful, from the Behaviour of one that is in actual Enjoyment, or one that is sensible thro' Sight and Taste, than by the dull Narration of one that is unexperienced & Insensible himself. I desire that this Matter may be examined by the strictest Reason. . . .

There never yet was a Time of remarkable pouring out of the Spirit, and great Revival of Religion, But that Example had a main Hand; so it was in the Time of the Reformation and so it evidently was in that great Out-pouring of the Spirit that was in the Apostles Days, in Jerusalem, and Samaria, & Ephesus, and other Parts of the World, as will be most manifest to any one that attends to the Accounts we have in the Acts of the Apostles. . . .

6. 'Tis no Sign that a Work that is wrought amongst a People is not from the Spirit of God, *That many that seem to be the Subjects of it, are guilty of great Imprudences & Irregularities in their Conduct.* We are to consider that the End for which God pours out his Spirit, is to make Men holy, and not to make them Politicians.[9] 'Tis no Wonder at all, that in a mixt Multitude of all sorts, wise and unwise, young & old, of weak and strong natural Abilities, that are under strong impressions of Mind, there are many that behave themselves imprudently. There are but few that know how to conduct them under vehement Affections of any Kind, whether they be of a temporal or spiritual Nature: to do so requires a great deal of Discretion, and strength & steadiness of Mind. A thousand Imprudences won't prove a Work not to be the Work of the Spirit of God. . . .

We have a remarkable Instance in the New Testament, of a People that partook largely of that great Effusion of the Spirit there was in the Apostles Days, among whom, there nevertheless abounded Imprudences and great Irregularities, and that is the Church of the *Corinthians*.[10] There is scarce any Church more celebrated in the New Testament for being blessed with large Measures of the Spirit of God, both in his ordinary Influences, in convincing and converting Sinners, and also in his extraordinary & miraculous Gifts; yet what manifold Imprudences, and great and sinful Irregularities, and strange Confusion did they run into, at the Lord's Supper, and in the Exercise of Church Discipline, and their indecent Manner of attending other Parts of publick Worship, and in Jarring and Contention about their Teachers, and even in the Exercise of their extraordinary Gifts of Prophecy, speaking with Tongues, and the like, wherein they spake and acted by the immediate Inspiration of the Spirit of God. . . .

And here in particular, it is no Evidence that a Work is not the Work of God, if many that are the Subjects of it, or are improved as instruments to carry it on, are guilty of too great a forwardness *to censure others as Unconverted.* . . . 'Tis observable that there never was a Time of great Reformation, to cause a Revival of much of a Spirit of *Zeal* in the Church of God, but that, it has been attended in some notable Instances, with Irregularity, running out some Way or other into an undue *Severity.* . . .

7. Nor are *many Errors in Judgment, and some Delusions of Satan intermix'd with the Work,* any Argument that the Work in general is not the Work of the Spirit of God. However great a pouring out of the Spirit there may be, 'tis not to be expected that the Spirit of God should be given now in the same Manner that it was to the Apostles, infallibly to guide them in Points of Christian Doctrine, so that what they taught might be relied on as a Rule to the Christian Church. . . .

8. If some such as were thought to be wrought upon, *fall away into gross Errors or scandalous Practices,* 'tis no Argument that the Work in general is not the Work of the Spirit of God. That there are some Counterfeits, is no Argument that nothing is true: such Things are always expected in a Time of Reforma-

tion. If we look into Church History, we shall find no Instance
of great Revival of Religion, but what has been attended with
many such Things. . . .

9. 'Tis no Argument that a Work is not from the Spirit
of God, *That it seems to be promoted by Ministers insisting
very much on the Terrors of God's Holy Law, and that with
a great deal of Pathos and Earnestness.*[11] If there be really a
Hell of such dreadful, and never ending Torments, as is generally supposed, that Multitudes are in great Danger of, and
that the bigger Part of Men in Christian Countries do actually
from Generation to Generation fall into, for want of a Sense
of the Terribleness of it, and their Danger of it, and so for
want of taking due Care to avoid it; then why is it not proper
for those that have the Care of Souls, to take great Pains to
make Men sensible of it? Why should not they be told as much
of the Truth as can be? If I am in Danger of going to Hell,
I should be glad to know as much as possibly I can of the
Dreadfulness of it: If I am very prone to neglect due Care to
avoid it, he does me the best Kindness, that does most to represent to me the Truth of the Case, that sets forth my Misery
and Danger in the liveliest Manner.

I appeal to every one in this Congregation, whether this
is not the very Course they would take in Case of Exposedness
to any great temporal Calamity? If any of you that are Heads
of Families, saw one of your Children in an House that was
all on Fire over it's Head, and in eminent Danger of being
soon consumed in the Flames, that seemed to be very insensible
of it's Danger, and neglected to escape, after you had often
spake to it, and called to it, would you go on to speak to it
only in a cold and indifferent Manner? Would not you cry
aloud, and call earnestly to it, and represent the Danger it
was in, and it's own Folly in delaying, in the most lively
Manner you was capable of? Would not Nature itself teach
this, and oblige you to it? If you should continue to speak to
it only in a cold Manner, as you are won't to do in ordinary
Conversation about indifferent Matters, would not those about
you begin to think you were bereft of Reason your self? . . .

When Ministers preach of Hell, and warn Sinners to avoid

it, in a cold Manner, tho' they may say in Words that it is
infinitely terrible; yet (if we look on Language as a Communication of our Minds to others) they contradict themselves;
for Actions, as I observed before, have a Language to convey
our Minds, as well as Words; and at the same Time that such
a Preacher's Words represent the Sinner's State as infinitely
dreadful, his Behaviour and Manner of speaking contradict it,
and shew that the Preacher don't think so; so that he defeats
his own Purpose; for the Language of his Actions, in such a
Case, is much more effectual than the bare Signification of
his Words.

Not that I think that the Law only should be preached:
Ministers may preach other Things too little. The Gospel is
to be preached as well as the Law, and the Law is to be
preached only to make Way for the Gospel, and in order to
an effectual preaching of that; for the main Work of Ministers
of the Gospel is to preach the Gospel: it is the End of the
Law; Christ is the End of the Law for Righteousness: So that
a Minister would miss it very much if he should insist so much
on the Terrors of the Law, as to forget his End, and neglect to
preach the Gospel; but yet the Law is very much to be insisted
on, and the preaching of the Gospel is like to be in vain
without it. . . .

Some talk of it as an unreasonable Thing to think to fright
Persons to Heaven; but I think it is a reasonable Thing to
endeavour to fright Persons away from Hell, that stand upon
the Brink of it, and are just ready to fall into it, and are
senseless of their Danger: 'tis a reasonable Thing to fright a
Person out of an House on Fire. The Word *Fright* is commonly used for sudden causless Fear, or groundless Surprize;
but surely a just Fear, that there is good Reason for, tho'
it be very great, is not to be spoken against under any such
Name.

Having thus shown, in some Instances, what are not Evidences that a Work that is wrought among a People, is not
a Work of the Spirit of God,

I now proceed in the *Second Place*, as was proposed, to
shew positively, What are the sure, distinguishing, Scripture

Evidences and Marks of a Work of the Spirit of God, by which
we may proceed in judging of any Operation we find in ourselves, or see among a People, without Danger of being misled.

And in this, as I said before, I shall confine my self wholly
to those Marks which are given us by the Apostle in the Chapter wherein is my Text, where this Matter is particularly
handled, and more plainly and fully than any where else in
the Bible. And in speaking to these Marks, I shall take them
in the Order in which I find them in the Chapter.

1. When that Spirit that is at work amongst a People is
observed to operate after such a Manner, as to raise their
Esteem of that *Jesus* that was born of *the Virgin,* and was crucified without the Gates of *Jerusalem;* [12] and seems more to
confirm and establish their Minds in the Truth of what the
Gospel declares to us of his being the Son of God, and the
Saviour of Men; 'tis a sure Sign that that Spirit is the Spirit
of God. . . .

2. When the Spirit that is at work *operates against the
Interest of Satan's Kingdom, which lies in encouraging and
establishing Sin, and cherishing Mens worldly Lusts;* this is a
sure Sign that 'tis a true, and not a false Spirit. . . .

And therefore if we see Persons made sensible of the
dreadful Nature of Sin, and of the Displeasure of God against
it, and of their own miserable Condition as they are in themselves, by Reason of Sin, and earnestly concerned for their
eternal Salvation, and sensible of their Need of God's Pity and
Help, and engaged to seek it in the Use of the Means that
God has appointed, we may certainly conclude that it is from
the Spirit of God, whatever Effects this Concern has on their
Bodies; tho' it causes them to cry out aloud, or to shriek, or
to faint, or tho' it throws them into Convulsions, or whatever
other Way the Blood and Spirits are moved. . . .

3. That Spirit that operates in such a Manner, as to *cause
in Men a greater Regard to the holy Scriptures, and establishes
them more in their Truth and Divinity,* is certainly the Spirit
of God. This Rule the Apostle gives us in the 6th Verse: *We
are of God; he that knoweth God heareth us: He that is not
of God, heareth not us: Hereby know we the Spirit of Truth,
and the Spirit of Error.* . . .

4. Another Rule to judge of Spirits may be drawn from those opposite Compellations given to the two opposite Spirits, in the last Words of the 6th Verse. THE SPIRIT OF TRUTH, and the SPIRIT OF ERROR. These Words do exhibit the two opposite Characters of the Spirit of God, and other Spirits that counterfeit his Operations. And therefore, if by observing the Manner of the Operation of a Spirit that is at work among a People, we see that it operates as a *Spirit of Truth,* leading Persons to *Truth,* convincing them of those Things that are true, we may safely determine that 'tis a right and true Spirit. . . .

5. If the Spirit that is at work among a People *operates as a Spirit of Love to God and Man,* 'tis a sure Sign that 'tis the Spirit of God. This Sign the Apostle insists upon from the 6th Verse to the End of the Chapter: *Beloved, let us love one another; for Love is of God, and every one that loveth is born of God, and knoweth God.* . . . In these Verses *Love* is spoken of as if it were that wherein the very Nature of the Holy Spirit consisted; or as if divine Love dwelling in us, and the Spirit of God dwelling in us, were the same Thing. . . . There is sufficient said in this Passage of St. *John,* that we are upon, of the Nature and Motive of a truly Christian Love, thoroughly to distinguish it from all such Counterfeits. It is Love that arises from an Apprehension of the wonderful Riches of free Grace, and Sovereignty of God's Love to us, in Christ Jesus; being attended with a Sense of our own utter Unworthiness, as in our 'selves the Enemies and Haters of God & Christ, and with a Renunciation of all our own Excellency and Righteousness. See Verses 9, 10, 11 & 19. . . .

Having thus fulfil'd what I at first proposed, in considering what are the certain, distinguishing Marks, by which we may safely proceed in judging of any Work that falls under our Observation, whether it be the Work of the Spirit of God or no—I now proceed to the

Application

I. From what has been said,[13] I will venture to draw this *Inference,* viz. *That that extraordinary Influence that has lately*

*appeared on the Minds of the People abroad in this Land,
causing in them an uncommon Concern and Engagedness of
Mind about the Things of Religion, is undoubtedly, in the
general, from the Spirit of God.*[14] There are but two Things that
need to be known in order to such a Work's being judged of,
viz *Facts* and *Rules.* The *Rules* of the Word of God we have
had laid before us; and as to *Facts*, there are but two Ways
that we can come at them, so as to be in a Capacity to compare them with the Rules, either by our own Observation, or
by Information from others that have had Opportunity to observe. . . . But when the Work is spread over great Part of
a Country, in Places distant one from another among People
of all Sorts, and all Ages, and in Multitudes of Persons, of
sound Mind, good Understanding, and known Integrity; there
would be the greatest Absurdity in Supposing that, by all the
Observation that can be made by all that is heard from them
and seen in them, for many Months together, by those that
are most intimate with them in these Affairs, and have long
been acquainted with them, that yet it can't be determined
what Kind of Influence the Operation they are under, has
upon People's Minds, whether it tends to awaken their Consciences, or to stupify them; whether it tends to incline them
more to seek their Salvation, or neglect it; whether it seems
to confirm them in a Belief of the Scriptures, or to lead them
to Deism; whether it makes them have more Regard to the
great truths of Religion, or less. . . . But much more unreasonable it would be, when such Professions are made, not by a
particular Person only, but a great Part of a People in a Land,
to suppose that they all agree in professing what indeed they
do not feel in their Souls. . . .

And as I [15] am One that, by the Providence of God, have
for some Months past, been much amongst those that have
been the Subjects of that Work, that has of late been carried
on in the Land; and particularly, have been abundantly in
the Way of seeing & observing those extraordinary Things that
many Persons have been much stumbled at; such as Persons
crying out aloud, shrieking, being put into great Agonies of
Body, and deprived of their bodily Strength, and the like; and

that in many different Towns; and have been very particularly conversant with great Numbers of such, both in the Time of their being the Subjects of such extraordinary Influences, and afterwards, from Time to Time, and have seen the Manner and Issue of such Operations, and the Fruits of them, for several Months together; many of them being Persons that I have long known, and have been intimately acquainted with them in Soul Concerns, before and since: So I look upon my self called on this Occasion to give my Testimony, that . . . this Work has all those Marks that have been spoken of; in very many Instances, in every Article; and particularly in many of those that have been the Subjects of such extraordinary Operations, all those Marks have appeared in a very great Degree.

Those in whom have been these uncommon Appearances, have been of two Sorts; either these that have been in great Distress, in an Apprehension of their Sin and Misery; or those that have been overcome with a sweet Sense of the Greatness, Wonderfulness and Excellency of divine Things. . . .

Those that are in such Extremity, commonly express a great Sense of their exceeding Wickedness, the Multitude and Aggravations of their actual Sins, and the dreadful Pollution, Enmity and Perverseness of their Hearts, and a dreadful Obstinancy and hardness of Heart; a Sense of their great Guilt in the Sight of God; and the Dreadfulness of the Punishment that Sin exposes to: Very often they have a lively Idea of the horrible Pit of eternal Misery; and at the same Time it appears to them, that a Great God that has them in his Hands, is exceeding Angry with them; his Wrath appears amazingly terrible to them. . . . They have been brought as it were to lie at God's Foot; and after great Agonies, a little before Light has arisen, they have been composed and quiet, in a Kind of Submission to a Just and Sovereign God; but their bodily Strength much spent; and sometimes their Lives, to Appearance almost gone and then Light has appeared, and a glorious Redeemer, with his wonderful all-sufficient Grace, has been represented to them, often, in some sweet Invitation of Scripture. Sometimes the Light comes in suddenly, sometimes more gradually, filling their Souls with Love, Admiration, Joy & Self-Abasement; drawing forth their

Hearts in Longing after the excellent lovely Redeemer, and
Longings to lie in the Dust before him; and Longings that
others might behold him, and embrace him, and be delivered
by him; and Longings to live to his Glory: but sensible that
they can do nothing of themselves; appearing Vile in their own
Eyes, and having much of a Jealousy over their own Hearts.[16]
And all the Appearances of a real Change of Heart have
followed. . . .

Some object against it, as great Confusion, when there is a
Number together, in such Circumstances, making a Noise; and
say, God can't be the Author of it, because he is the God of
Order, not of Confusion. . . . But if God is pleased to convince
the Consciences of Persons, so that they can't avoid great outward Manifestations, even to the interrupting, and breaking off
those publick Means they were attending, I don't think this is
Confusion, or an unhappy Interruption, any more than if a
Company should meet on the Field to pray for Rain, and should
be broken off from their Exercise by a plentiful Shower. . . .[17]

Providence has cast my Lot in a Place where the Work of
God has formerly been carried on: I had the Happiness to be
settled in that Place two Years with the venerable STODDARD;
and was then acquainted with a Number that, during that
Season, were wro't upon, under his Ministry, and have been
intimately acquainted with the Experiences of many others,
that were wro't upon before under his Ministry, in a Manner
agreeable to his Doctrine, and the Doctrine of all orthodox.
Divines; and of late that Work has been carried on there, with
very much of these uncommon Opperations: but 'tis apparent to
all to be the same Work, not only that was wro't there six or
seven Years ago, but elder Christians there know it to be the
same Work that was carried on there, in the former Pastor's
Days, tho' there be some new Circumstances. And certainly we
must throw by all the Talk of Conversion and Christian Experience; and not only so, but we must throw by our Bibles, and
give up revealed Religion, if this be not in general the Work of
God. . . .

The Imprudences and Errors that have attended this Work,
are the less to be wonder'd at, if it be considered, that it is

chiefly young Persons that have been the Subjects of it, who have less Steadiness and Experience, and are in the Heat of Youth, and much more ready to run to Extreams. . . . And doubtless it has been one Occasion of much of the Misconduct there has been, that in many Places, People that are the Subjects of this Work of God's Spirit, see plainly that their Ministers have an ill Opinion of the Work; and therefore with just Reason, durst not apply themselves to 'em as their Guides in this Work; and so are without Guides: [18] and no Wonder that when a People are as Sheep without a Shepherd, they wander out of the Way. . . . And if a People have Ministers that favour the Work, and rejoyce in it, yet 'tis not to be expected that, either People or Ministers should know so well how to conduct themselves in such an extraordinary State of Things, while it is new, and what they never had any Experience of before, as they may, after they have had Experience, and Time to see the Tendency, Consequences and Issue of Things. The happy Influence of Experience is very manifest at this Day, in the People among whom God has settled my Abode. The Work of God that has been carried on there this Year, has been much purer than that which was wrought there six Years before: It has seem'd to be more purely spiritual; freer from natural and corrupt Mixtures, and any Thing favouring of enthusiastick Wildness & Extravagance. . . .

II. Let us all be hence warned, *by no Means to oppose, or do any Thing, in the least to clog or hinder that Work that has lately been carried on in the Land, but on the contrary, to do our utmost to promote it.* Now Christ is come down from Heaven into this Land, in a remarkable & wonderful Work of his Spirit, it becomes all his professed Disciples to acknowledge him, and give him Honour.

. . . .

Whether what has been said in this Discourse be enough to convince all that have heard it, that the Work that is now carried on in the Land, is the Work of God, or not, yet I hope that for the future, they will at least hearken to the Caution of *Gamaliel* that has been now mentioned; for the future not to oppose it, or say any Thing against it, or any Thing that has so much as an indirect Tendency to bring it into Discredit, least they should

be found to be Opposers of the Holy Ghost. There is no Kind of
Sins so hurtful and dangerous to the Souls of Men, as those that
are committed against the Holy Ghost. We had better speak
against God the Father, or the Son, than to speak against the
Holy Spirit in his gracious Operations on the Hearts of Men:
nothing will so much tend for ever to prevent our having any
Benefit of his Operations in our own Souls. . . .[19]

I come now in the

III. and last Place, to apply my self to those that are the
Friends of this Work, and have been Partakers of it, and are
zealous to promote it. Let me earnestly exhort such *to give
diligent heed to themselves to avoid all Errors & Misconduct, and
whatsoever may darken and obscure the Work, and give Occasion to those that stand ready to reproach it.* . . .

Some of the true Friends of the Work of God's Spirit have
err'd in giving too much heed to Impulses and strong Impressions
on their Minds as tho' they were immediate Significations from
Heaven, to them, of something that should come to pass, or
something that it was the Mind & Will of God that they should
do, which was not signified or revealed any where in the Bible
without those Impulses.

. . . .

And another Thing I would beg the dear Children of God
more fully to consider of, is; How far, and upon what Grounds,
the Rules of the holy Scriptures will truly justify their passing
Censures upon others that are professing Christians, as Hypocrites and ignorant of any Thing of real Religion.

. . . .

I know by Experience that there is a great Aptness in Men,
that think they have had some Experience of the Power of Religion, to think themselves sufficient to discern and determine
the State of others Souls, by a little Conversation with them; and
Experience has taught me that 'tis an Error. I once did not
imagine that the Heart of Man had been so unsearchable as I
find it is. I am less charitable, and less uncharitable than once I
was. I find more Things in wicked Men that may Counterfeit,
and make a fair Shew of Piety, and more Ways that the remaining Corruption of the Godly may make them appear like carnal
Men, Formalists and dead Hypocrites, than once I knew of. The

longer I live, the less I wonder that God challenges it as his Prerogative to try the Hearts of the Children of Men, and has directed that this Business should be let alone *till the Harvest.* . . .[20]

And another Thing that I would intreat the zealous Friends of this glorious Work of God to avoid, is managing the Controversy with Opposers with too much Heat, and Appearance of an angry Zeal; and particularly insisting very much in publick Prayer and Preaching, on the Persecution of Opposers. If their Persecution were ten Times so great as it is, methinks it would not be best to say so much about it. It becomes Christians to be like Lambs, not to be apt to complain and cry when they are hurt; to be dumb and not open their Mouth, after the Example of our dear Redeemer; and not to be like Swine, that are apt to scream aloud when they are touch'd. . . . Whatsoever has the Appearance of a great Innovation, that tends much to shock and surprize Peoples Minds, and to set them a talking and disputing, tends greatly to hinder the Progress of the Power of Religion. . . . Therefore that which is very much beside the common Practice, unless it be a Thing in it's own Nature of considerable Importance, had better be avoided. Herein we shall follow the Example of one, who had the greatest Success in propagating the Power of Religion in the World, of any Man that ever lived, that he himself gives us an Account of, 1 *Cor.* 9:20, 21, 22, 23. *Unto the Jews, I became as a Jew, that I might gain the Jews: to them that are under the Law, as under the Law, that I might gain them that are under the Law: To them that are without Law, (being not without Law to God, but under Law to Christ,) that I might gain them that are without Law: To the weak, became I as weak, that I might gain the weak: I am made all Things to all Men, that I might by all Means, save some. And this I do for the Gospel's sake, that I might be partaker thereof with you.*[21]

INTERROGATIVE NOTES

1. Do you think that Edwards's "laying out" of the Text serves sufficiently well to introduce the topic and to open the listeners to persuasion? How successfully does he fuse his topic with the authority

of the Bible? Today when a speech is delivered upon a noteworthy occasion, the speaker almost inevitably makes some references to the situation. What might have been Edwards's reasons for making no such references? In the introduction, Edwards explains that his design is to show the "true" evidences of a work of the spirit of God and that as a means of preparing the way he will first describe "signs" which are not reliable evidence. What are some of the assets and liabilities of such a use of definition by negation? Inasmuch as the section on negative signs proves to be considerably longer and much more vividly concrete than the one on true signs, do you think that Edwards did enough to prepare his listeners for this development?

2. How effectively do you think that Edwards handles this generation gap? How successful is his attempt to turn back upon the conservatives their own reliance upon continuity with the past?

3. By moving backward to the days of the apostles and forward to the end of the world, does Edwards succeed in developing an impression of all-inclusiveness? If so, does he accomplish this basically through logical or psychological means? Or, both?

4. As you read through the sermon, note the numerous times that Edwards refers to the nature of man as support for his theology and his rhetoric. (To understand better Edwards's references, you may wish to review the discussion in Part One concerning the morphology of conversion and the nature of man.)

5. In the following passage, observe Edwards's procedure of stating a basic premise, following it with familiar material, and then moving to a hypothetical particularization of the basic premise. In this case, do you think this procedure worked? Compare this passage with similar ones in his "Future Punishment" (Reading Number one) and with the readily available "Sinners in the Hands of an Angry God."

6. Inasmuch as Edwards exploits affirmative evidence from the Scriptures whenever possible, in answering this objection is he attempting to camouflage the weakness of his Scriptural proof?

7. This passage provides an important clue to Edwards's techniques of persuasion. As he does elsewhere in this speech, and in "Future Punishments," Edwards is attempting here to move his hearers swiftly from one strong emotion to its opposite. Empathizing as closely as possible with the listeners, estimate the impact of this persuasion. In a psychology text, check the modern theory concerning the effect upon the system caused by swift and extreme changes in emotions.

8. In defending the influence of emotional behavior upon other persons, Edwards attempts to subsume this controversial behavior under the hallowed principle of the "means" (i.e., that God employs various means to bring man to salvation, such as preaching, prayer, and so on), argues that nonverbal communication may have rational symbolic values, and that "example" has been an important part of all revivals from the days of the apostles to the present. According to natural scientists, absolute proof is achieved when a particular is classified

under a general covering law. Do you believe that Edwards has achieved such demonstration by his attempt to subsume "example" under the general principle of "means"?

9. To what extent, if any, is Edwards guilty here of distortion and camouflage?

10. Note carefully Edwards's citation of the church at Corinth so that you can contrast it with that of Charles Chauncy's usage in the next reading, "Enthusiasm Described and Caution'd Against."

11. What psychological and logical elements of strength exist in Edwards's defense of emotional preaching? What elements of weakness? Does he open himself to counterattacks?

12. Is Edwards using suitable economy of language here? How would you define "economy of language"? What effect is Edwards seeking?

13. Has Edwards lived up to his stated purpose of providing "true" and "certain" marks by which the presence of grace could be determined ("My Design therefore at this Time is to shew what are the true, certain, and distinguishing Evidences of a Work of the Spirit of God, by which we may proceed safely in judging of any Operation we find in ourselves, or see in others. . . .")? How does his stand compare to that of Solomon Stoddard, Edwards's grandfather and his predecessor in the Northampton pulpit (see Part One)? Since Stoddardism had been widely accepted in the Connecticut Valley, what influence might this difference have had upon the listeners? If we hypothesize that the difference may have had slight significance at the time of the speech, could this difference have a residual effect which influenced later behavior (remember that Edwards was dismissed from his pulpit in 1750)? Does Edwards come close to advocating "good works"? Would the application of the "marks" as measuring criteria be easy or difficult?

14. In this main head, Edwards states a basic conclusion, introduces the criteria necessary to prove this proposition of "fact," and applies the criteria. Does he state the criteria so that he seems to set up a pattern of absolute proof? How well do you think that his supporting evidence matches the criteria?

15. Drawing upon your knowledge of Edwards and his relationship to his audience, how persuasive were the logical elements of this appeal to *ethos*? The psychological elements?

16. Does this reference to Calvinist absolutism stand out distinctly? Or, does Edwards focus on it only peripherally? What might have been some of the reasons why Edwards would wish to de-emphasize absolute values in this speech?

17. Does Edwards really answer the question? Or, does he merely seem to? Does he change the question?

18. From both a logical and psychological standpoint, how persuasive is Edwards's attempt to "turn the tables" by blaming conservative ministers for the disorders?

19. For a threat like this to be effective, what conditions must be present?

20. Is Edwards contradicting his earlier statements concerning censoriousness?

21. Do you find summarizing qualities present in the Application, or "inferences" segment of the speech? Do you find a significant change in tone or mood from the earlier segments? Does the style of the Application seem better directed to a reading or listening audience? To exhortation or dehortation? To immediate or long-range effect?

Enthusiam Described and Caution'd Against

Charles Chauncy

A founder of the American Academy of Arts and Sciences and a member of the Harvard Board of Overseers, Chauncy was Edwards's peer as a scholar, albeit his inferior as an original or profound thinker. In many ways he was a paradox: he was disinterested in religious miracles, but during the Revolutionary War he was convinced that, if they were needed, God would send battalions of angels to help the Colonists fight the British; he proclaimed the dominion of reason in religion, but in political matters his emotionalism sometimes transcended good sense; he was gentle and indulgent by nature— and he preached a benign religion, but he was callous to human suffering and was antidemocratic in his class consciousness. When aroused, Chauncy was a highly effective warrior. The first of the Boston ministers to oppose the Awakening, he spoke out vigorously against the prevailing emotionalism. When James Davenport accosted him in his study and demanded proof of his conversion, Chauncy responded by preaching and publishing his "Enthusiasm Described." *

Like Edwards's "Distinguishing Marks," Chauncy's "Enthusiasm Described" was presented during a college commencement—the ceremonies of Harvard in 1742. A slashing attack upon the particular extremes of Davenport, it was also a general attack upon emotionalism in religion. Furthermore, to some extent it went beyond the defense of the traditional balance between reason and emotion to present a new and greater emphasis upon the rational in religion.

* For additional orientation, see Part One: The Developing Exigence. The text comes from Charles Chauncy, *Enthusiasm Described and Caution'd Against* (Boston, 1742).

1 CORINTHIANS 14:37

If any man among you think himself to be a PROPHET *or*
SPIRITUAL, *let him acknowledge that the Things that I*
write unto you are the Commandments of the LORD.

Many Things were amiss in the *Church* of *Corinth,* when
Paul wrote this Epistle to them.[1] There were envyings, strife and
divisions among them, on account of their ministers. Some cried
up one, others another: one said, I am of Paul, another I am of
APPOLLOS. They had form'd themselves into parties, and each
party so admired the teacher they followed, as to reflect unjust
contempt on the other.[2]

Nor was this their only fault. A spirit of pride prevailed exceedingly among them. They were conceited of their gifts, and
too generally dispos'd to make an ostentatious shew of them.
From this vain glorious temper . . . to the disturbance, rather
than edification of the church . . . they spake not by turns, but
several at once, in the same place of worship, to the introducing
such confusion, that they were in danger of being tho't mad.

Nor were they without some pretence to justify these disorders. Their great plea was, that in these things they were
guided by the Spirit, acted under his immediate influence and
direction. This seems plainly insinuated in the words I have read
to you. *If any man think himself to be a prophet, or Spiritual,*
let him acknowledge that the things that I write unto you are the
commandments of the Lord. . . . 'Tis all imagination, meer pretence, unless you pay a due regard to the commandments I have
here wrote to you. . . . You are nothing better than *Enthusiasts;*
your being acted by the SPIRIT, immediately guided and influenced by him, is meer pretence; you have no good reason to
believe any such thing.[3]

From the words thus explained, I shall take occasion to
discourse to you upon the following Particulars.

I. I shall give you some account of *Enthusiasm,* in its *nature*
and *influence.*

II. Point you to a rule by which you may judge of persons,
whether they are under the influence of *Enthusiasm.*

III. Say what may be proper to guard you against this unhappy turn of mind.

The whole will then be follow'd with some suitable
Application.

I. I am in the first place, to give you some account[4] of
Enthusiasm. . . . The word, from it's Etymology, carries in it a
good meaning, as signifying *inspiration from* GOD: in which
sense, the prophets under the old testament, and the apostles
under the new, might properly be called *Enthusiasts.* For they
were under a divine Influence, spake as moved by the HOLY
GHOST, and did such things as can be accounted for in no way,
but by recurring to an immediate extraordinary power, present
with them.

But the word is more commonly used in a bad sense, as
intending an *imaginary,* not a *real* inspiration: according to
which sense, the *Enthusiast* is one, who has a conceit of himself
as a person favoured with the extraordinary presence of the
Deity. He mistakes the workings of his own passions for divine
communications, and fancies himself immediately inspired by the
SPIRIT of GOD, when all the while, he is under no other
influence than that of an over-heated imagination.

The cause of this *enthusiasm* is a bad temperament of the
blood and spirits; 'tis properly a disease, a sort of madness. . . .
And various are the ways in which their enthusiasm discovers
itself.

Sometimes, it may be seen in their countenance. A certain
wildness is discernable in their general look and air; especially
when their imaginations are mov'd and fired.

Sometimes, it strangely loosens their tongues, and gives them
such an energy, as well as fluency and volubility in speaking, as
they themselves, by their utmost efforts, can't so much as imitate,
when they are not under the enthusiastick influence.

Sometimes, it affects their bodies, throws them into convulsions and distortions, into quakings and tremblings. . . .
Sometimes, it will unaccountably mix itself with their conduct,
and give it such a tincture of that which is freakish or furious,
as none can have an idea of, but those who have seen the behaviour, of a person in a phrenzy.

Sometimes, it appears in their imaginary peculiar intimacy with heaven. They are, in their own opinion, the special favourites of GOD, have more familiar converse with him than other good men, and receive immediate, extraordinary communications from him. The tho'ts which suddenly rise up in their minds, they take for suggestions of the SPIRIT; their very fancies are divine illuminations; nor are they strongly inclin'd to any thing, but 'tis an impulse from GOD, a plain revelation of his will. . . .

But in nothing does the enthusiasm of these persons discover it self more, than in the disregard they express to the Dictates of reason. They are above the force of argument, beyond conviction from a calm and sober address to their understandings. As for them, they are distinguish'd persons; GOD himself speaks inwardly and immediately to their souls. "They see the light infused into their understandings, and cannot be mistaken; 'tis clear and visible there, like the light of bright sunshine; shews it self and needs no other proof but its own evidence. They feel the hand of GOD moving them within, and the impulses of his SPIRIT; and cannot be mistaken in what they feel. Thus they support themselves, and are sure reason hath nothing to do with what they see and feel. What they have a sensible experience of, admits no doubt, needs no probation." And in vain will you endeavour to convince such persons of any mistakes they are fallen into. They are certainly in the right; and know themselves to be so. They have the SPIRIT opening their understandings and revealing the truth to them. They believe only as he has taught them: and to suspect they are in the wrong is to do dishonour to the SPIRIT; 'tis to oppose his dictates, to set up their own wisdom in opposition to his, and shut their eyes against that light with which he has shined into their souls. They are not therefore capable of being argued with; you had as good reason with the wind.

And as the natural consequence of their being thus sure of every thing, they are not only infinitely stiff and tenacious, but impatient of contradiction, censorious and uncharitable: they encourage a good opinion of none but such as are in their way of thinking and speaking.[5] Those, to be sure, who venture to de-

bate with them about their errors and mistakes, their weaknesses and indiscretions, run the hazard of being stigmatiz'd by them as poor unconverted wretches, without the SPIRIT, under the government of carnal reason, enemies to GOD and religion, and in the broad way to hell.

They are likewise positive and dogmatical, vainly fond of their own imaginations, and invincibly set upon propagating them: And in the doing of this, . . . they sometimes exert themselves with a sort of extatic violence: And 'tis this that gives them the advantage, among the less knowing and judicious, of those who are modest, suspicious of themselves, and not too assuming in matters of conscience and salvation. The extraordinary fervour of their mind, accompanied with uncommon bodily motions, and an excessive confidence and assurance, gains them great reputation among the populace; who speak of them as men of GOD in distinction from all others, and too commonly hearken to, and revere their dictates as tho' they really were, as they pretend, immediately communicated to them from the DIVINE SPIRIT.

This is the nature of *Enthusiasm,* and this is operation, in a less or greater degree, in all who are under the influence of it. 'Tis a kind of religious Phrenzy, and evidently discovers it self to be so, whenever it rises to any great height. . . .

But I come

II. In the second place, to point you to a *rule* by which you may judge of persons, whether they are *enthusiasts,* meer pretenders to the immediate guidance and influence of the SPIRIT. And this is, in general, *a regard to the bible, an acknowledgment that the things therein contained are the commandments of GOD.* This is the rule in the text. And 'tis an infallible rule of tryal in this matter: We need not fear judging amiss, while we keep closely to it.[6]

'Tis true, it wont certainly follow, that a man, pretending to be a *prophet,* or *Spiritual,* really is so, if he owns the *bible,* and receives the truths therein revealed as the mind of GOD: But the conclusion, on the other hand; is clear and certain; if he pretends to be conducted by the SPIRIT, and disregards the scripture, pays no due reverence to *the things there delivered as the*

commandments of GOD, he is a meer pretender, be his pretences ever so bold and confident, or made with ever so much seeming seriousness, gravity, or solemnity.

And the reason of this is obvious; viz that the things contained in the scripture were . . . received from God, and committed to writing under his immediate, extraordinary influence and guidance. And the divine, ever-blessed SPIRIT is consistent with himself. He cannot be supposed to be the author of any *private* revelations that are contradictory to the *public standing* ones. . . . 'Tis therefore as true, that those are *enthusiastical,* who pretend to the SPIRIT, and at the same time express a disregard to the scripture, as that the SPIRIT is the great revealer of the thing, therein declared to us. And we may depend upon the certainty of this conclusion. We have warrant to do so from the *inspired PAUL.* . . .

But the *rule* in the text is yet more particular. It refers especially to the *things wrote by the apostle* PAUL, and which he wrote to the *church* of *Corinth,* to rectify the *disorders* that had crept in among them. . . . And here suffer me to make particular mention of some of the things, the apostle has wrote in *this Epistle,* which, whoever will not acknowledge, in *deed* as well as *word,* to be the *commandments of GOD,* they are not guided by the SPIRIT, but vainly pretend to be so.

The first thing, in this kind, I would mention, is that which relates to *Ministers;* condemning an undue preference of one to another, the holding one in such admiration as to reflect disgrace on another. This was one of the disorders the Apostle takes notice of, as prevailing in the *church* of *Corinth;* and he is particular in his care to give check to this unchristian spirit, which had crumbled them into parties, and introduced among them faction and contention. . . .

Another thing the apostle is particular in writing upon, is the *commandment* of *charity.* And this he declares to be a matter of such essential importance in true christianity, that if a man is really destitute of it, he is nothing in the sight of GOD; Nay, tho' his pretences, his attainments, his gifts, be ever so extraordinary or miraculous; still, if he is without charity he will certainly be rejected of GOD and the LORD JESUS CHRIST.

This is beautifully represented in the three first verses of the 13th chapter of this Epistle, in some of the boldest figures. "Tho' I speak, says the apostle, with the tongues of men and of angels, and have not charity, I am become as sounding brass, or a tinkling cymbal. And tho' I have the gift of prophecy, and understand all mysteries and all Knowledge; and tho' I have all faith, so that I could remove mountains, and have not charity, I am nothing. And tho' I bestow all my goods to feed the poor, and tho' I give my body to be burned, and have not charity, it profiteth me nothing.". . .

And in vain may any pretend to be under the extraordinary guidance of the SPIRIT, while in their practice they trample upon this law of christian love. Men may talk of their *impulses* and *impressions*, conceive of them as the call of GOD, and go about, as moved by them, from place to place, imagining they are sent of GOD, and immediately commissioned by him: But if they are censorious and uncharitable; if they harbour in their minds evil surmisings of their brethren; if they slander and reproach them; if they claim a right to look into their hearts, make it their business to judge of their state, and proclaim them hypocrites, carnal unregenerate sinners, when at the same time they are visibly of a good conversation in CHRIST; I say, when this is the practice of any, they do not acknowledge what the inspired PAUL has here *wrote as the commandment of God.* . . . Charity, my brethren, is the commandment of the gospel by way of eminence. 'Tis the grand mark by which christians are to distinguish themselves from all others. . . .

Another thing the apostle bespeaks this church upon, is that self-conceit which appear'd among them in the exercise of spiritual gifts. . . .[7] 'Tis evident from what the apostle here writes, and indeed from the current strain of this whole chapter, that there is in the body of CHRIST, the Church, a distinction of members; some intended for one use, others for another; and that it would bring confusion into the *body mystical,* for one member to be employed in that service which is adapted to another, and is its proper business.

'Tis not therefore the pretence of being moved by the SPIRIT, that will justify *private christians* in quitting their own

proper station, to act in that which belongs to another. Such a practice as this naturally tends to destroy that order, GOD has constituted in the church, and may be followed with mischiefs greater than we may be aware of. . . . And 'tis owing to such pretences as these, that encouragement has been given to the rise of such numbers of *lay-exhorters and teachers,* in one place and another, all over the land. But if 'tis one of the things wrote by the apostles as the *commandment of* GOD, that there should be *officers* in the church, an *order of men* to whom it should belong, as their *proper, stated work,* to exhort and teach, this cannot be the business of others. . . . And indeed, if the SPIRIT has bid men to *abide in their own callings,* 'tis not conceivable he should influence them to *leave their callings.* . . .

The last thing I shall mention as written by the apostle, is that which obliges to a *just decorum in speaking* in the *house of* GOD. It was an extravagance these *Corinthians* had fallen into, their speaking many of them together, and upon different things, while in the same place of worship. *How is it, brethren,* says the apostle? *When ye come together, every one hath a psalm; hath a doctrine; hath a tongue; hath a revelation; hath an interpretatien.* It was this that introduced the confusion and noise, upon which the apostle declares, if an unbeliever should come in among them, he would take them to be mad. And the *commandment* he gives them to put a stop to this disorder, is, that they should *speak in course, one by one,* and so as that *things might be done to edifying.* . . .

The disorder of EXHORTING, and PRAYING, and SINGING, and LAUGHING, *in the same house of worship, at one and the same time,* is as great as was that, the apostle blames in the *church of Corinth:* And whatever the persons, guilty of such gross irregularity may imagine, and however they may plead their being under the influence of the SPIRIT, and mov'd by him, 'tis evidently a breach upon common order and decency; yea, a direct violation of the *commandment* of GOD, written on purpose to prevent such disorders. . . . In these, and all other instances, let us compare men's pretences to the SPIRIT by the SCRIPTURE: And if their conduct is such as can't be reconcil'd with an *acknowledgment of the things therein revealed, as the*

commandments of GOD, their pretences are vain, they are *prophets* and *Spiritual,* only in their own proud imaginations.[8] I proceed now to

III. The third thing, which is to caution you against giving way to *enthusiastic impressions.* And here much might be said,

I might warn you from the *dishonour* it reflects upon the SPIRIT OF GOD. And perhaps none have more reproach'd the blessed SPIRIT, than men pretending to be under his extraordinary guidance and direction. The veryest fancies, the vainest imaginations, the strongest delusions, they have father'd on him. There is scarce any absurdity in *principle,* or irregularity in *practice,* but he has been made the patron of it. . . .

I might also warn you from the damage it has done in the world. . . . It has, in one word, been a pest to the church in all ages, as great an enemy to real and solid religion, as perhaps the grossest *infidelity.*

I might go on and warn you from the danger of it to yourselves. If you should once come under the influence of it, none can tell whither it would carry you. There is nothing so wild and frantick, but you may be reconcil'd to it. And if this shou'd be your case, your recovery to a right mind would be one of the most difficult things in nature. . . .

But as the most suitable guard against the first tendencies towards *enthusiasm,* let me recommend to you the following words of counsel.

1. Get a true understanding of the *proper work of the* SPIRIT; and don't place it in those things wherein the gospel does not make it to consist. The work of the SPIRIT is different now from what it was in the first days of christianity. Men were then favoured with the extraordinary presence of the SPIRIT. He came upon them in miraculous gifts and powers; as a spirit of prophecy, of knowledge, of revelation, of tongues, of miracles: But the SPIRIT is not now to be expected in these ways.[9] His grand business lies in preparing men's minds for the grace of GOD, by true *humiliation,* from an apprehension of sin, and the necessity of a *Saviour;* then in working in them *faith* and *repentance,* and such a *change* as shall *turn them from the power of sin and Satan unto* GOD. . . .

Herein, in general, consists the work of the SPIRIT. It does not lie in giving men *private revelations*, but in opening their minds to understand the *publick ones* contained in the scripture. It does not lie in *sudden impulses* and *impressions*, in *immediate calls* and *extraordinary missions*. . . .

2. Keep close to the *Scripture*, and admit of nothing for an impression of the SPIRIT, but what agrees with that unerring rule. . . . And whatever you are moved to, reject the motion, esteem it as nothing more than a vain fancy, if it puts you upon any method of *thinking*, or *acting*, that can't be evidently reconcil'd with the *revelations* of GOD in *his word*. . . .

3. Make use of the *Reason* and *Understanding* [10] GOD has given you.[11] This may be tho't an ill-advis'd direction, but 'tis as necessary as either of the former. Next to the *Scripture*, there is no greater enemy to *enthusiasm*, than *reason*. 'Tis indeed impossible a man should be an *enthusiast*, who is in the just exercise of his understanding; and 'tis because men don't pay a due regard to the sober dictates of a well inform'd mind, that they are led aside by the delusions of a vain imagination. Be advised then to shew yourselves men, to make use of your reasonable powers; and not act as the *horse* or *mule*, as tho' you had no understanding.

'Tis true, you must not go about to set up your own *reason* in *opposition* to *revelation*: Nor may you entertain a tho't of making *reason* your *rule* instead of *Scripture*. The *bible*, as I said before, is the *great rule* of religion, the grand test in matters of salvation: But then, you must use your reason in order to understand the *bible*: Nor is there any other possible way, in which, as a reasonable creature, you shou'd come to an understanding of it.

You are, it must be acknowledged, in a corrupt state. The fall has introduc'd great weakness into your reasonable nature. You can't be too sensible of this; nor of the danger you are in of making a wrong judgment, thro' prejudice, carelessness, and the undue influence of sin and lust. And to prevent this, you can't be too solicitous to get your *nature Sanctified:* Nor can you depend too strongly upon the divine grace to assist you in your search after truth: And 'tis in the way of due dependance on GOD, and

the influences of his SPIRIT, that I advise you to the use of your reason: And in this way, you must make use of it. How else will you know what is a revelation from GOD? What shou'd hinder your entertaining the same tho't of a *pretended* revelation, as of a *real* one, but your reason discovering the falshood of the one, and the truth of the other? And when in the enjoyment of an undoubted revelation from GOD, as in the case of the *scripture,* How will you understand its meaning, if you throw by your reason? How will you determine, that this, and not that, is its true sense, in this and the other place? Nay, if no reasoning is to be made use of, are not all the senses that can be put on scripture equally proper? Yea, may not the most contrary senses be receiv'd at the same time since reason only can point out the inconsistency between them? And what will be sufficient to guard you against the most monstrous extravagancies, in *principle* as well as *practice,* if you give up your understandings? What have you left, in this case, to be a check to the wantoness of your imaginations? What shou'd hinder your following every idle fancy, 'till you have lost yourselves in the wilds of falshood and inconsistency?

You may, it is true, misuse your reason: And this is a consideration, that shou'd put you upon a due care, that you may use it well; but no argument why you shou'd not use it at all: And indeed, if you shou'd throw by your reason as a useless thing, you would at once put your selves in the way of all manner of delusion.

But, it may be, you will say, you have committed yourselves to the *guidance* of the SPIRIT; which is the best preservative. Herein you have done well; nothing can be objected against this method of conduct: Only take heed of mistakes, touching the SPIRIT's *guidance.* Let me enquire of you, how is it the SPIRIT preserves from delusion? Is it not by opening the understanding, and enabling the man, in the due use of his reason, to perceive the truth of the things of GOD and religion? Most certainly: And, if you think of being led by the SPIRIT, without understanding, or in opposition to it, you deceive yourselves. The SPIRIT of GOD deals with men as *reasonable* creatures: And they ought to deal with themselves in like manner. And while

they do thus, making a wise and good use of the understanding, GOD has given them, they will take a proper means to prevent their falling into delusions; nor will there be much danger of their being led aside by *enthusiastic* heat and imagination.

4. You must not lay too great stress upon the *workings* of your *passions* and *affections*. These will be excited in a less or greater degree, in the business of religion: And 'tis proper they shou'd. The passions, when suitably mov'd, tend mightily to awaken the *reasonable powers,* and put them upon a lively and vigorous exercise. And this is their proper use: And when ad-dress'd to, and excited to this purpose, they may be of good service: whereas we shall mistake the right use of the passions, if we place our religion *only* or *chiefly,* in the heat and fervour of them. The *soul* is the *man:* [12] And unless the *reasonable nature* is suitably wro't upon, the *understanding* enlightned, the *judgment* convinc'd, the *will* perswaded, and the *mind* intirely chang'd, it will avail but to little purpose; tho' the passions shou'd be set all in a blaze. This therefore you shou'd be most concern'd about. And if while you are sollicitous that you may be in transports of affection, you neglect your more noble part, your reason and judgment, you will be in great danger of being carried away by your imaginations. This indeed leads directly to *Enthusiasm:* And you will in vain, endeavour to preserve your-selves from the influence of it, if you a'nt duly careful to keep your passions in their proper place under the government of a well inform'd understanding. While the passions are uppermost, and bear the chief sway over a man, he is in an unsafe state: None knows what he may be bro't to. You can't therefore be too careful to keep your passions under the regimen of a *sober judgment.* 'Tis indeed a matter of necessity, as you would not be led aside by delusion and fancy.

5. In the last place here, you must not forget to go to GOD by *prayer.* . . . And if he shall please to undertake for you, no delusion shall ever have power over you, to seduce you; but, possessing a sound mind, you shall go on in the uniform, steady service of your maker and generation, till of the mercy of GOD, thro' the merits of the REDEEMER, you are crowned with eternal life.[13]

But I shall now draw towards a close, by making some suitable *application* of what has been said,[14] And,

1. Let us beware of charging GOD *foolishly*, from what we have heard of the *nature*, and *influence* of *enthusiasm*. This may appear a dark article in GOD'S government of the world; but it stands upon the same foot with his permission of other evils, whether *natural* or *moral*.

. . . .

2. Let none, from what has been offered, entertain prejudices in their minds against the *operations* of the SPIRIT. There is such a thing as his influence upon the hearts of men. No consistent sense can be put upon a great part of the *bible*, unless this be acknowledged for a truth: Nor is it any objection against its being so, that there has been a great deal of *enthusiasm* in the world, many who have mistaken the motions of their own passions for divine operations. This, it must be acknowledged, shou'd make us cautious. . . . But at the same time, 'tis no reason, why we shou'd think the worse of the blessed SPIRIT, or of those influences that are really his . . . lest we shou'd grieve the *good* SPIRIT, and he shou'd leave us to perish in a state of alianation from GOD, and true holiness.

. . . .

3. Let not any think *ill* of religion, because of the *ill* representation that is made of it by *enthusiasts*. . . . There is such a thing as real religion,[15] let the conduct of men be what it will; and 'tis, in it's nature, a sober, calm, reasonable thing: Nor is it an objection of any weight against the sobriety or reasonableness of it, that there have been *enthusiasts*, who have acted as tho' it was a wild, imaginary business. We should not make our estimate of religion as exhibited in the behaviour of men of a *fanciful* mind; to be sure, we should not take up an ill opinion of it, because in the example they give of it, it don't appear so amiable as we might expect. This is unfair. We shou'd rather judge of it from the conduct of men of a *sound judgment;* whose lives have been such a uniform, beautiful transcript of that which is just and good, that we can't but think well of religion, as display'd in their example. . . .

4. Let us esteem those as *friends* to religion, and not *ene-*

mies, who warn us of the danger of *enthusiasm,* and would put us upon our guard, that we be not led aside by it.[16] . . . This land had, in all probability, been over-run with confusion and distraction, if they acted under the influence of the same *heat* and *zeal,* which some others have been famous for.

. . . .

The good LORD give us all wisdom; and courage, and conduct, in such a Day as this! And may both *ministers* and *people* behave after such a manner, as that religion may not suffer; but in the end, gain advantage, and be still more universally established.

And, may that grace of GOD, which has appeared to all men, bringing salvation, teach us effectually, to deny ungodliness and worldly lusts, and to live soberly, and righteously, and godlily in the world: so may we look with comfort for the appearing of our SAVIOUR JESUS CHRIST: And when he shall appear in the glory of his FATHER, and with his holy angels, we also shall appear with him, and go away into everlasting life: Which GOD, of his infinite mercy grant may be the portion of us all; for the sake of CHRIST JESUS.

INTERROGATIVE NOTES

1. In relation to Edwards's "Distinguishing Marks" (Reading Number Two), would you characterize Chauncy's strategy in this speech as presenting purely a refutative counterattack? A defense of conditions which existed before the revival? A counterproposal representing a new emphasis upon the rational in religion? A combination of approaches? In view of Chauncy's role as a leader of the emerging opposition to emotional religion, how well do you think he selected his strategy? Within the confines of his strategy, how well does he pattern his arguments?

2. Compare Chauncy's use of the church of Corinth with that of Edwards in his "Distinguishing Marks" (see note no. 10, Reading Number Two). To what extent does Chauncy agree with Edwards concerning the nature of the disturbances in the Corinth church? How does he bend this data to fit his different conclusions? Is this citation more important to Chauncy's case?

3. In his "laying out" of the Text, Chauncy is attempting to promote the

acceptance of his basic premise so that he can then reason deductively from the established "universal truth" to the particular application or conclusion. What means does he use to substantiate his premise?

4. In developing this head, Chauncy first states the point, then he defines "enthusiasm" by explaining what it is not and what it is, suggests the cause of enthusiasm, illustrates the various manifestations of enthusiasm, indicates its evil influence, and, finally, summarizes the thought. Does this development seem overly structured? In fleshing out this development does Chauncy direct his appeal exclusively to the reasoning of the listeners? Is his development deceptive in that it gives the appearance of appealing to the intellect when, in reality, it appeals strongly to the emotions as well?

5. In the following paragraphs, note carefully the methodology of Chauncy's attack upon the irrationality, censoriousness, and emotional preaching of the revivalists. In the Inquiry section of our volume, we shall return to this point.

6. Chauncy is here attempting to establish an infallible general principle or premise which will permit him to reason deductively—and with certainty—to particular derivatives of this premise. How effective is his defense of the basic principle? Why did he believe that this defense was necessary? If one accepts Chauncy's covering law, does one logically have to accept as spiritual aberrations the specific items discussed in the following paragraphs?

7. In developing this point, to what extent—if any—does Chauncy give evidence of an antidemocratic sentiment? Have you detected any such flavor previously in this speech?

8. Chauncy makes extensive use of internal summaries to restate and to refocus attention upon the essential push of his major arguments. Here he not only reiterates the basic thought of this main head but he also attempts to link the point to the fundamental premise underlying his entire case. Does Chauncy carry out his development so that his technique is unobtrusive? Or, does it stand out badly?

9. In comparison to Edwards's views, do you find a fundamentally different concept of religion suggested here in phrases such as "in preparing men's minds" and "in opening their minds"? In what ways —if any—does Chauncy attempt to make rationality in religion seem attractive? Necessary?

10. What evidence do you find in this and in succeeding sections to demonstrate that Chauncy accepts the terminology and the concepts of faculty psychology?

11. In the next few pages you will find a capsulated statement of Chauncy's argument for rational religion. What kinds of persons would be most apt to respond affirmatively to such appeals? To respond negatively? Estimate the clarity and modernity of his arguments.

12. Chauncy's phrase "The *soul* is the *man*" is critically important to his argument. Read this paragraph carefully to appreciate the thrust of

his composition. This topic will come to our attention again in the Inquiry section.

13. Without rereading the speech, recall your impressions concerning Chauncy's use of slanted language (as in this sentence his reference to "sound mind" and "uniform, steady service"), figurative language, homey expressions, idiomatic speech, and vivid concreteness. Does his style seem to be fresh? Lively? Forceful?

14. Does Chauncy appear to be completely sincere in the applications which he advances? Do his applications seem contrived in part, at least, as backhanded slaps at his opponents?

15. In this definition of "real religion," does Chauncy give the impression of speaking in a coolly rational manner while, in reality, he wishes to evoke the emotions? Perhaps without his being conscious of it, has he conjoined logical and emotional appeals?

16. What are the needs of his argument that prompted Chauncy to include this point?

Concerning the Nature of the Affections, and Their Importance in Religion

Jonathan Edwards

During the winter of 1742–43, in response to the widespread opposition which had developed to the excesses of the revival, Edwards delivered a series of sermons defending and explaining the role of emotion in religion. "Concerning the Nature of the Affections" * is the first of the lectures in this series. Missing from this speech are the impelling emotional appeals and the sulfurous fumes which were so overpowering in "Future Punishments" and which were present to a lesser extent in the "Distinguishing Marks." Missing, too, are the stridency, the abrasiveness, the confidence, and the clarion calls to action. Appearing to recognize that the chief peril to his cause was the misunderstanding of his supporters, in this series Edwards seems to address particularly his allies, explaining the role of emotion in religion and cautioning against excesses. Although the tone throughout the sermons is ostensibly expository, the style is affectingly directed to the senses, and the implicit thrust is evocative.

Possibly "the most profound explanation of the religious psychology in all American literature," these sermons represent Edwards's mature position concerning the relation of the emotions to religion. Affections are the substance of religion. By their nature, saving affections are reasonable and rational. They cannot be experienced, however, through the censoring agency of the Understanding which— as a disinterested and distant spectator—passes impersonal, objective judgments. Of central significance to his confrontations with the antirevivalists, Edwards called for the involvement, the engagement, of the reason as an integral part of the whole man's experiencing of religion.

---

* Along with the other lectures in this series, "The Nature of the Affections" was published in 1746 under the title, *A Treatise Concerning Religious Affections.* The text of our copy comes from the *Treatise.* For further orientation, see Part One: The Developing Exigence.

1 PETER 1:8

Whom having not seen, ye love: In whom, though now ye see him not, yet believing, ye rejoice with Joy unspeakable, and full of Glory.

In these Words, the Apostle represents the State of the Minds of the Christians he wrote to, under the Persecutions they were then the subjects of.[1] These Persecutions are what he has Respect to, in the two preceeding Verses, when he speaks of *the Trial of their Faith,* and of *their being in Heaviness through manifold Temptations.*

Such Trials are of threefold Benefit to true Religion: Hereby the truth of it is manifested, and it appears to be indeed *true Religion:* They, above all other Things, have a Tendency to distinguish between true Religion and false, and to cause the Difference between them evidently to appear. Hence they are called by the Name of *Trials,* in the Verse nextly preceeding the Text, and in innumerable other Places: They try the Faith and Religion of Professors, of what Sort it is; as apparent Gold is tried in the Fire, and manifested, whether it be true Gold or no. And the Faith of true Christians being thus tried and proved to be true, is *found to Praise, and Honour, and Glory;* as in that preceeding Verse.

And then, These Trials are of further Benefit to true Religion; they not only manifest the *Truth* of it, but they make it's genuine *Beauty* and *Amiableness* remarkably to appear. True Vertue never appears so lovely, as when it is most oppressed: And the divine Excellency of real Christianity, is never exhibited with such Advantage, as when under the greatest Trials: Then it is that true Faith appears much more precious than Gold; and upon this Account, is *found to Praise, and Honour, and Glory.*

And again, Another Benefit that such Trials are of to true Religion, is, that they purify and increase it. They not only manifest it to be true, but also tend to refine it, and deliver it from those Mixtures of that which is false, which incumber and impede it; that nothing may be left but that which is true. They tend to cause the Amiableness of true Religion to appear to the best Advantage, as was before observed; and not only so, but

they tend to increase it's Beauty, by establishing and confirming it, and making it more lively and vigourous, and purifying it from those Things that obscured it's Lustre and Glory. As Gold that is tried in the Fire, is purged from it's Alloy, and all Remainders of Dross, and comes forth more solid and beautiful; so true Faith being tried as Gold is tried in the Fire, becomes more precious; and thus also is *found unto Praise, and Honour, and Glory.* The Apostle seems to have Respect to each of these Benefits, that Persecutions are of to true Religion, in the Verse preceeding the Text.

And in the Text, the Apostle observes how true Religion operated in the Christians he wrote to, under their Persecutions, whereby these Benefits of Persecution appeared in them; or what manner of Operation of true Religion, in them, it was, whereby their Religion, under Persecution, was manifested to be *true* Religion, and eminently appeared in the genuine *Beauty* and *Amiableness* of true Religion, and also appeared to be *increased* and *purified,* and so was like to be *found unto Praise, and Honour, and Glory, at the Appearing of Jesus Christ.* And there were two Kinds of Operation, or Exercise of true Religion, in them, under their Sufferings, that the Apostle takes Notice of in the Text, wherein these Benefits appeared.

1. *Love to Christ; Whom having not seen, ye love.* The World was ready to wonder, what strange Principle it was, that influenc'd them to expose themselves to so great Sufferings, to forsake the Things that were seen, and renounce all that was dear and pleasant, which was the Object of Sense: They seem'd to the Men of the World about them, as though they were beside themselves, and to act as tho' they hated themselves; there was nothing in their View, that could induce them thus to suffer, and support them under, and carry them thro' such Trials. But altho' there was nothing that was seen, nothing that the World saw, or that the Christians themselves ever saw with their bodily Eyes, that thus influenced and supported 'em; yet they had a supernatural Principle of Love to something *unseen;* they loved Jesus Christ, for they saw him spiritually, whom the World saw not, and whom they themselves had never seen with bodily Eyes.

2. *Joy in Christ.* Tho' their outward Sufferings were very

grievous, yet their inward spiritual Joys were greater than their Sufferings, and these supported them, and enabled them to suffer with Chearfulness.

There are two Things which the Apostle takes Notice of in the Text concerning this Joy. 1. The Manner in which it rises, the Way in which Christ, tho' unseen, is the Foundation of it, *viz.* By Faith; which is the Evidence of Things not seen; *In whom, though now ye see him not, yet* beleiving, *ye rejoice——*. 2. The Nature of this Joy; *unspeakable, and full of Glory.*[2] *Unspeakable* in the *Kind* of it; very different from worldly Joys, and carnal Delights; of a vastly more pure, sublime and heavenly Nature, being something supernatural, and truly divine, and so ineffably excellent; the Sublimity, and exquisite Sweetness of which, there were no Words to set forth. Unspeakable also in *Degree;* it pleasing God to give 'em this holy Joy, with a liberal Hand, and in large Measure, in their State of Persecution.

Their Joy was *full of Glory:* Altho' the Joy was unspeakable, and no Words were sufficient to describe it; yet something might be said of it, and no Words more fit to represent it's Excellency, than these, that it was *full of Glory;* or, as it is in the Original, *glorified Joy.* In rejoicing with this Joy, their Minds were filled, as it were, with a glorious Brightness, and their Natures exalted and perfected: It was a most worthy, noble Rejoicing, that did not corrupt and debase the Mind, as many carnal Joys do; but did greatly beautify and dignify it: It was a Prelibation of the Joy of Heaven, that raised their Minds to a Degree of heavenly Blessedness: It fill'd their Minds with the Light of God's Glory, and made 'em themselves to shine with some Communication of that Glory.

Hence the Proposition of Doctrine, that I would raise from these Words is this,

DOCT. *True Religion, in great Part, consists in holy Affections.*

We see that the Apostle, in observing and remarking the Operations and Exercises of Religion, in the Christians he wrote to, wherein their Religion appeared to be true and of the right Kind, when it had it's greatest Trial of what Sort it was, being tried by Persecution as Gold is tried in the Fire, and when their Religion not only proved true, but was most pure, and cleansed

from it's Dross and Mixtures of that which was not true, and when Religion appeared in them most in it's genuine Excellency and native Beauty, and was found to Praise, and Honour, and Glory; he singles out the religious Affections of *Love* and *Joy*, that were then in exercise in them: These are the Exercises of Religion he takes Notice of, wherein their Religion did thus appear true and pure, and in it's proper Glory.

Here I would,

I. Shew what is intended by the *Affections*,

II. Observe some Things which make it evident, that a great Part of true Religion lies in the Affections.

I. It may be enquired, what the Affections of the Mind are? I answer, The Affections are no other, than the more vigorous and sensible Exercises of the Inclination and Will of the Soul.[3]

God has induced the Soul with two Faculties: [4] One is that by which it is capable of Perception and Speculation, or by which it discerns and views and judges of Things; which is called the Understanding. The other Faculty is that by which the Soul don't merely perceive and view Things, but is some Way inclin'd with respect to the Things it views or considers; either is inclined to 'em, or is disinclined, and averse *from 'em;* or is the Faculty by which the Soul don't behold Things, as an indifferent unaffected Spectator, but either as liking or disliking, pleas'd or displeas'd, approving or rejecting. This Faculty is called by various Names: It is sometimes called the *Inclination:* And, as it has respect to the Actions that are determined and governed by it, is called the *Will:* And the Mind, with regard to the Exercises of this Faculty, is often called the *Heart.*

The Exercises of this Faculty are of two Sorts; either those by which the Soul is carried out towards the Things that are in view, in *approving* of them, being pleased with them, and inclined to them; or those in which the Soul opposes the Things that are in view, in *disapproving* them, and in being displeased with them, averse from them, and rejecting them.

And as the Exercises of the Inclination and Will of the

Soul are various in their *Kinds,* so they are much more various
in their *Degrees.* There are some Exercises of Pleasedness or
Displeasedness, Inclination or Disinclination, wherein the Soul
is carried but a little beyond a State of perfect Indifference.
And there are other Degrees above this, wherein the Approbation or Dislike, Pleasedness or Aversion, are stronger; wherein
we may rise higher and higher, 'till the Soul comes to act vigorously and sensibly, and the Actings of the Soul are with that
Strength that (thro' the Laws of the Union which the Creator
has fix'd between Soul and Body) the Motion of the Blood and
animal Spirits begins to be sensibly alter'd; whence oftentimes
arises some bodily Sensation, especially about the Heart and
Vitals, that are the Fountain of the Fluids of the Body: From
whence it comes to pass, that the Mind, with regard to the
Exercises of this Faculty, perhaps in all Nations and Ages, is
called *the Heart.* And it is to be noted, that they are these more
rigorous and sensible Exercises of this Faculty, that are called
the *Affections.*

The *Will,* and the *Affections* of the Soul, are not two Faculties; the Affections are not essentially distinct from the Will,
nor do they differ from the meer Actings of the Will and Inclination of the Soul, but only in the Liveliness and Sensibleness
of Exercise.

It must be confessed, that Language is here somewhat
imperfect, and the Meaning of Words in a considerable Measure
loose and unfixed, and not precisely limited by Custom, which
governs the Use of Language. In some Sense, the Affection of
the Soul differs nothing at all from the Will and Inclination,
and the Will never is in any Exercise any further than it is
affected; it is not moved out of a State of perfect Indifference,
any otherwise than as it is *affected* one Way or other, and
acts nothing voluntarily any further. But yet there are many
Actings of the Will and Inclination, that are not so commonly
called *Affections:* In every Thing we do, wherein we act voluntarily, there is an Exercise of the Will and Inclination, 'tis our
Inclination that governs us in our Actions: But all the actings
of the Inclination and Will, in all our common Actions of Life,
are not ordinarily called Affections. Yet, what are commonly

called Affections are not essentially different from them, but only in the Degree and Manner of Exercise. In every Act of the Will whatsoever, the Soul either likes or dislikes, is either inclined or disinclined to what is in view: These are not essentially different from those Affections of *Love* and *Hatred:* That Liking or Inclination of the Soul to a Thing, if it be in a high Degree, and be vigorous and Lively, is the very same Thing with Affection of *Love:* And that Disliking and Disinclining, if in a great Degree, is the very same with *Hatred.* In every Act of the Will *for,* or *towards* something not present, the Soul is in some Degree inclined to that Thing; and that Inclination, if in a considerable Degree, is the very same with the Affection of *Desire.* And in every Degree of the Act of the Will, wherein the Soul approves of something Present, there is a Degree of Pleasedness; and that Pleasedness, if it be in a considerable Degree, is the very same with the Affection of *Joy* or *Delight.* And if the Will disapproves of what is present, the Soul is in some Degree displeased, and if that Displeasedness be great, 'tis the very same with the Affection of *Grief* or *Sorrow.*

Such seems to be our Nature, and such the Laws of the Union of Soul and Body, that there never is in any Case whatsoever, any lively and vigorous Exercise of the Will or Inclination of the Soul, without some Effect upon the Body, in some Alteration of the Motion of it's Fluids, and especially of the animal Spirits.[5] And on the other Hand, from the same Laws of the Union of Soul and Body, the Constitution of the Body, and the Motion of it's Fluids, may promote the Exercise of the Affections. But yet, it is not the Body, but the Mind only, that is the proper Seat of the Affections.[6] The Body of Man is no more capable of being really the Subject of Love or Hatred, Joy or Sorrow, Fear or Hope, than the Body of a Tree, or than the same Body of Man is capable of thinking and understanding. As 'tis the Soul only that has Ideas, so 'tis the Soul only that is pleased or displeased with it's Ideas. As 'tis the Soul only that thinks, so 'tis the Soul only that loves or hates, rejoices or is grieved at what it thinks of.[7] Nor are these Motions of the animal Spirits, and Fluids of the Body, any thing properly belonging to the Nature of the Affections; tho' they always

accompany them, in the present State; but are only Effects or Concomitants of the Affections, that are entirely distinct from the Affections themselves, and no Way essential to them; so that an unbodied Spirit may be as capable of Love and Hatred, Joy or Sorrow, Hope or Fear, or other Affections, as one that is united to a Body.

The *Affections* and *Passions* are frequently spoken of as the same; and yet, in the more common Use of Speech, there is in some Respect a Difference; and *Affection* is a Word, that in it's ordinary Signification, seems to be something more extensive than *Passion;* being used for all vigorous lively Actings of the Will or Inclination; but Passion for those that are more sudden, and whole Effects on the animal Spirits are more violent, and the Mind more overpower'd, and less in its own Command.

As all the Exercises of the Inclination and Will, are either in approving and liking, or disapproving and rejecting; so the Affections are of two Sorts; they are those by which the Soul is carried out to what is in view, cleaving *to* it, or *seeking* it; or those by which it is averse *from* it, and *opposes* it.

Of the former Sort are *Love, Desire, Hope, Joy, Gratitude, Complacence.* Of the latter Kind, are *Hatred, Fear, Anger, Grief,* and such like; which it is needless now to stand particularly to define.

And there are some Affections wherein there is a Composition of each of the aforementioned Kinds of Actings of the Will; as in the Affection of *Pity,* there is something of the *former Kind,* towards the Person suffering, and something of the *Latter,* towards what he suffers. And so in *Zeal,* there is in it high *Approbation* of some Person or Thing, together with vigorous *Opposition* to what is conceived to be contrary to it.

There are other mixt Affections that might be also mention'd, but I hasten to the

IId. Thing proposed, Which was to observe some Things that render it evident, that true Religion, in Great Part, consists in the Affections. And here,

1. What has been said of the Nature of the Affections, makes this evident, and may be sufficient, without adding any

thing further, to put this Matter out of Doubt: For who will deny that true Religion consists, in a great Measure, in vigorous and lively Actings of the *Inclination* and *Will* of the Soul, or the fervent Exercises of the *Heart*.

That Religion which God requires, and will accept, don't consist in weak, dull and lifeless Wouldings, raising us but a little above a State of Indifference: God, in his Word, greatly insists upon it, that we be in good Earnest, *fervent in Spirit,* and our Hearts vigorously engaged in Religion: Rom. 12:11. *Be ye fervent in Spirit, serving the Lord.* Deut. 10:12. *And now* Israel, *What doth the Lord thy God require of thee, but to fear the Lord thy God, to walk in all his Ways, and to love him, and to serve the Lord thy God, with all thy Heart, and with all thy Soul?* And Chap. 6:4, 5. *Hear, O* Israel; *the Lord our God is one Lord; and thou shalt love the Lord thy God, with all thy Heart, and with all thy Soul, and with all thy Might.* 'Tis such a fervent, vigorous Engagedness of the Heart in Religion, that is the Fruit of a real Circumcision of the Heart, or true Regeneration, and that has the Promises of Life; Deut. 30:6. *And the Lord thy God will circumcise thine Heart, and the Heart of thy Seed, to love the Lord thy God, with all thy Heart, and with all thy Soul, that thou mayest live.*

If we ben't in good earnest in Religion, and our Wills and Inclinations ben't strongly exercised, we are nothing. The Things of Religion are so great, that there can be no Suitableness in the Exercises of our Hearts, to their Nature and Importance, unless they be lively and powerful. In nothing, is Vigour in the Actings of our Inclinations so requisite, as in Religion; and in nothing is Lukewarmness so odious. True Religion is evermore a powerful Thing; and the Power of it appears, in the first Place, in the inward Exercises of it in the Heart, where is the principal and original Seat of it. Hence true Religion is called the *Power of Godliness,* in Distinction from the external Appearances of it, that are *the Form* of it, 2 Tim. 3:5. *Having a Form of Godliness, but denying the Power of it.* The Spirit of God, in those that have sound and solid Religion, is a Spirit of powerful holy Affection; and therefore, God is said *to have given them the Spirit of Power, and*

of Love, and of a sound Mind, 2 Tim. 1:7. And such, when they
receive the Spirit of God, in his sanctifying and saving Influences, are said to be *baptized with the Holy Ghost, and with
Fire;* by reason of the Power and Fervour of those Exercises
the Spirit of God excites in their Hearts, whereby their Hearts,
when Grace is in exercise, may be said to *burn within them;*
as is said of the Disciples, *Luke* 24:32.

The Business of Religion is, from Time to Time, compared
to those Exercises, wherein Men are wont to have their Hearts
and Strength greatly exercised and engaged; such as Running,
Wrestling or Agonizing for a great Prize or Crown, and Fighting
with strong Enemies that seek our Lives, and Warring as those
that by Violence take a City or Kingdom.

And tho' true Grace has various Degrees, and there are
some that are but Babes in Christ, in whom the Exercise of the
Inclination and Will towards divine and heavenly Things, is
comparatively weak; yet every one that has the Power of Godliness in his Heart, has his Inclinations and Heart exercised
towards God and divine Things, with such Strength and Vigour, that these holy Exercises do prevail in him above all
carnal or natural Affections, and are effectual to overcome
them: For every true Disciple of Christ, *loves him above Father
or Mother, Wife and Children, Brethren and Sisters, Houses
and Lands; yea, than his own Life.* From hence it follows, that
wherever true Religion is, there are vigorous Exercises of the
Inclination and Will, towards divine Objects: But by what was
said before, the vigorous, lively and sensible Exercises of the
Will, are no other than the Affections of the Soul.[8]

2. The Author of the human Nature has not only given
Affections to Men, but has made 'em very much the Spring of
Men's Actions.[9] As the Affections do not only necessarily belong
to the human Nature, but are a very great Part of it; so (inasmuch as by Regeneration, Persons are renewed in the whole
Man, and sanctified thro'out) holy Affections do not only necessarily belong to true Religion, but are a very great Part of
that. And as true Religion is of a practical Nature, and God
hath so constituted the human Nature, that the Affections are
very much the Spring of Men's Actions, this also shews, that
true Religion must consist very much in the Affections.

Such is Man's Nature, that he is very unactive, any otherwise than he is influenc'd by some Affection, either *Love or Hatred, Desire, Hope, Fear* or some other. These Affections we see to be the Springs that set Men a going, in all the Affairs of Life, and engage them in all their Pursuits: These are the Things but put Men forward, and carry 'em along, in all their worldly Business; and especially are Men excited and animated by these, in all Affairs, wherein they are earnestly engaged, and which they pursue with Vogour. We see the World of Mankind to be exceeding busy and active; and the Affections of Men are the Springs of the Motion: Take away all *Love* and *Hatred,* all *Hope* and *Fear,* all *Anger, Zeal* and affectionate *Desire,* and the World would be, in a great Measure, motionless and dead; there would be no such Thing as Activity amongst Mankind, or any earnest Pursuit whatsoever. 'Tis Affection that engages the covetous Man, and him that is greedy of worldly Profits, in his Pursuits; and it is by the Affections, that the ambitious Man is put forward in his Pursuit of worldly Glory; and 'tis the Affections also that actuate the voluptuous Man, in his Pursuit of Pleasure and sensual Delights: The World continues, from Age to Age, in a continual Commotion and Agitation, in a Pursuit of these Things: but take away all Affection, and the Spring of all this Motion would be gone, and the Motion it self would cease. And as in worldly Things, Worldly Affections are very much the Spring of Mens Motion and Action; so in religious Matters, the Spring of their Actions are very much religious Affections: He that has doctrinal Knowledge and Speculation only, without Affection, never is engaged in the Business of Religion.

3. Nothing is more manifest *in Fact,* than that the Things of Religion take hold of Men's Souls, no further than they *affect* them. There are Multitudes that often hear the Word of God, and therein hear of those Things that are infinitely great and important, and that most nearly concern them, and all that is heard seems to be wholly ineffectual upon them, and to make no Alteration in their Disposition or Behaviour; and the Reason is, they are not affected with what they hear. There are many that often hear of the glorious Perfections of God, his almighty Power, and boundless Wisdom, his infinite Majesty, and that

Holiness of God, by which he is of purer Eyes than to behold
Evil, and cannot look on Iniquity, and the Heavens are not
pure in his Sight, and of God's infinite Goodness and Mercy,
and hear of the great Works of God's Wisdom, Power and
Goodness, wherein there appear the admirable Manifestations
of these Perfections; they hear particularly of the unspeakable
Love of God and Christ, and of the great Things that Christ
has done and suffer'd, and of the great Things of another World,
of eternal Misery, in bearing the Fierceness and Wrath of almighty God, and of endless Blessedness and Glory in the Presence of God, and the Enjoyment of his dear Love; they also
hear the peremptory Commands of God, and his gracious Coun-
sels and Warnings, and the sweet Invitations of the Gospel; I
say, they often hear these Things, and yet remain as they were
before, with no sensible Alteration on them, either in Heart or
Practice, because they are not affected with what they hear;
and never will be so 'till they are affected. I am bold to assert,
that there never was any considerable Change wrought in the
Mind or Conversation of any one Person, by any thing of a
religious Nature, that ever he read, heard or saw, that had not
his Affections mov'd. Never was a natural Man engaged earnestly to seek his Salvation: Never were any such brought to
cry after Wisdom, and lift up their Voice for Understanding,
and to wrestle with God in Prayer for Mercy; and never was
one humbled, and bro't to the Foot of God, from any thing
that ever he heard or imagin'd of his own Unworthiness and
Deservings of God's Displeasure; nor was ever one induced to
fly for Refuge unto Christ, while his Heart remain'd unaffected.
Nor was there ever a Saint awakened out of a cold, lifeless
Frame, or recovered from a declining State in Religion, and
brought back from a lamentable Departure from God, without
having his Heart affected. And in a Word, there never was any
Thing considerable brought to pass in the Heart or Life of any
Man living, by the Things of Religion, that had not his Heart
deeply affected by those Things.

4. The holy Scriptures do every where place Religion very
much in the Affections: such as Fear, Hope, Love, Hatred,
Desire, Joy, Sorrow, Gratitude, Compassion and Zeal.

The Scriptures place much of Religion in godly *Fear;* insomuch that 'tis often spoken of as the Character of those that are truly religious Persons, that *they tremble at God's Word, that they fear before him,* that *their Flesh trembles for Fear of him,* and that *they are afraid of his Judgments,* that *his Excellency makes them afraid, and his Dread falls upon them;* and the like: And a Compellation commonly given the Saints in Scripture, is, *Fearers of God,* or *they that fear the Lord.* And because the Fear of God is a great Part of true Godliness, hence true Godliness in general, is very commonly called by the Name of *the Fear of God;* as every one knows, that knows any thing of the Bible.

So *Hope* in God and in the Promises of his Word, is often spoken of in the Scripture, as a very considerable Part of true Religion. 'Tis mention'd as one of the three great Things of which Religion consists, 1 Cor. 13:13. Hope in the Lord is also frequently mentioned as the Character of the Saints: Psal. 146:5. *Happy is he that hath the God of* Jacob *for his Help, whose Hope is in the Lord his God.* Jer. 17:7. *Blessed is the Man that trusteth in the Lord, whose Hope the Lord is.* Psal. 31:24. *Be of good Courage, and he shall strengthen your Heart, all ye that Hope in the Lord.* And the like in many other Places. Religious Fear and Hope are, once and again, joined together, as jointly constituting the Character of the true Saints. Psal. 33:18. *Behold the Eye of the Lord is upon them that* Fear *him, upon them that* Hope *in his Mercy.* Psal. 147:11. *The Lord taketh Pleasure in them that* Fear *him, in those that* Hope *in his Mercy.* Hope is so great a Part of true Religion, that the Apostle says *we are saved by Hope,* Rom. 8:24. And this is spoken of as the Helmet of the christian Soldier, 1 Thes. 5:8. *And for an Helmet, the Hope of Salvation,* and the sure and stedfast Anchor of the Soul, which preserves it from being cast away by the Storms of this evil World, Heb. 6:19. *Which Hope we have, as an Anchor of the Soul both sure and stedfast, and which entreth into that within the Veil.* 'Tis spoken of as a great Fruit and Benefit which true Saints receive by Christ's Resurrection, 1 Pet. 1:3. *Blessed be the God and Father of our Lord Jesus Christ,* which according to his abun-

dant Mercy, *hath begotten us again unto a lively Hope, by the Resurrection of Jesus Christ from the Dead.*

The Scriptures place Religion very much in the Affection of *Love,* in Love to God, and the Lord Jesus Christ, and Love to the people of God, and to Mankind. The Texts in which this is manifest, both in the Old Testament, and New, are innumerable. But of this more afterwards.

The contrary Affection of *Hatred* also, as having Sin for its Object, is spoken of in Scripture, as no inconsiderable Part of true Religion. It is spoken of as that by which true Religion may be known and distinguished, Prov. 8:13. *The Fear of the Lord is to hate Evil.* And accordingly the Saints are called upon to give Evidence of their Sincerity by this, Psal. 97:10. *Ye that fear the Lord hate Evil.* And the Psalmist often mentions it as an Evidence of his Sincerity; Psal. 101:2, 3. *I will walk within my House with a perfect Heart; I will set no wicked Thing before mine Eyes: I hate the Work of them that turn aside.* Psal. 119:104. *I hate every false way.* So Verse 128. Again Psal. 139:21. *Do I not hate them, O Lord, that hate thee.*

So holy *Desire,* exercised in Longings, Hungrings and Thirstings after God and Holiness, is often mention'd in Scripture as an important Part of true Religion; Isai. 26:8. *The Desire of our Soul is to thy Name, and to the Remembrance of thee.* Psal. 27:4. *One Thing have I desired of the Lord, and that will I seek after; that I may dwell in the House of the Lord, all the Days of my Life, to behold the Beauty of the Lord, and to enquire in his Temple.* Psal. 42:1, 2. *As the Heart panteth after the Water-brooks, so panteth my Soul after thee, O God; My Soul thirsteth for God, for the living God: When shall I come and appear before God?* Psal. 63:1, 2. *My Soul thirsteth for thee, my Flesh longeth for thee, in a dry and thirsty Land, where no Water is, to see thy Power and thy Glory, so as I have seen thee in the Sanctuary.* Psal. 84:1, 2. *How amiable are thy Tabernacles, O Lord of Hosts! My Soul longeth, yea, even fainteth, for the Courts of the Lord; my Heart and my Flesh crieth out for the living God.* Psal. 119:20. *My Soul breaketh for the Longing it hath unto thy Judgments,*

at all Times. So Psal. 73:25. and 143:6, 7. and 130:6. Cant. 3:1, 2. and 6:8. Such a holy Desire and Thirst of Soul is mentioned, as one of those great Things which renders or denotes a Man truly blessed, in the Beginning of Christ's Sermon on the Mount, Matth. 5:6. *Blessed are they that do hunger and thirst after Righteousness, for they shall be filled.* And this holy Thirst is spoken of, as a great Thing in the Condition of a Participation of the Blessings of eternal Life, Rev. 21:6. *I will give unto him that is athirst, of the Fountain of the Water of Life freely.*

The Scriptures speak of holy *Joy*, as a great Part of true Religion. So is it represented in the Text. And as an important Part of Religion, it is often exhorted to, and press'd, with great Earnestness; Psal. 37:4. *Delight thy self in the Lord, and he shall give thee the Desires of thine Heart.* Psal. 97:12. *Rejoice in the Lord, ye Righteous.* So Psal. 33:1. *Rejoice in the Lord, O ye Righteous.* Matth. 5:12. *Rejoice, and be exceeding glad.* Phil. 3:1. *Finally Brethren, rejoice in the Lord.* And Chap. 4:4. *Rejoice in the Lord alway, and again I say rejoice.* 1 Thes. 5:16. *Rejoice evermore.* Psal. 149:2. *Let Israel rejoice in him that made him; let the Children of* Zion *be joyful in their King.* This is mention'd among the principal Fruits of the Spirit of Grace, Gal. 5:22. *The Fruit of the Spirit is Love, Joy,* &c. - - - - The Psalmist mentions his holy Joy, as an Evidence of his Sincerity, Psal. 119:14. *I have rejoiced in the Way of thy Testimonies, as much as in all Riches.*

Religious *Sorrow*, Mourning, and Brokenness of Heart, are also frequently spoken of as a great Part of true Religion. These Things are often mentioned as distinguishing Qualities of the true Saints, and a great Part of their Character; Matth. 5:4. *Blessed are they that mourn; for they shall be comforted.* Psal. 34:18. *The Lord is nigh unto them that are of a broken Heart, and saveth such as be of a contrite Spirit.* Isai. 61:1, 2. *The Lord hath anointed me* - - - - *to bind up the Broken-hearted* - - - - *to comfort all that mourn.* This godly Sorrow, and Brokenness of Heart is often spoken of, not only, as a great Thing in the distinguishing Character of the Saints, but that in them, which is peculiarly acceptable and pleasing to God; Psal. 51:17. *The Sacrifices of God are a broken Spirit; a broken and a*

contrite Heart, O God, thou wilt not despise. Isai. 57:15. *Thus saith the high and lofty One that inhabiteth Eternity, whose Name is Holy: I dwell in the high and holy Place, with him also that is of a humble and contrite Spirit, to revive the Spirit of the Humble, and to revive the Heart of the contrite ones.* Chap. 66:2. *To this Man will I look, even to him that is poor, and of a contrite Spirit.*

Another Affection often mentioned, as that in the Exercise of which much of true Religion appears, is *Gratitude;* especially as exercised in Thankfulness and Praise to God. This being so much spoken of in the Book of Psalms, and other Parts of the holy Scriptures, I need not mention particular Texts.

Again, The holy Scriptures do frequently speak of *Compassion* or *Mercy,* as a very great and essential Thing in true Religion; insomuch that good Men are in Scripture denominated from hence; and a merciful Man, and a good Man, are equivalent Terms in Scripture; Isai. 57:1. *The Righteous perisheth, and no Man layeth it to Heart; and* merciful Men *are taken away.* And the Scripture chooses out this Quality, as that by which, in a peculiar Manner, a righteous Man in decypher'd; Psal. 37:21. *The Righteous sheweth* Mercy, *and giveth;* and Ver. 26. *He is ever* merciful, *and lendeth.* And Prov. 14:3. *He that honoureth the Lord, hath Mercy on the Poor.* And Col. 3:12. *Put ye on, as the Elect of God, Holy and Beloved,* Bowels of Mercies, &c. This is one of those great Things, by which those who are truly Blessed are described by our Saviour, Matth. 5:7. *Blessed are the Merciful, for they shall obtain Mercy.* And this Christ also speaks of, as one of the Weightier Matters of the Law, Matth. 23:23. *Wo unto you Scribes and Pharisees, Hypocrites; for ye pay Tythe of Mint, and Annise, and Cummin, and have omitted the weightier Matters of the Law, Judgment,* Mercy, *and Faith.* To the like Purpose is that, Mich. 6:8. *He hath shewed thee, O man, what is good: And what doth the Lord require of thee, but to do Justice, and love* Mercy, *and walk humbly with thy God?* And also that, Hos. 6:6. *For I desired* Mercy, *and not Sacrifice.* Which seems to have been a Text much delighted in by our Saviour, by his Manner of citing it once and again; Matth. 9:13. and 12:7.

Zeal is also spoken of, as a very essential Part of the Religion of true Saints. 'Tis spoken of as a great Thing Christ had in view, in giving himself for our Redemption; Tit. 2:14. *Who gave himself for us, that he might redeem us from all Iniquity, and purify unto himself a peculiar People,* zealous *of good Works.* And this is spoken of, as the great Thing wanting in the luke-warm *Laodiceans,* Rev. 3:15, 16, 19.

I have mentioned but a few Texts, out of an innumerable Multitude, all over the Scripture, which place Religion very much in the Affections. But what has been observed, may be sufficient to shew that they who would deny that much of true Religion lies in the Affections, and maintain the Contrary, must throw away what we have been wont to own for our Bible, and get some other Rule, by which to judge of the Nature of Religion.[10]

5. The Scriptures do represent true Religion, as being summarily comprehended in *Love,* the Chief of the Affections, and Fountain of all other Affections.

So our blessed Saviour represents the Matter, in answer to the Lawyer, who asked him, which was the great Commandment of the Law. Matth. 22:37, 38, 39, 40. *Jesus said unto him, Thou shalt love the Lord thy God, with all thy Heart, and with all thy Soul, and with all thy Mind: This is the first, and great Commandment; and the second is like unto it, Thou shalt love thy Neighbour as thy self. On these two Commandments hang all the Law and the Prophets.* Which last Words signify as much, as that these two Commandments comprehend all the Duty prescribed, and the Religion taught in the Law and the Prophets. And the Apostle *Paul* does from Time to Time make the same Representation of the Matter; as in Rom. 13:8. *He that loveth another, hath fulfilled the Law.* And Ver. 10. *Love is the fulfilling of the Law.* And Gal. 5:14. *For all the Law is fulfilled in one Word, even in this, Thou shalt love thy Neighbour as thy self.* So likewise in 1 Tim. 1:5. *Now the End of the Commandment is Charity, out of a pure Heart, &c.* So the same Apostle speaks of Love, as the greatest Thing in Religion, and as the Vitals, Essence and Soul of it; without which, the greatest Knowledge and Gifts, and the most glaring Pro-

fession, and every thing else which appertains to Religion, are vain and worthless; and represents it as the Fountain from whence proceeds all that is good, in 1 Cor. 13, thro'out; for that which is there rendered *Charity,* in the Original is αγαπη, the proper English of which is *Love.*

Now altho' it be true, that the Love thus spoken of, includes the whole of a sincerely benevolent Propensity of the Soul, towards God and Man; yet it may be considered, that it is evident from what has been before observed, that this Propensity or Inclination of the Soul, when in sensible and vigorous Exercise, becomes *Affection,* and is no other than affectionate Love. And surely it is such vigourous and fervent Love which Christ speaks of, as the Sum of all Religion, when he speaks of Loving God with all our Hearts, with all our Souls, and with all our Minds, and our Neighbour as ourselves, as the Sum of all that was taught and prescribed in the Law and the Prophets.

Indeed it cannot be supposed, when this Affection of Love is here, and in other Scriptures, spoken of as the Sum of all Religion, that hereby is meant the Act, exclusive of the Habit, or that the Exercise of the Understanding is excluded, which is implied in all reasonable Affection. But it is doubtless true, and evident from these Scriptures, that the *Essence* of all true Religion lies in holy Love; and that in this divine Affection, and an habitual Disposition to it, and that Light which is the Foundation of it, and those Things which are the Fruits of it, consists the *Whole* of Religion.

From hence it clearly and certainly appears, that great Part of true Religion consists in the Affections. For Love is not only one of the Affections, but it is the first and chief of the Affections, and the Fountain of all the Affections. From *Love* arises *Hatred* of those Things which are contrary to what we love, or which oppose & thwart us in those Things that we delight in: And from the various Exercises of Love and Hatred, according to the Circumstances of the Objects of these Affections, as present or absent, certain or uncertain, probable or improbable, arise all those other Affections of *Desire, Hope, Fear, Joy, Grief, Gratitude, Anger,* &c. From a vigorous, affec-

tionate, and fervent *Love to God*, will necessarily arise other *religious* Affections: hence will arise an intense *Hatred* and Abhorrence of Sin, *Fear* of Sin, and a *Dread* of God's Displeasure, *Gratitude* to God for his Goodness, *Complacence* and *Joy* in God when God is graciously and sensibly present, and *Grief* when he is absent, and a joyful *Hope* when a future Enjoyment of God is expected, and fervent *Zeal* for the Glory of God. And in like manner, from a fervent *Love to Men*, will arise all other vertuous Affections towards Men.

6. The Religion of the most eminent Saints we have an Account of in the Scripture, consisted much in holy *Affections*.

I shall take particular Notice of three eminent Saints, which have express'd the Frame and Sentiments of their own Hearts, and so described their own Religion, and the Manner of their Intercourse with God, in the Writings which they have left us, that are a Part of the sacred Canon.

The *first* Instance I shall take notice of, is *David*, that *Man after God's own Heart;* who has given us a lively Portraiture of his Religion, in the Book of *Psalms*. Those holy Songs of his, he has there left us, are nothing else but the Expressions and Breathings of devout and holy *Affections;* such as an humble and fervent *Love* to God, *Admiration* of his glorious Perfections and wonderful Works, earnest *Desires*, Thirstings and Pantings of Soul after God, *Delight* and *Joy* in God, a sweet and melting *Gratitude* to God for his great Goodness, an holy *Exultation* and Triumph of Soul in the Favour, Sufficiency and Faithfulness of God, his *Love* to, and *Delight* in the Saints the excellent of the Earth, his great *Delight* in the Word and Ordinances of God, his *Grief* for his own and others Sins, and his fervent *Zeal* for God, and against the Enemies of God and his Church. And these Expressions of holy Affection, which the Psalms of *David* are every where full of, are the more to our present Purpose, because those Psalms are not only the Expressions of the Religion of so eminent a Saint, that God speaks of as so agreeable to his Mind; but were also, by the Direction of the Holy Ghost, penn'd for the Use of the Church of God in its publick Worship, not only in that Age, but in after Ages; as being fitted to express the Religion of all Saints, in all Ages,

as well as the Religion of the Psalmist. And it is moreover to be observed, that *David*, in the Book of Psalms, speaks not as a private Person, but as the *Psalmist of Israel*, as the subordinate Head of the Church of God, and Leader in their Worship and Praises; and in many of the Psalms, speaks in the Name of Christ, as personating him in these Breathings forth of holy Affection, and in many other Psalms, he speaks in the Name of the Church.

Another Instance I shall observe, is the Apostle *Paul;* who was, in many Respects, the Chief of all the Ministers of the New Testament; being above all others, a chosen Vessel unto Christ, to bear his Name before the Gentiles, and made the chief Instrument of propagating and establishing the christian Church in the World, and of distinctly revealing the glorious Mysteries of the Gospel, for the Instruction of the Church in all Ages; and (as has not been improbably thought by some) the most eminent Servant of Christ, that ever lived, received to the highest Rewards in the heavenly Kingdom of his Master. By what is said of him in the Scripture, he appears to have been a Person that was full of Affection. And 'tis very manifest, that the Religion he expresses in his Epistles, consisted very much in holy Affections. It appears by all his Expressions of himself, that he was, in the Course of his Life, enflamed, actuated and entirely swallowed up, by a most ardent *Love* to his glorious Lord, esteeming all Things as Loss, for the Excellency of the Knowledge of him, and esteeming them but Dung that he might win him. He represents himself, as overpower'd by this holy Affection, and as it were compelled by it to go forward in his Service, thro' all Difficulties and Sufferings, 2 Cor. 5:14, 15. And his Epistles are full of Expressions of an overflowing Affection towards the People of Christ: He speaks of his *dear Love* to them, 2 Cor. 12:19. Phil. 4:1. 2. Tim. 1:2. Of his *abundant Love,* 2 Cor. 2:4. And of his *affectionate and tender Love,* as of a Nurse towards her Children, 1 Thes. 2:7, 8. *But we were gentle among you; even as a Nurse cherisheth her Children; so being affectionately desirous of you, we were willing to have imparted unto you, not the Gospel of God only, but also our own Souls, because ye were dear unto us.* So also he

speaks of his *Bowels of Love*, Phil. 1:8. Philem. 5:12, and 20. So he speaks of his *earnest Care* for others, 2 Cor. 8:16. and of his *Bowels of Pity* or *Mercy* towards them, Phil. 2:1. and of his Concern for others, even to *Anguish of Heart*, 2 Cor. 2:4. *For out of much Affliction, and Anguish of Heart, I wrote unto you, with many Tears; not that ye should be grieved; but that ye might know the Love which I have more abundantly unto you.* He speaks of the *great Conflict* of his Soul for them, Col. 2:1. He speaks of *great and continual Grief* that he had *in his Heart* from *Compassion* to the *Jews*, Rom. 9:2. He speaks of *his Mouth's being open'd, and his Heart enlarged* towards Christians, 2 Cor. 6:11. *O ye* Corinthians, *our Mouth is open unto you, our heart is enlarged!* He often speaks of his *affectionate and longing Desires*, 1 Thes. 2:8. Rom. 1:11. Phil. 1:8. and Chap. 4:1. 2 Tim. 1:4. The same Apostle is very often, in his Epistles, expressing the Affection of *Joy*, 2 Cor. 1:12. and Chap. 7:7. And Ver. 9. and 16. Phil. 1:4. and Chap. 2:1, 2. and Chap. 3:3. Col. 1:24. 1 Thes. 3:9. He speaks of his *rejoicing with great Joy*, Phil. 4:10. Philem. 1:7. of his *joying and rejoicing*, Phil. 2:1, 7. and of his *rejoicing exceedingly*, 2 Cor. 7:13. And of his being *filled with Comfort, and being exceeding joyful*, 2 Cor. 7:4. He speaks of himself as *always rejoicing*, 2 Cor. 6:10. So he speaks of the *Triumphs* of his Soul, 2 Cor. 2:14. And of *his glorying in Tribulation*, 2 Thes. 1:4. and Rom. 5:3. He also expresses the Affection of *Hope;* in Phil. 1:20. he speaks of his *earnest Expectation*, and *his Hope*. He likewise expresses an Affection of *Godly Jealousy*, 2 Cor. 11:2, 3. And it appears by his whole History, after his Conversion, in the *Acts*, and also by all his *Epistles*, and the Accounts he gives of himself there, That the Affection of *Zeal*, as having the Cause of his Master, and the Interest and Prosperity of his Church, for its Object, was mighty in him, continually inflaming his Heart, strongly engaging to those great and constant Labours he went through, in instructing, exhorting, warning and reproving Others, *traveling in Birth with them;* conflicting with those powerful and innumerable Enemies who continually opposed him, wrestling with Principalities and Powers, not fighting as one who beats the Air, running the Race set before him, continually pressing

forwards through all Manner of Difficulties and Sufferings; so that others thought him quite beside himself. And how full he was of Affection, does further appear by his being so full of Tears: In 2 Cor. 2:4. he speaks of his *many Tears*, and so Acts 20:19. And of his *Tears* that he shed *continually, Night and Day*, Ver. 31.

Now if any one can consider these Accounts given in the Scripture of this great Apostle, and which he gives of himself, and yet not see that his Religion consisted much in Affection, must have a strange Faculty of managing his Eyes, to shut out the Light which shines most full in his Face.

The other Instance I shall mention, is of the Apostle *John*, that beloved Disciple, who was the nearest and dearest to his Master of any of the Twelve, and was by him admitted to the greatest Privileges of any of them: Being not only one of the three who were admitted to be present with him in the Mount at his Transfiguration, and at the raising of Jairus's Daughter, and whom he took with him when he was in his Agony, and one of the three spoken of by the Apostle *Paul*, as the three main Pillars of the christian Church; but was favour'd above all, in being admitted to lean on his Master's Bosom, at his last Supper, and in being chosen by Christ, as the Disciple to whom he would reveal his wonderful Dispensation towards his Church, to the End of Time; as we have an Account in the Book of Revelation: And to shut up the Canon of the New-Testament, and of the whole Scripture; being preserved much longer than all the rest of the Apostles, to set all Things in Order in the christian Church, after their Death.

It is evident by all his Writings, (as is generally observed by Divines) that he was a Person remarkably full of Affection: His Addresses to those whom he wrote to, being inexpressibly tender and pathetical, breathing nothing but the most fervent Love; as tho' he were all made up of sweet and holy Affection. The Proofs of which can't be given without Disadvantage, unless we should transcribe his whole Writings.

7. He whom God sent into the World, to be the Light of the World, and Head of the whole Church, and the perfect Example of true Religion and Vertue, for the Imitation of all,

the Shepherd whom the whole Flock should follow wherever he goes, even the Lord Jesus Christ, was a Person who was remarkably of a tender and affectionate Heart; and his Vertue was express'd very much in the Exercises of holy Affections. He was the greatest Instance of Ardency, Vigour and Strength of *Love*, to both God and Man, that ever was. It was these Affections which got the Victory, in that mighty Struggle and Conflict of his Affections, in his Agonies, when *he prayed more earnestly, and offered strong Crying and Tears*, and wrestled in Tears and in Blood. Such was the Power of the Exercises of his holy Love, that they were stronger than Death, and in that great Struggle, overcame those strong Exercises of the natural Affections of Fear and Grief, when he was sore amazed, and his Soul was exceeding sorrowful, even unto Death. And he also appear'd to be full of Affection, in the Course of his Life. We read of his great *Zeal*, fulfilling that in the 69th Psalm, *the Zeal of thine House hath eaten me up*, John 2:17. We read of his *Grief* for the Sins of Men, Mark 3:5. *He looked round about on them with Anger, being grieved for the Hardness of their Hearts*. And his breaking forth in Tears and Exclamations, from the Consideration of the Sin and Misery of ungodly Men, and on the Sight of the City of *Jerusalem*, which was full of such Inhabitants, Luke 19:41, 42. *And when he was come near, he beheld the City, and wept over it, saying, If thou hadst known, even thou, at least in this thy Day, the Things which belong unto thy Peace! but now they are hid from thine Eyes*. With Chap. 13:34. *O Jerusalem, Jerusalem, which killest the Prophets, and stonest them that are sent unto thee, How often would I have gathered thy Children together, as a Hen doth gather her Brood under her Wings, and ye would not!* We read of Christ's earnest *Desire*, Luke 22:15. *With Desire have I desired to eat this Passover with you, before I suffer*. We often read of the Affection of *Pity* or *Compassion* in Christ, Matth. 15:32. and 18:34. Luke 7:13. and of his *being moved with Compassion*, Matth. 9:36. and 14:14. and Mark 6:34. And how tender did his Heart appear to be, on occasion of *Mary's* and *Martha's* Mourning for their Brother, and coming to him with their Complaints and Tears: Their Tears soon drew Tears from his

Eyes: He was affected with their Grief, and *wept* with them; tho' he knew their Sorrow should so soon be turned into Joy, by their Brother's being raised from the Dead; see John 11. And how ineffably affectionate was that last and dying Discourse, which Jesus had with his eleven Disciples the Evening before he was crucified? when he told them he was going away, and foretold them the great Difficulties and Sufferings they should meet with in the World, when he was gone; and conforted and counseled 'em, as his dear little Children, and bequeathed to them his holy Spirit, and therein his Peace, and his Comfort and Joy, as it were in his last Will and Testament, in the 13th, 14th, 15th, and 16th Chapters of John; and concluded the Whole with that affectionate intercessory Prayer for them, and his whole Church in Chap. 17. Of all the Discourses ever penn'd, or utter'd by the Mouth of any Man, this seems to be the most affectionate, and affecting.

8. The Religion of Heaven consists very much in Affection.

There is doubtless true Religion in Heaven, and true Religion in it's utmost Purity and Perfection. But according to the Scripture Representation of the heavenly State, the Religion of Heaven consists chiefly in holy and mighty *Love* and *Joy*, and the Expression of these in most fervent and exalted Praises. So that the Religion of the Saints in Heaven consists in the same Things with that Religion of the Saints on Earth, which is spoken of in our Text, viz. *Love*, and *Joy unspeakable, and full of Glory*. Now it would be very foolish to pretend, that because the Saints in Heaven ben't united to Flesh and Blood, and have no animal Fluids to be moved, (through the Laws of Union of Soul and Body) with those great Emotions of their Souls, that therefore their exceeding Love and Joy are no Affections. - - - - We are not speaking of the Affections of the Body, but of the Affections of the Soul, the chief of which are *Love* and *Joy*. When these are in the Soul, whether that be in the Body or out of it, the Soul is affected and moved. And when they are in the Soul, in that Strength in which they are in the Saints in Heaven, the Soul is mightily affected and moved, or, which is the same Thing, has great Affections. 'Tis

true, we don't experimentally know what Love and Joy are in a
Soul out of a Body, or in a glorified Body; i.e. we han't had
Experience of Love and Joy in a Soul in these Circumstances;
but the Saints on Earth do know what divine Love and Joy in
the Soul are, & they know what Love & Joy are of the same
Kind, with the Love and Joy which are in Heaven, in separate
Souls there. The Love and Joy of the Saints on Earth, is the
Beginning and Dawning of the Light, Life, and Blessedness of
Heaven, and is like their Love and Joy there; or rather, the
same in Nature, tho' not the same with it, or like to it, in Degree
and Circumstances. This is evident by many Scriptures, as
Prov. 4:18. John 4:14. and Chap. 6:40, 47, 50, 51, 54, 58. 1 John
3:15. 1 Cor. 13:8, 9, 10, 11, 12. 'Tis unreasonable therefore to
suppose, that the Love and Joy of the Saints in Heaven, not only
differ in Degree and Circumstances, from the holy Love and Joy
of the Saints on Earth, but is so entirely different in Nature, that
they are no Affections; and meerly because they have no Blood
and animal Spirits to be set in Motion by them, which Motion
of the Blood and animal Spirits is not of the Essence of these
Affections, in Men on the Earth, but the Effect of them; altho'
by their Reaction they may make some circumstantial Difference
in the Sensation of the Mind.[11] There is a Sensation of the Mind
which loves and rejoices, that is antecedent to any Effects on the
Fluids of the Body; and this Sensation of the Mind, therefore
don't depend on these Motions in the Body, and so may be in
the Soul without the Body. And wherever there are the Exercises of Love and Joy, there is that Sensation of the Mind,
whether it be in the Body, or out; and that inward Sensation,
or kind of spiritual Sense, or Feeling, and Motion of the Soul, is
what is called Affection; The Soul when it thus feels, (if I may
so say) and is thus moved, is said to be affected, and especially
when this inward Sensation and Motion, are to a very high
Degree, as they are in the Saints in Heaven. If we can learn any
thing of the State of Heaven from the Scripture, the Love and
Joy that the Saints have there, is exceeding great and vigorous;
impressing the Heart with the strongest and most lively Sensation, of inexpressible Sweetness, mightily moving, animating,
and engaging them, making them like to a Flame of Fire. And

if such Love and Joy ben't Affections, then the Word *Affection* is
of no Use in Language.- - - -Will any say, that the Saints in
Heaven, in beholding the Face of their Father, and the Glory of
their Redeemer, and contemplating his wonderful Works, and
particularly his laying down his Life for them, have their Hearts
nothing moved and affected, by all which they behold or
consider?

Hence therefore the *Religion of Heaven*, consisting chiefly in
holy Love and Joy, consists very much in Affection: And therefore
undoubtedly, *true Religion* consists very much in Affection. The
Way to learn the true Nature of any Thing, is to go where that
Thing is to be found in it's Purity and Perfection. If we would
know the Nature of true Gold, we must view it, not in the Oar,
but when it is refined. If we would learn what true Religion is,-
we must go where there is true Religion, and nothing but true
Religion, and in it's highest Perfection, without any Defect or
Mixture. All who are truely religious are not of this World, they
are Strangers here, and belong to Heaven; they are born from
above, Heaven is their native Country, and the Nature which
they receive by this heavenly birth, is an heavenly Nature, they
receive *an Anointing from Above;* that Principle of true Religion
which is in them, is a Communication of the Religion of Heaven;
their Grace is the Dawn of Glory; and God fits them for that
World by conforming them to it.

9. This appears from the Nature and Design of the Ordinances and Duties, which God hath appointed, as Means and
Expressions of true Religion.

To instance in the Duty of Prayer: 'Tis manifest, we are
not appointed, in this Duty, to declare God's Perfections, his
Majesty, Holiness, Goodness, and Allsufficiency, and our own
Meanness, Emptiness, Dependence, and Unworthiness, and our
Wants and Desires, to inform God of these Things, or to incline
his Heart, and prevail with him to be willing to shew us Mercy;
but suitably to affect our own Hearts with the Things we express,
and so to prepare us to receive the Blessings we ask. And such
Gestures, and Manner of external Behaviour in the Worship
of God, which Custom has made to be Significations of Humility
and Reverence, can be of no further Use, than as they have

some Tendency to affect our own Hearts, or the Hearts of others. And the Duty of singing Praises to God, seems to be appointed wholly to excite and express religious Affections. No other Reason can be assigned, why we should express our selves to God in Verse, rather than in Prose, and do it with Musick, but only, that such is our Nature and Frame, that these Things have a Tendency to move our Affections.

The same thing appears in the Nature and Design of the Sacraments, which God hath appointed. God, considering our Frame, hath not only appointed that we should be told of the great Things of the Gospel, and of the Redemption of Christ, and instructed in them by his Word; but also that they should be, as it were, exhibited to our View, in sensible Representations, in the Sacraments, the more to affect us with them.

And the impressing divine Things on the Hearts and Affections of Men, is evidently one great and main End for which God has ordained, that his Word delivered in the holy Scriptures, should be opened, applied, and set home upon Men, in Preaching. And therefore it don't answer the Aim which God had in this Institution, meerly for Men to have good Commentaries and Expositions on the Scripture, and other good Books of Divinity; because, altho' these may tend, as well as Preaching, to give Men a good doctrinal or speculative Understanding of the Work of God, yet they have not an equal Tendency to impress them on Men's Hearts and Affections. God hath appointed a particular, and lively Application of his Word, to Men, in the Preaching of it, as a fit Means to affect Sinners, with the Importance of the Things of Religion, and their own Misery, and Necessity of a Remedy, and the Glory and Sufficiency of a Remedy provided; and to stir up the pure Minds of the Saints, and quicken their Affections, by often bringing the great Things of Religion to their Remembrance, and setting them before them in their proper Colours, tho' they know them, and have been fully instructed in them already; 2 Pet. 1:12, 13. And particularly, to promote those two Affections in them, which are spoken of in the Text, *Love* and *Joy: Christ gave some Apostles, and some Prophets, and some Evangelists, and some Pastors and Teachers, that the Body of Christ might be edified in Love*, Eph. 4:11, 12,

16. The Apostle, in instructing and counselling *Timothy*, concerning the Work of the Ministry, informs him that the great End of that Word which a Minister is to preach, is *Love* or *Charity*, 1 Tim. 1:3, 4, 5. And another Affection which God has appointed Preaching as a Means to promote in the Saints, is *Joy;* and therefore Ministers are called *Helpers of their Joy,* 2 Cor. 1:24.

10. 'Tis an Evidence that true Religion, or Holiness of Heart, lies very much in the Affection of the Heart, that the Scriptures place the Sin of the Heart very much in *Hardness of Heart.* Thus the Scriptures do every where. It was Hardness of Heart, which excited Grief and Displeasure in Christ towards the Jews, Mark 3:5. *He looked round about on them with Anger, being grieved for the Hardness of their Hearts.* It is from Men's having such a Heart as this, that they treasure up Wrath for themselves. Rom. 2:5. *After thy Hardness and impenitent Heart, treasurest up unto thy self Wrath, against the Day of Wrath, and Revelation of the righteous Judgment of God.* The Reason given why the House of *Israel* would not obey God, was that they were hardhearted, Ezek. 3:7. *But the House of* Israel *will not hearken unto thee; for they will not hearken unto me: For all the House of* Israel *are impudent and hard-hearted.* The Wickedness of that perverse rebellious Generation in the Wilderness, is ascribed to the Hardness of their Hearts; Psal. 95:7, - - - 10. *To Day, if ye will hear my Voice, harden not your Heart, as in the Provocation, and as in the Day of Temptation in the Wilderness; when your Fathers tempted me, proved me, and saw my Work: Forty Years long was I grieved with this Generation, and said it is a People that do err in their Heart,* &c. - - - This is spoken of as what prevented *Zedekiah's* turning to the Lord, 2 Chron. 36:13. He *stiffened his Neck, and hardened his Heart, from turning to the Lord God of* Israel. This Principle is spoken of, as that from whence Men are without the Fear of God, and depart from God's Ways; Isai. 63:17. *O Lord, why hast thou made us to err from thy Ways, and hardened our Heart from thy Fear?* And Men's rejecting Christ, and opposing Christianity, is laid to this Principle; Acts 19:9. *But when divers were hardned, and believed not, but spake Evil of that Way before the Multitude;* - - - - God's leaving Men to the Power of the Sin and Corruption

of the Heart, is often express'd by God's hardening their Hearts; Rom. 9:18. *Therefore hath he Mercy on whom he will have Mercy, and whom he will he hardeneth.* John 12:40. *He hath blinded their Minds, and hardened their Hearts.* And the Apostle seems to speak of *an evil Heart, that departs from the living God,* and *a hard Heart,* as the same Thing, Heb. 3:8. *Harden not your Heart, as in the Provocation,* &c. Verse 12, 13. *Take heed Brethren, lest there be in any of you an evil Heart of Unbelief in departing from the living God; but exhort one another daily, while it is called to Day; lest any of you be hardened through the Deceitfulness of Sin.* And that great Work of God in Conversion, which consists in delivering a Person from the Power of Sin, and mortifying Corruption, is express'd, once and again, by God's *taking away the Heart of Stone, and giving an Heart of Flesh,* Ezek. 11:19. and Chap. 36:26.

Now by a hard Heart, is plainly meant an unaffected Heart, or a Heart not easy to be moved with vertuous Affections, like a Stone, insensible, stupid, unmoved and hard to be impressed. Hence the hard Heart is called a *stony* Heart, and is opposed to an *Heart of Flesh,* that has feeling, and is sensibly touch'd and moved. We read in Scripture of a *hard Heart,* and a *tender Heart:* And doubtless we are to understand these, as contrary the one to the other. But what is a tender Heart, but a Heart which is easily impressed with what ought to affect it? God commends *Josiah,* because his Heart was tender; and 'tis evident by those Things which are mention'd as Expressions and Evidences of this Tenderness of Heart, that by his Heart being tender is meant, his Heart being easily moved with religious and pious Affection; 2 Kings 22:19. *Because thine Heart was tender, and thou hast humbled thy self before the Lord, when thou heardst what I spake against this Place, and against the Inhabitants thereof, that they should become a Desolation, and a Curse, and hast rent thy Clothes, and hast wept before me; I also heard thee, saith the Lord.* And this is one thing, wherein it is necessary we should *become as little Children, in order to our entring into the Kingdom of God,* even that we should have our Hearts tender, and easily affected and moved in spiritual and divine Things, as little Children have in other Things.

'Tis very plain in some Places, in the Texts themselves, that

by Hardness of Heart is meant a Heart void of Affection. So to
signify the *Ostrich's* being without natural Affection to her
Young, it is said, Job. 39:16. *She hardeneth her Heart against
her young Ones, as though they were not hers.* So a Person
having a Heart unaffected in Time of Danger, is express'd by
his hardening his Heart, Prov. 28:14. *Happy is the Man that
feareth alway; but he that hardneth his Heart shall fall into
Mischief.*

Now therefore since it is so plain, that by a hard Heart, in
Scripture, is meant a Heart destitute of pious Affections, and
since also the Scriptures do so frequently place the Sin and
Corruption of the Heart in Hardness of Heart; it is evident,
that the Grace and Holiness of the Heart, on the contrary, must,
in a great Measure, consist in its having pious Affections, and
being easily susceptive of such Affection. Divines are generally
agreed, that Sin radically and fundamentally consists in what
is negative, or privative, having its Root and Foundation in a
Privation or Want of Holiness. And therefore undoubtedly, if it
be so that Sin does very much consist in Hardness of Heart, and
so in the Want of pious Affections of Heart; Holiness does consist very much *in those pious Affections.*

I am far from supposing that all Affactions do shew a tender
Heart: Hatred, Anger, Vain-glory, and other selfish and self-
exalting Affections, may greatly prevail in the hardest Heart. But
yet it is evident that *Hardness of Heart,* and *Tenderness of
Heart,* are Expressions that relate to the Affections of the Heart,
and denote the Heart's being susceptible of, or shut up against,
certain Affections, of which I shall have Occasion to speak more
afterwards.

Upon the Whole, I think it clearly and abundantly evident,
that true Religion lies very much in the Affections. Not that I
think these Arguments prove, that Religion in the Hearts of the
truly Godly, is ever in exact Proportion to the Degree of
Affection, and present Emotion of the Mind. For undoubtedly,
there is much Affection in the true Saints which is not spiritual:
Their religious Affections are often mixed; all is not from Grace,
but much from Nature. And tho' the Affections have not their
Seat in the Body, yet the Constitution of the Body, may very

much contribute to the present Emotion of the Mind. And the Degree of Religion is rather to be judged of by the Fixedness and Strength of the Habit that is exercised in Affection, whereby holy Affection is habitual, than by the Degree of the present Exercise: And the Strength of that Habit is not always in Proportion to outward Effects and Manifestations, or inward Effects, in the Hurry and Vehemence, and sudden Changes of the Course of the Thoughts of the Mind. But yet it is evident, that Religion consists so much in Affection, as that without holy Affection there is no true Religion: And no Light in the Understanding is good, which don't produce holy Affection in the Heart; no Habit or Principle in the Heart is good, which has no such Exercise; and no external Fruit is good, which don't proceed from such Exercises.[12]

Having thus considered the Evidence of the Proposition laid down, I proceed to some Inferences.

I. We may hence learn how great their Error is, who are for discarding all religious Affections, as having nothing solid or substantial in them.

There seems to be too much of a Disposition this Way, prevailing in this Land at this Time. Because many who, in the late extraordinary Season, appeared to have great religious Affections, did not manifest a right Temper of Mind, and run into many Errors, in the Time of their Affection, and the Heat of their Zeal; and because the high Affections of many seem to be so soon come to nothing, and some who seemed to be mightily raised and swallowed with Joy and Zeal, for a While, seem to have returned like the Dog to his Vomit: Hence religious Affections in general are grown out of Credit, with great Numbers, as tho' true Religion did not at all consist in them. Thus we easily, and naturally run from one Extreme to another. A little while ago we were in the other Extreme; there was a prevalent Disposition to look upon all high religious Affections, as eminent Exercises of true Grace, without much inquiring into the Nature and Source of those Affections, and the Manner in which they arose: If Persons did but appear to be indeed very much moved and raised, so as to be full of religious Talk, and express themselves with great Warmth and Earnestness, and to be *fill'd*, or to

be *very full*, as the Phrases were; it was too much the Manner, without further Examination, to conclude such Persons were full of the Spirit of God, and had eminent Experience of his gracious Influences. This was the Extreme which was prevailing three or four Years ago. But of late, instead of *esteeming* and *admiring* all religious *Affections, without Distinction*, it is a Thing much more prevalent, to *reject* and *discard* all *without Distinction*. Herein appears the Subtilty of *Satan*. While he saw that *Affections* were much in Vogue, knowing the greater Part of the Land were not versed in such Things, and had not had much Experience of great *religious Affections*, to enable them to judge well of 'em, and distinguish between true and false; then he knew he could best play his Game, by sowing Tares amongst the Wheat, and mingling *false Affections* with the Works of God's Spirit: He knew this to be a likely Way to delude and eternally ruin many Souls, and greatly to wound Religion in the Saints, and entangle them in a dreadful Wilderness, and by and by, to bring all Religion into Disrepute. But now, when the ill Consequences of these *false Affections* appear, and 'tis become very apparent, that some of those Emotions which made a glaring Shew, and were by many greatly admired, were in Reality Nothing; the Devil sees it to be for his Interest to go another Way to Work, and to endeavour to his utmost to propagate and establish a Perswasion, that all Affections and sensible Emotions of the Mind, in Things of Religion, are nothing at all to be regarded, but are rather to be avoided, and carefully guarded against, as Things of a pernicious Tendency. This he knows is the Way to bring all Religion to a meer lifeless Formality, and effectually shut out the Power of Godliness, and every Thing which is spiritual, and to have all true Christianity turn'd out of Doors. For altho' to true Religion, there must indeed be something else besides Affection; yet true Religion consists so much in the Affections, that there can be no true Religion without them. He who has no religious Affection, is in a State of spiritual Death, and is wholly destitute of the powerful, quickening, saving Influences of the Spirit of God upon his Heart. As there is no true Religion, where there is nothing else but Affection; so there is no true Religion where there is no *religious*

Affection. As on the one Hand, there must be Light in the Understanding, as well as an *affected* fervent Heart, where there is Heat without Light, there can be nothing divine or heavenly in that Heart; so on the other Hand, where there is a Kind of Light without Heat, a Head stored with Notions and Speculations, with a cold and unaffected Heart, there can be nothing divine in that Light, that Knowledge is no true spiritual Knowledge of divine Things. If the great Things of Religion are rightly understood, they will affect the Heart. The Reason why Men are not affected by such infinitely great, important, glorious, and wonderful Things, as they often hear and read of, in the Word of God, is undoubtedly because they are blind; if they were not so, it would be impossible, and utterly inconsistent with human Nature, that their Hearts should be otherwise, than strongly impress'd, and greatly moved by such Things.

This Manner of slighting all religious *Affections*, is the Way exceedingly to harden the Hearts of Men, and to encourage 'em in their Stupidity and Senselessness, and to keep 'em in a State of spiritual Death as long as they live, and bring 'em at last to Death eternal. The prevailing Prejudice against *religious Affections* at this Day, in the Land, is apparently of awful Effect, to harden the Hearts of Sinners, and damp the Graces of many of the Saints, and stund the Life and Power of Religion, and preclude the Effect of Ordinances, and hold us down in a State of Dulness and Apathy, and undoubtedly causes many Persons greatly to offend God, in entertaining men and low Thoughts of the extraordinary Work he has lately wrought in this Land.

And for Persons to despise and cry down all religious *Affections*, is the Way to shut all Religion out of their own Hearts, and to make thorough Work in ruining their Souls.

They who condemn high Affections in others, are certainly not likely to have high Affections themselves. And let it be consider'd, that they who have but little religious Affection, have certainly but little Religion. And they who condemn others for their *religious Affections*, and have none themselves, have no Religion.

There are false *Affections*, and there are true. A Man's having *much Affection*, don't prove that he has any true Re-

ligion: But if he has *no Affection*, it proves that he has no true
Religion. The right Way, is not to reject all Affections, nor to
approve all; but to distinguish between Affections, approving
some, and rejecting others; separating between the Wheat and
the Chaff, the Gold and the Dross, the Precious and the Vile.

2. If it be so, that true Religion lies much in the *Affections*,
hence we may infer, that such Means are to be desired, as
have much of a Tendency to move the Affections. Such Books,
and such a Way of Preaching the Word, and Administration of
Ordinances, and such a Way of worshipping God in Prayer,
and singing Praises, is much to be desired, as has a Tendency
deeply to affect the Hearts of those who attend these Means.

Such a Kind of Means, would formerly have been highly ap-
proved of and applauded by the Generality of the People of the
Land, as the most excellent and profitable, and having the
greatest Tendency to promote the Ends of the Means of Grace.
But the prevailing Taste seems of late strangely to be alter'd:
That pathetical Manner of Praying and Preaching, which
would formerly have been admir'd and extoll'd, and that for this
Reason, because it had such a Tendency to move the Affections,
now, in great Multitudes, immediately excites Disgust, and
moves no other Affections, than those of Displeasure and
Contempt.

Perhaps, formerly the Generality (at least of the common
People) were in the Extreme, of looking too much to an affectionate Address, in publick Performances: But now, a very
great Part of the People, seem to have gone far into a contrary
Extreme. Indeed there may be such Means, as may have a great
Tendency to stir up the Passions of weak and ignorant Persons,
and yet have no great Tendency to Benefit their Souls. For tho'
they may have a Tendency to excite Affections, they may have
little or none to excite gracious Affections, or any Affections
tending to Grace. But undoubtedly, if the Things of Religion,
in the Means used, are treated according to their Nature, and
exhibited truly, so as tends to convey just Apprehensions, and a
right Judgment of them; the more they have a Tendency to
move the Affections, the better.

3. If true Religion lies much in the Affections, hence we

may learn, what great Cause we have to be ashamed and confounded before God, that we are no more affected with the great Things of Religion. It appears from what has been said, that this arises from our having so little true Religion.[13]

God has given to Mankind Affections, for the same Purpose which he has given all the Faculties and Principles of the human Soul for, *viz.* that they might be subservient to Man's chief End, and the great Business for which God has created him, that is the Business of Religion. And yet how common is it among Mankind, that their Affections are much more exercised and engaged in other Matters, than in Religion! In Things which concern Men's worldly Interest, their outward Delights, their Honour and Reputation, and their natural Relations, they have their Desires eager, their Appetites vehement, their Love warm and affectionate, their Zeal ardent; in these Things their Hearts are tender and sensible, easily moved, deeply impress'd, much concerned, very sensibly affected, and greatly engaged; much depress'd with Grief at worldly Losses, and highly raised with Joy at worldly Successes and Prosperity. But how insensible and unmoved are most Men, about the great Things of another World! How dull are their Affections! How heavy and hard their Hearts in these Matters! Here their Love is cold, their Desires languid, their Zeal low, and their Gratitude small. How they can sit and hear of the infinite Height and Depth and Length and Breadth of the Love of God in Christ Jesus, of his giving his infinitely dear Son, to be offered up a Sacrifice for the Sins of Men, and of the unparallel'd Love of the innocent, holy and tender Lamb of God, manifested in his dying Agonies, his bloody Sweat, his loud and bitter Cries, and bleeding Heart, and all this for Enemies, to redeem them from deserved, eternal Burnings, and to bring to unspeakable and everlasting Joy and Glory; and yet be cold, and heavy, insensible, and regardless! Where are the Exercises of our Affections proper, if not here? What is it that does more require them? And what can be a fit Occasion of their lively and vigorous Exercise, if not such an one as this? Can any Thing be set in our View, greater and more important? Any Thing more wonderful and surprising? Or more nearly concerning our Interest? Can we suppose the wise Creator

implanted such Principles in the human Nature as the Affections, to be of Use to us, and to be exercised on certain proper Occasions, but to lie still on such an Occasion as this? Can any Christian, who believes the Truth of these Things, entertain such Thoughts?

If we ought ever to exercise our Affections at all, and if the Creator han't unwisely constituted the human Nature, in making these Principles a Part of it, when they are vain and useless; then they ought to be exercised about those Objects which are most worthy of them. But is there any Thing, which Christians can find in Heaven or Earth, so worthy to be the Objects of their Admiration and Love, their earnest and longing Desires, their Hope, and their Rejoicing, and their fervent Zeal, as those Things that are held forth to us in the Gospel of Jesus Christ? In which, not only are Things declared most worthy to affect us, but they are exhibited in the most affecting Manner. The Glory and Beauty of the blessed Jehovah, which is most worthy in itself, to be the Object of our Admiration and Love, is there exhibited in the most affecting Manner that can be conceived of, as it appears shining in all its Lustre, in the Face of an incarnate, infinitely loving, meek, compassionate, dying Redeemer. All the Vertues of the Lamb of God, his Humility, Patience, Meekness, Submission, Obedience, Love & Compassion, are exhibited to our View, in a manner the most tending to move our Affections, of any that can be imagined; as they all had their greatest Trial, and their highest Exercise, and so their brightest Manifestation, when he was in the most affecting Circumstances; even when he was under his last Sufferings, those unutterable and unparallel'd Sufferings, he endured, from his tender Love and Pity to us. There also, the hateful Nature of our Sins is manifested in the most affecting Manner possible; as we see the dreadful Effects of them, in what our Redeemer, who undertook to answer for us, suffered for them. And there we have the most affecting Manifestations of God's Hatred of Sin, and his Wrath and Justice in punishing it; as we see his Justice in the Strictness and Inflexibleness of it, and his Wrath in its Terribleness, in so dreadfully punishing our Sins, in One who was infinitely dear to him, and loving to us. So has

God disposed Things, in the Affair of our Redemption, and in his glorious Dispensations, revealed to us in the Gospel, as tho' every Thing were purposely contrived in such a Manner, as to have the greatest, possible Tendency to reach our Hearts in the most tender Part, and move our Affections most sensibly and strongly. How great Cause have we therefore to be humbled to the Dust, that we are no more affected!

INTERROGATIVE NOTES

1. As compared to Edwards's other speeches in this volume, do you find that a different mood seems to characterize this one? If so, based upon your reading of Part One and the headnote to this sermon, how do you account for this difference?

2. Edwards's methodology parallels the recommendations of the sixteenth-century academic reformer Peter Ramus, who was highly regarded by the New England Puritans: he has made a universal statement, defined it, and divided it into its parts, preferably two in number; then he has refined the thought by further definitions and divisions. Does this pattern of organization cause his approach to be flat and obtrusive? Does it promote understandability? In any part of this speech, does Edwards depart from the didactic approach by using the implicative or indirect methods? Can you suggest reasons why, or why not?

3. By "sensible," Edwards means "through the senses." If time permits, seek the origins of Edwards's psychology in John Locke's *An Essay Concerning Understanding*.

4. How is Edwards here overthrowing the traditional concept of the faculties and the compartmentalization of the mind? Does he make thoroughly clear the distinguishing qualities of his concepts concerning the nature of man and the central significance of these concepts to the issue of emotion in religion? If not, can you suggest reasons why he might have deliberately chosen to veil part of his thinking?

5. Consult a modern text in psychology to estimate the modernity of this view. The text will use language such as "motivation" or "drive" which "positively correlates" with "activation" or "tension."

6. Why is it critical to Edwards's theory of divine affections (heavenly affections) that he associate the affections with the mind or soul and that he disassociate them from the body? That he make "animal spirits" the unessential effect rather than a constituent of the affections? Throughout the sermon is he consistent in this matter of "nonessential product" vs. "component element." Why does he chiefly

use the term "soul" here instead of "mind" which he uses elsewhere, as in the beginning of his treatment of the Doctrine?

7. Perhaps without his consciously recognizing it, is Edwards here admitting the primacy of the intellect?

8. If Edwards's basic premise in this section is accepted, does his conclusion automatically follow: true faith evokes strong emotions?

9. In these passages, and in those later on in the speech, does Edwards seem to be saying that the emotions provide the starting point, the initiating mechanism, in the process of conversion? Is he saying that the emotions must be aroused before the mind will rationally accept? Does he later contradict his expressions here? Does he seem to contradict his position earlier (see note no. 6 above) that animal spirits are the unessential result of affections?

10. Note that in developing subhead no. 4, Edwards first states a general thesis which includes a listing of derivative particulars; then he develops each of the particulars, relating each to the basic premise; he explains that for support he has used only a small representative sampling of a great amount of Biblical evidence, and he applies the supportive evidence to the basic premise by means of a terse homey thrust. Since his proof involves the apodictic demonstration of the Bible, were his listeners logically compelled to accept his use of Scriptural evidence, as well as the extension of his basic contention? Why, or why not?

11. Does Edwards make clear what he means by the qualification: "although by their reaction they may make some circumstantial difference in the sensation of the mind"? What do you think his meaning is? Does he differentiate clearly between the animal spirits which are the effect of divine affections and those which are merely animal spirits, without antecedent divine intervention? How does this view comport with his implications elsewhere (see note no. 9 above) that animal spirits may initiate mental functions which, in turn, may lead to conversion and to holy affections?

12. After you have reviewed the nine subheads which serve as the basic structure of the Reasons segment, estimate the logical and psychological potential of this development. Do you believe that Edwards planned a steadily rising level of tension which would peak in subhead no. 9, with the summary representing a brief falling action before the climax in the Application? Is there a suggestion of anticlimax in subhead no. 9? Do you believe that there are several peaks of logical-emotional appeal? If so, identify this series. Do you believe that his argument is based on an "emerging conceptualization" in which the formulations gradually evolve through a sequential development of key fragments?

13. In the Application, Edwards's reasoning is based on this sequence: because true religion consists much in the affections, it follows that if

a man has no affections he has no true religion; therefore, such means are to be desired which have much tendency to move the affections; and, therefore, persons have great cause to be ashamed that they are no more affected with the great things of religion. Is this an inexorable chain of logical connectives? Are specious links present? Are necessary links missing?

Natural Religion

Ebenezer Gay

Disliking the inscrutability and the unpredictability of Calvin's God, Ebenezer Gay sought to find order and harmony in the universe. From the earliest days of his ministry, he emphasized the rational, multi-dimensional search for answers to religious questions, and when the emotionalism of the revival swept over his community of Hingham, he denounced the extravagances. If he cannot rightly be called the father of American Unitarianism, Gay should be famed for epitomizing New England Liberalism in his "Natural Religion." *

Presented at Harvard College more than a decade after the Awakening had subsided, "Natural Religion" was one of the lectures in the Dudleian series on natural religion. Antithetic to Edwards's view that "Our people do not so much need to have their heads stored, as to have their hearts touched," Gay's lecture carried the implications of rational religion much further than did Chauncy's "Enthusiasm Described." In addressing his elite audience upon a distinguished occasion, Gay introduced new dimensions to the issue of emotion in religion. Attempting to keep within the acceptable boundaries of Calvinist thought, Gay nevertheless greatly expanded the role of reason in man, in God, and in the relationship between God and man; also, he suggested that man may be the steersman of his spiritual destiny. Too, whereas Chauncy accepted a useful, though limited, role for the emotions under the strict supervision of an informed Understanding, Gay—except for a fleeting genuflection—ignored the emotions. In contradistinction to Edwards's unitive psychology, Gay considered that the cognitive faculties were separated from the emotions and were restrictive masters controlling spontaneous affective responses.

Conforming to his de-emphasis of both the emotions and the faculty of Imagination which gives rise to emotionalism, Gay spoke

---

* The text of our lecture comes from Ebenezer Gay, *Natural Religion, as Distinguished from Revealed* (Boston, 1759). See Part One: The Developing Exigence.

directly and clearly to the intellect in an uncompromisingly dull and bloodless style.

ROMANS 2:14, 15

For when the Gentiles, which have not the Law, do by Nature the Things contained in the Law; these having not the Law, are a Law unto themselves: Which shew the Work of the Law written in their Hearts, their Conscience also bearing witness, and their Thoughts the mean while accusing, or else excusing one another.[1]

The Belief of GOD's Existence is most essentially fundamental to all Religion, and having been at the first of the *Dudleian* Lectures established;[2] the moral Obligation which it induceth upon the Nature of Man, may be the Subject of our present Inquiry.

A DEVOUT *Hermit* being asked,[3] How he could profit in Knowledge, living in a Desart, without Men and Books? answered, "I have one Book which I am always studying, and turning over Day and Night: The Heavens, the Earth and the Waters, are the Leaves of which it consists." The Characters of the Deity are plainly legible in the whole Creation around us: And if we open the Volume of our own Nature, and look within, we find there a Law written;—a Rule of virtuous Practice prescribed.

RELIGION and Law (divine) are Words of promiscuous Use; denoting in the general Signification thereof, *An Obligation lying upon Men to do those Things which the Perfections of God, relative unto them, do require to them.* In this Definition (whether exact and full, or not,) I mean to imply all Things incumbent on such reasonable Creatures as Men are, toward all Beings with which they are concerned, GOD, the supreme, one another, and themselves; and which are incumbent on them, by vertue of the Perfections of God, in the Relation there is betwixt Him and them: other Obligation which can be supposed to any of the same Things, not being of the religious Kind. And in the doing those Things to which Religion is the Obligation, are

included, besides the actual Performance, the Principles, Motives and Ends thereof; all that is necessary to render any Acts of Men, whether internal or external, such as the Perfections of the Deity require.

RELIGION is divided into natural and revealed:—Revealed Religion, is that which GOD hath made known to Man by the immediate Inspiration of his Spirit, the Declarations of his Mouth, and Instructions of his Prophets: *Natural,* that which bare Reason discovers and dictates: As 'tis delineated by the masterly Hand of St. Paul, the Apostle of the Gentiles, in the Words of holy Scripture now read—Which I take as a proper and advantageous Introduction to my intended Discourse on this Head, Viz.

THAT *Religion is, in some measure, discoverable by the Light, and practicable to the Strength, of Nature;* [4] and is so far fitly called *Natural* by Divines and learned Men. The Religion which is possible to be discover'd by the Light, and practis'd by the Power of Nature, consists in rend'ring all those inward and outward Acts of Respect, Worship and Obedience unto God, which are suitable to the Excellence of his all-perfect Nature, and our Relation to Him, who is our Creator, Preserver, Benefactor, Lord, and Judge;—And in yielding to our Fellow-Men that Regard, Help and Comfort, which their partaking of the same Nature, and living in Society with us, give them a Claim to;—And in managing our Souls and Bodies, in their respective Actions and Enjoyments, in a way agreeable to our *Make,* and conducive to our Ease and Happiness; And doing all from a Sense of the Deity, imposing the Obligation, and approving the Discharge of it. [5] For 'tis a Regard to Him in every moral Duty that consecrates it, and makes it truly an Act of Religion. These Things, indeed, are contained in the Revelation of God, which affords the chief Assistance to our knowing and doing of them; and yet they belong to the Religion of Nature, so far as Nature supplies any Light and Strength to the Discovery and Practice of them. [6]

I. THAT Religion is in some measure, discoverable by the Light of Nature. [7] The Obligation lying on us to do those Things which the Perfections of GOD, as related to us, require, is dis-

cernable in the Light of natural Reason.[8] This Faculty of the
human Soul, exercised in the Contemplation of the universal
Frame of Nature, or of any Parts thereof; and in the Observation of the general Course of Providence, or of particular
Events therein, may convince Men of the Existence and Attributes of God, the alwise, powerful and good Maker, Upholder,
and Governor of all Things. It may be questioned whether the
reasoning Faculty, as it is in the Bulk of Mankind, be so acute
and strong, as . . . to prove all other Perfections do belong to
God in an infinite Degree. . . . Yet it is plain to the lowest
Capacity of those who, with a little Attention, survey the Works
of God, that He is a Being of such Perfection: And that, since
He is their Maker, Owner, and Benefactor, to whom they are
indebted for all that they are, and have, and on whom they depend for all they need, or can enjoy; they are bound to yield
unto Him, in the Temper of their Minds, and Manner of their
Behaviour, toward Him, and his Creatures they are concerned
with, all that Regard which Religion founded in the Nature of
God, and in the Nature of Man, and the Relation there is between them implies. . . . Their Souls may know right well, how
wonderfully God hath made them with Powers and Faculties
superior to any bodily Endowments; which should not therefore
be subjected to the Sway of bruitish Appetites and blind
Passions. Reason may know it's divine Right to govern, to maintain it's Empire in the Soul, regulating the Passions and Affections; directing them to proper Objects, and stinting them to just
Measures. Nature affords considerable Light for the Discovery,
and Arguments for the Proof, of such Parts of Religion. There is
an essential Difference between Good and Evil, Right and
Wrong, in many Cases that relate to moral Conduct toward our
Maker, Mankind, and Ourselves, which the Understanding (if
made use of) cannot but discern. The obvious Distinction is
founded in the Natures and Relations of Things: And the Obligation thence arising to chuse the Good, and do that which is
Right, is not (as I conceive) antecedent to any Law or Institution, enjoining this upon us. It primarily originates from the
Will and Appointment of the Author of those Natures, and
Founder of those Relations, which are the Grounds and

Reasons of it. And his Will is signified by his apparently wise and good Constitution of Things, in their respective Natures and Relations. The Law of Nature is given by the God of Nature, who is Lord of all. He enacted it by creating and establishing a World of Beings in such Order, as he hath done. He publishes it to rational Creatures (as is necessary to it's binding them) in making them capable to learn from his Works, what is good, and what is required of them. Natural Conscience is his Voice, telling them their Duty. This (in part) is the *work of the Law in their Hearts.*—'Tis the Engravement of it there, answerable to the Writing of it on Tables, in order to it's being made known: And so Men are *a Law unto themselves,* are supply'd with a Rule of Actions within their own Breasts. The Righteousness which is of Nature (to adopt the Language of Inspiration) speaketh on some such wise, as doth that which is of Faith: *Say not in thine Heart who shall ascend into Heaven; or who shall descend into the Deep,* to bring us the Knowledge of our Duty? *The Word is nigh thee, even in thy Heart,* shewing thee what thou oughtest to do: *Conscience also bearing witness,* testifying for or against Men, according as they obey or disobey the Word of Reason, which is the Word of God: And so *their Thoughts*—the general Notions of Good and Evil in them, make them either to accuse themselves as Transgressors of a known Law, or else excuse them, as not having culpably done any Thing against it. In the due Exercise of their natural Faculties, Men are capable of attaining some Knowledge of God's Will, and their Duty, manifested in his Works, as if it were written in legible Characters on the Tables of their Hearts. And 'tis on this Account, that any Part of Religion is called Natural; and stands distinguished, in *Theology,* from that which is revealed.[9]

II. THAT Religion is, in some Measure, practicable to the Strength of Nature.[10] There is doing, as well as knowing, by Nature, the Things contained in the Law of it. Knowing them is but in order to the doing them: And the Capacity to know them would be in vain, (which nothing in Nature is) if there was no Ability to do them. Whoever observes the divine Workmanship in human Nature, and takes a Survey of the Powers and Faculties with which it is endowed, must needs see that it was

designed and framed for the Practice of Virtue: That Man is not merely so much lumpish Matter, or a *mechanical* Engine, that moves only by the Direction of an impelling Force; but that he hath a Principle of Action within himself, and is an Agent in the Strict and proper Sense of the Word. The special Endowment of his Nature, which constitutes him such, is the Power of Self-determination, or Freedom of Choice; his being possessed of which is as self-evident, as the Explanation of the Manner of it's operating, is difficult: He feels himself free to act one Way, or another: And as he is capable of distinguishing between different Actions, of the moral Kind; so is he likewise of chusing which he will do, and which leave undone. Further to quality our Nature for Virtuous or religious Practice (which necessarily must be of Choice) the Author of it hath annexed a secret Joy or Complacence of Mind to such Practice, and as sensible a Pain or Displicence to the contrary. . . . The Spirit of Man being thus formed within him, it is (according to the original Design and wise Contrivance of our Maker) naturally disposed toward Religion: It hath an Inclination thereto implanted in it, which under the Direction of right Reason, is an inward Spring of Motion and Action, when Reason alone would not give sufficient Quickness and Vigour in pursuing it's Dictates.

THERE may be something in the intelligent moral World analogous to Attraction in the material System [11]—something that inclines and draws Men toward God, the Centre of their Perfection, and consummate Object of their Happiness; and which, if it's Energy were not obstructed, would as certainly procure such Regularity in the States and Actions of all intelligent Beings in the spiritual World, as that of Attraction doth in the Positions and Motions of all the Bodies in the material World. . . . In Him there is an infinite Desire and Ardor of possessing and enjoying Himself, and his own infinite Perfections, in order to render Him happy. . . . There must therefore be an Image of this his infinite Desire after Happiness in all his intelligent Creatures—a Desire after Happiness in a Re-union with Him. . . . This Principle was most certainly implanted in the Creation of intelligent Beings, in the very Fund and Substance of their Natures, tho there remains but few Footsteps and Instances of

it's Being or Effects.—It wonderfully analogises with that of
Attraction in the material World: As to the SUPREME INFI-
NITE, it may very properly be called, his *Attraction* of them;
and as to them, their *Central Tendency,* or Gravitation (so to
speak) toward Him. . . . There is in common Nature, which all
partake of, a Propension to Acts, not only of human Kindness,
but also of divine Worship; which excites to the Performance
of them, when proper Occasions of doing them occur, without
previous, express Deliberation and Determination concerning
them: And to forbear them is a painful Restraint upon Nature;
and to do the contrary, is thwarting it's Inclination, and wresting
it from it's Bent. . . . His Formation of them qualifys them, in
a measure, for religious Practice; as his Regeneration, or Reno-
vation of them doth more so. And his fitting them by Nature
therefor, is a Work of his, to which the Work of Sanctification, in
his furnishing them with Grace to evangelical Obedience,
Beareth Analogy. The former is the Work of the Law written in
their Hearts, that they may do, as well as know, what it enjoins:
The latter is the Impression of the Gospel upon them, that, thro'
Christ's strengthening them, they may do what it requires. And
by doing the Things contained in the Law of Nature, Men *shew*
the Work of the Law written in their Hearts, and are a Law unto
themselves, as truly and plainly, as regenerate Christians, by
doing the Things contained in the Gospel, are *manifestly de-*
clared to be the Epistle of Christ, written, not with Ink, but with
the Spirit of the living God, not in Tables of Stone, but in fleshly
Tables of the Heart. The Scriptures thus describing the Religion
of Nature and of Christ, clearly distinguish between them; as
the former may be practiced by the Strength of Nature, and the
latter by the Strength of Christ,—his Spirit helping the In-
firmities of our Nature.

How far the Duties of Religion are possible to be performed
by the Strength of Nature, in a lapsed State; and to what
Measure of divine Approbation and Acceptance, Reason, unen-
lightened by Revelation, may not be able to determine.—The
Law of Nature is purely a Law of Works, and requires perfect
Obedience, which the Transgressors of it, as all Men are, cannot
yield to it: And whether that which is wanting in their Obedi-

ence, may be supplied by Repentance and Humility in them, and by Mercy and Pardon in God, cannot be certainly known without a Revelation of his Will, on which it wholly depends. The Goodness of God, in the general Course of his Providence, toward sinful Mankind, sheweth Him to be placable, and leadeth them to Repentance; but doth not assure them of Pardon upon it, much less of the Reward of eternal Life, for imperfect, tho' it should be sincere, Obedience. . . . And their Thoughts excusing and approving of them for doing, in some Measure, what the Law requires, implies a Hope, which may not be altogether vain, that they shall be accepted. Thô it should be, as one saith, "That all the moral Virtues are so many Cyphers—unavailing Nothings, unless the Deity be placed as the principal Figure at the Head of them; "yet if practiced out of any Sense of Duty to God, and with a View to pleasing Him, as it is possible they may be, and have been, shall we say, they are meerly splendid Vices in his Eyes; and that the most humble Prayers of natural Men are Blasphemies in his Ears? May there not be such a conscientious doing *by Nature The Things contained in the Law* of it, as, thrô the Riches of divine Bounty and Goodness, shall in some low Measure, compar'd with doing the same by Grace, be acceptable and rewardable? May not a *God of Knowledge, by whom Actions are weighed,* discern some Good in those done by the Strength of Nature, and approve the honest, thô weak, Efforts thereof, to serve him; and thereupon, besides outward Favours (of which He is liberal to all both good and bad Men) grant the Succours of his Grace, enabling them to do the same, and other Things to better Acceptance, and to the obtaining a greater Reward, even that which the Christian Revelation proposes; and is thereby differenced and distinguished from natural Religion?

AND, now, if what hath been so imperfectly spoken, be according to the Truth in Nature, and not inconsistent with the Christian Verity, the proper Use and Improvement of it is, *To form a just Estimate of Natural Religion;* and guard against the dangerous Extremes in our Regards to it—Not to have a debasing, nor a too exalted Notion of it.[12]

1. We should not depreciate and cry down Natural Religion,

on Pretence of advancing the Honour of Revealed—as if they were two opposite Religions, and could no more stand together in the same Temple than Dagon and the Ark of God. Whatever Distinction we observe between them, there is no Contrariety in the one to the other: They subsist harmoniously together, and mutually strengthen and confirm each other. Revealed Religion is an *Additional* to Natural; built, not on the Ruins, but on the strong and everlasting Foundations of it. Nothing therefore can be vainer and more preposterous, than the Attempt to . . . represent the former as insignificant to the grand Purpose of Religion, and chief End of Man; the glorifying and enjoying God:—As availing nothing towards Man's Recovery from a sinful State, and his Attainment unto Holiness and Happiness:—As if his knowing and doing *by Nature the Things contained in the Law* of it, could be no more acceptable to his Maker, nor profitable to himself, than his Ignorance and Neglect of them: And whatever Improvement and Progress he made in natural Religion, he was not a Step nearer the Kingdom of God; nor a fairer Candidate for Heaven than a *Heathen-Man, or a Publican.* The Law of Nature, like that of *Moses,* may be serviceable unto Men, *as a School-Master to bring them to Christ,* for higher Instruction; especially where the Means of such are afforded; and so usher them into a State of Grace. Notwithstanding the Insufficiency of natural Religion to their Salvation, yet it may, in some Measure, prepare them to be Partakers of the Benefit, without any Diminution of the Glory of the Gospel, which is the Grant of it, or Detraction from the Merits of our blessed Redeemer, who is the Author of it. It is only by Grace that sinful Men can be saved; yet, by making some good Use of their rational Powers (weakened as they be) in the Study and Practice of natural Religion, they may be in a better Preparation of Mind to comply with the Offers and Operations of divine Grace, than if they wholly give up themselves to the Conduct of sensual Appetites & Passions. Whether those Offers & Operations of divine Grace are designed for, and ever vouchsafed to such as are not favoured with Revelation; and it be possible for them to obtain Mercy, in the Day when God by Jesus Christ shall judge the Things which they have done, *according to the*

Gospel; is a Point which Revelation only can determine; and is not my Province to discuss.

In the Preference we give to revealed Religion, we should not for the sake of any particular Truth we apprehend to be deliver'd in it, hastily renounce a Principle of natural Religion, seeming contrary thereto. . . . To say, in Defence of any religious Tenets, reduced to Absurdity, that the Perfections of God, his Holiness, Justice, Goodness, are quite different Things in Him, from what, in an infinitely lower Degree, they are in Men, is to overthrow all Religion both natural and revealed; and make our Faith, as well as Reason vain.—For, if we have no right Notions of the Deity, (as 'tis certain, upon this Supposition, we have none), as we worship, so we believe, we know not what, or why. We don't know what Respects are due from us to the Perfections of God; or that any are required of us by Him. For, as well as any other moral Perfections, Truth may be quite different in God, from what it is in Men; and so there may be nothing of that which we conceive of as such, in his Assertions and Promises.—He may declare one Thing, and mean another; promise one Thing, and do another:—God may be True and Faithful, and yet deceive us; as well as Holy and Just, and do that which is not Right. Revelation gives us the same (tho' clearer) Ideas of the Attributes of God, which we have from Nature and Reason: And if it taught any Thing contrary thereto, it would unsay what it saith, and destroy it's own Credibility. To set the Gifts of God at variance, is to frustrate the good Design and deprive ourselves of the Benefit of them. Vehemently to decry Reason, as useless, or as a blind Guide, leading Men into Error and Hell; and to run down natural Religion as mere *Paganism,* derogates from the Credit of revealed, subverts our Faith in it, and Dissolves our Obligation to practice it.

2. We should not magnify and extol natural Religion, to the Disparagement of Revealed. We cannot say, that the Light and Strength of Nature, how great soever, in it's original State of Rectitude, had no Assistance from Revelation. . . . Had Man, with all his natural Endowments in their perfect Order and Strength, been placed in this World, and no Notice given him of it's Maker, might he not have stood wondring some Time at the

amazing Fabrick, before he would have thence, by Deductions of Reason, argued an invisible Being, of eternal Power, Wisdom and Goodness, to be the Author of it and him; to whom he was therefore obliged to pay all Regards suitable to such glorious Excellencies? . . . Yet his falling into Sin, and effacing the divine Image in his Soul, greatly alter'd the Case, with respect to him, and his Posterity, and made Revelation a necessary Supplement of supernatural Light and Strength, for the Discovery and Performance of acceptable and available Religion. . . .

REASON, as well as Revelation, teacheth us, that human Nature, in it's original Constitution, and as it came out of the Hands of a good Creator, must be Perfect in it's Kind, and that it since, by our Abuse of it, is wofully impaired. It might not approach quite so near the Angelical, yea, Divine Nature in it's integral State, as some imagine; nor might it by the Sin of the *Protoplast* fall quite so low, as others affirm; and become a strange heterogeneous Compound of two other Natures, retaining nothing of Humanity in it. . . . Even in it's lapsed Estate: There are still in it, as received by Derivation from apostate Parents, "some *legible Characters, Out-lines,* and *Lineaments* of it's Beauty; some *magnificent Ruins,* which shew what it had been, enough to demonstrate the original Impression of the divine Image and Law." It is, however disorder'd and debilitated, a rational Nature, capable of religious Knowledge and Practice.

. . . .

And the Grace of God appears in assisting Reason by Revelation in those Discoveries, which it possibly could, but never did, nor would make, without such Help. — And the same is true, with respect to the Performances of Duty: *In thy Light we see Light.* It is in the Light of Revelation, added to that of Nature, that Things are so plain and easy to our discerning, as that we are ready to think bare Reason must discover them to all Mankind. . . . By Means of Revelation we have the right Use of Reason, in Matters of Religion: And, by the due Exercise of Reason, so excited and directed, we have the inestimable Benefit of Revelation. Both are *good Gifts,* — Rays from *the*

Father of Lights, to *enlighten every Man that cometh into the World.*—The Mind hath great Satisfaction in observing the harmonious Agreement between them, and the Objects of religious Knowledge and Faith appear the more beautiful and amiable in this double Light: And the better we understand and practice the Religion of Nature, the wiser and better Christians shall we be.

In a just Sense of this, and with a pious View to the Establishment of Religion, natural and revealed, and the Propagation of it in this Land, free from impure Mixtures of Heathenish and Popish Errors and Superstitions, by the Ministry of able, authorized Preachers, was the Anniversary-Lecture, here founded by the Honourable Judge DUDLEY, whose Memory must be ever precious in this Society, as his Praise will be in our Churches, as well as Courts.

AND this Discourse may lead the Students of the College, such especially as are design'd for the Work of the Ministry, to reflect on the great Advantage of a liberal Education, to open and enlarge their Minds for the Knowledge, and dispose their Hearts to the Love and Practice, and fit them to be Preachers of Religion. . . . All the Skill you here acquire in Arts and Sciences, may be serviceable to you in the Profession of *Theology:* And the better Scholars you go from this Place, the abler Divines will you prove, and the more Good may you do in the World. . . . How reproachful will it be to you, and not a little dishonourable to this School of the Prophets, if . . . you should then have need that one teach you the Rudiments of natural Religion . . . ? It concerns us all to make Proficiency in Religion . . . That having the Foundations of it well laid in our Minds, by convincing Reasons, and authentic Testimonies of Scripture, we go on to Perfection. Which that we may do;—Let us, as the Discourse now had, admonishes us, have a due Respect both to natural and revealed Religion. . . . Let us faithfully improve all the Light and Strength which natural Reason and divine Revelation supply . . . and to make continual Advance in Religion, 'till we come unto a *perfect Man*, in the redintegrated State of Nature—*unto the Measure of the Stature of the Fulness of CHRIST.*

INTERROGATIVE NOTES

1. Does this speech make for dull and difficult reading? What specific characteristics of style and content account for your answer? For speech composition of this type to be successful, what qualities must be present in the audience?
2. Does this reference to the speaking occasion seem to get the sermon off to a somewhat different start from the other speeches in this volume? Do the references to the Dudley lectures here *and in the close of the sermon* seem to give a modern touch which is lacking in the other speeches?
3. Does this allusion to "a devout hermit" seem to constitute a stylistic development which is not found in the speeches by Chauncy and Edwards? In what ways is it an important logical and psychological means of preparing the audience for the substance that follows?
4. This sentence is intended to serve as Gay's statement of purpose for the entire sermon. How well does the remainder of the speech adhere to this purpose?
5. Note the length of this sentence. Do you find that the understandability and the readability of this speech are affected by the length of the sentences? By the structure of the sentences? By the choice of language? By the degree of impersonality? By the degree of abstraction? If so, how?
6. In beginning this treatment of the Doctrine, Gay makes a purpose statement; he offers a long and involved definition, which refines further the definitions previously offered (Why has Gay emphasized definitions to such an extent thus far?); he relates the definitions to religion and ties the definitions to the purpose statement. In Gay's carrying out this pattern of development, do you feel that he has emphasized the rational over the emotional aspects to such an extent that his style seems tedious?
7. Notice that his subject sentence is the first half of the purpose statement (see note no. 4 above). As you continue your reading of this speech, do you find that the traditional format of definition-division-explanation is exaggerated—or is emphasized to about the same extent as in the other speeches in this volume? Later, how does Gay introduce the second main head of the Doctrine?
8. Do you find evidence in this paragraph that Gay has made any attempt to break the thought into easily digestible parts? Read the paragraph out loud. Does the style possess the instant intelligibility demanded of good oral communication?
9. Drawing upon your reading of Part One, what is Gay asserting in main head no. I, concerning man, nature, and religion, that is centrally significant to the issue of emotion vs. reason? In terms of argumenta-

tive development, is Gay attempting to prepare the listener to accept God as the formulator of the laws of nature, including those which condition man to respond spiritually in accord with his nature? Which faculty serves as the key of Gay's conception? Why is this particular faculty essential to Gay's paradigm of religion? (You may wish to review the treatment of faculty psychology contained in the introductory essay.) Is Gay significantly enlarging the scope of man's rational nature, enabling man to understand God's will and to respond—through self-determination—to it? In what ways does this main head serve to prepare the listener for that part of the argument which is yet to be presented?

10. In this passage is Gay attacking the determinism of Calvinism? In comparison to predestination, does Gay's approach seem to be mechanistic? Or, liberating?

11. How effective do you think that this figurative analogy would be for his particular audience? (Gay is referring here, of course, to the Newtonian scheme of the universe.) Recognizing that Harvard College was the elite center of learning and of "liberal" religious attitudes, do you believe that the listeners would be informed about Newton's system of attraction-repulsion, force-counterforce, mathematical certitude, and so on? Would they probably be psychologically receptive to this allusion? Is the thrust of this analogy mechanistic? If so, does it clash with, or complement, his discussion of determinism (see notes no. 9 and 10 above).

12. In this transition, Gay links the previous development to the Application and indicates the two major subdivisions of the Application. Why did he feel that it was unnecessary to summarize the preceding contents? Would Gay's transition be too obviously a signpost for the modern audience? In binding the parts of the speech together, how does Gay's methodology compare with that of Edwards and Chauncy?

PART THREE

Inquiry

Now that you have read Part One and the speeches and have answered the interrogative notes, it is time to rethink—to turn to account—your various experiences. To facilitate this end, the Inquiry section has been designed to particularize the general thrust of our entire study concerning the issue of emotion in religion, that is, to encourage you to consider the rhetorical problems confronted by each speaker, the options available to him, the choices he makes, and the wisdom of his choices. In order that you may exploit various lines of inquiry, your attention will be directed to illustrative instances in the speeches. For example, according to our reference system, if you should encounter this bracketed information, [3:10], you should turn to the tenth of the interrogative notes suffixed to the third reading, Chauncy's "Enthusiasm Described," and then should refer to the appropriate passages in the text. Our following suggestive comments and inquiries are clustered under three somewhat overlapping headings: strategies of argument, strategies of style and composition, and strategies of disposition.

Strategies of Argument

As our method of attack, let us consider the strategies of argument according to four criteria: consistency, clarity, persuasiveness, and modernity.

Concerning the *consistency and clarity of argument,* both Chauncy and Gay should be given satisfactory marks. In his "Enthusiasm Described," Chauncy is basically lucid and congruous in his analysis of the psychological nature of man [3:10] and of man's relationship with God [3:9]. Nevertheless, he could be charged with inconsistency of a sort: he celebrates reason and denigrates emotion, but in his efforts to make the

175

apposition impelling he reinforces his logical argument with emotional elements of style and composition [3:4 and 15]. Too, he sometimes seems to use ambiguous words and phrases for their emotional values. Thus, within the context of the sermon, his assertion that "the *soul* is the *man*" may be evocative, but it is either meaningless or it signifies that emotions do not comprise a part of man [3:12]. In his "Natural Religion," Gay discusses clearly and consistently the relationship between nature, man, and God, as well as the primacy of reason [5:9]. He does not etch sharply, however, the equation of natural vs. revealed religion, nor does he specify clearly either the extent to which one may influence his chance for salvation [5:9 and 10] or how man's basic nature is an "inclination" under control of the Understanding—a view incompatible with that of Edwards (see text in 5, immediately above placement of note no. 11). Nevertheless, while remaining respectful of the prevailing currents of Calvinism, he employs—as does Chauncy—the strategy of clear and forthright argument.

On the other hand, does one always know where Edwards stands? Is his argument clear, accurate, and consistent? If not, are his aberrations unintentional? Do they represent a pattern of duplicity? Are they so significant that they call into question the *validity* of his case?

Consider the consistency and clarity of Edwards's policies toward church membership. For nearly twenty years after he first went to Northampton as the handpicked assistant and future successor of his grandfather, Solomon Stoddard, he had continued to accept the open admission policies which Stoddard had long before established in the Valley. About 1744, however, during the course of serious disputes with the town over his salary and over the teenager "bad book episode," Edwards apparently shifted to the position that no one should be admitted to communion without a profession of faith and experience. For the next four years no inhabitant of the shocked and resentful town applied for admission to his church. In December 1748, when he refused membership to a candidate unwilling or unable to make a public profession, the congregation began a movement to dismiss Edwards, giving as the reason for separation: Ed-

wards had "departed from the principles which the great Mr. Stoddard brought in and practiced, and which he himself was settled upon, and a long time practiced." The premise upon which Stoddard had based his admissions policy was that no one could tell with certainty who were elected. In Edwards's "Distinguishing Marks" of 1741, however [2:13], he contradicted this premise of Stoddard's by offering five "certain marks" of salvation, and in his sermons on religious affections, 1742-43, he spelled out the seriousness of his split with Stoddardism. Thus, on the one hand, between 1727 and 1744—when he moved to his new system, Edwards had applied Stoddard's open admission policy. On the other hand, at least as early as September 1741, he had abandoned the basic premise which warranted the opening of church membership and the Lord's Supper to all except obvious sinners. Is it reasonable—or is it not—to charge Edwards with hypocrisy [2:13]?

Consider the consistency and clarity of Edwards's theological position. In his "Future Punishment" and "Distinguishing Marks," he preaches something close to universalism [1:15]. Ignoring absolutist principles [2:16], he brings salvation within the grasp of the earnest seeker. He condemns the unconverted for not possessing saving faith and he exhorts them to acquire it. Nevertheless, in his "The Nature of the Affections" and in the other sermons in his series on religious affections, it is apparent that all are damned—regardless of the purity of their lives or the sincerity of their efforts—except for the elect, those whom God has capriciously endowed with a saving spiritual predisposition. The ultimate, terrifying absolute statement of the helplessness of man appears in his *Freedom of the Will*, published in 1754. (This treatise is contained in his *Works*. An excellent modern edition is Paul Ramsey's *Jonathan Edwards: Freedom of the Will* [New Haven: Yale University Press, 1957]). Do you agree that in his "Future Punishment" he offers as much spiritual initiative to man as does Gay in his "Natural Religion" [5:9 and 10]? In "Future Punishment," is Edwards guilty—or not guilty—of using the strategy of deception? Designed ambiguity? Of seeking to achieve effect by whatever methods will work in a given situation?

Consider the consistency and clarity of Edwards's theories concerning the role of emotion in religion. In the first place, in its strategies of argument, style-composition, and disposition, his "Future Punishment" is meticulously and superbly designed to evoke maximum emotional response. Nevertheless, in his "Distinguishing Marks," preached five months later—and especially in his sermons on religious affections—Edwards recognizes that the preaching of some revivalists had produced undesirable emotional extravagances and that emotional responses are themselves extremely unreliable indexes of spirituality. Is Edwards guilty—or not guilty—of sustaining a remarkably swift change in beliefs concerning the emotions? Of expediency, in seeking in "Future Punishment" to gain power over his listeners without regard for the means? Inasmuch as he employs extremely potent emotional appeals in his "Distinguishing Marks" in juxtaposition with his cautions against emotionalism, is he guilty—or not guilty—of speaking out of both sides of his mouth? At the time he preached the "Future Punishment" and the "Distinguishing Marks" the revival was running full tide, but within a few months a riptide of reaction had set in and, in response to the current, Edwards forsook his horrific preaching. Is this, or is this not, an evidence of Edwards's opportunism?

In the second place, concerning the role of emotions in religion, is Edwards clear in his definitions relating to the emotions and is he consistent in the application of these definitions? As a suggestive beginning of such lines of inquiry, let us look at the following. If you had not read Part One, would you have recognized clearly that in "The Nature of the Affections" Edwards is discarding both the traditional Puritan psychology of the faculties and the compartmentalization of the mind [2:4; 4:4]? That Edwards is employing new concepts concerning the nature of man, in conjunction with new concepts concerning the nature of religion and the nature of rhetoric, to formulate a new morphology of conversion? That in this new morphology the Will is no longer dependent upon the Understanding for the initiation of, and the rational determination of, the mind's response? In "The Nature of the Affections," is it clear that the Will has become the inclination of the soul, in reality the soul

itself—man himself—as it responds to spiritual stimuli? (Contrast with Chauncy's view that "the *soul* is the *man*" [3:12].) That by every act of the Will the "soul is either inclined or disinclined to what is in view"? That all such movements of the soul, all such "sensible exercises of the Will are no other than the *affections* of the soul"? That a strong inclination toward God is virtually synonymous with strong emotions? And that strong emotions result in a strong movement of the "animal spirits"? Inasmuch as Edwards refers to the Understanding as a distinct and separate faculty, is it clear that he has relegated the Understanding to a kind of cooperative, but supplemental, advisory function [4:7]? Is it clear that man has ceased to be a fragmented being whose effector mechanism consists of a "response" circuit with sequential control stations (see Part One)? That man is now substantially a unified being who responds to spiritual stimuli according to his basic predisposition? And that, because of the nature of man-God-religion, this response must necessarily be emotional? If you experienced difficulty in following Edwards through the thickets of his psychological theories, do you think that, in comparison to you, his listeners—schooled as they were in faculty psychology—would have had more, or less, difficulty?

In pursuing further the clarity and consistency of Edwards's argument concerning the role of emotion in religion, let us look closely at what is possibly his most vulnerable point. Edwards states that [4:5] "any lively and vigorous exercise of the inclination" produces some effect upon the body, influencing the "motion of its fluids, and especially of the animal spirits." He continues that "from the same laws of union" the "motion" of the body fluids "may promote the exercise of the affections." How this reverse flow of effect might occur becomes even less clear when Edwards removes the "seat of the emotions" from the body and places it in the soul [4:6]; it is only the soul that is inclined, i.e., that loves, hates, etc. [4:7]. The "animal spirits" or the "motion" of the body fluids, are only the "concomitants of the affections." They are "entirely distinct from the affections [the inclinations of the soul] themselves" and are in "no way essential" to the emotions. Thus, an "unbodied spirit" is "as

capable" of emotions as a spirit "that is united to a body."

The foregoing poses some critical problems. What is an emotion? If love, for instance, is an emotion, what is love? If such "emotions" exist exclusively in the soul, how are they felt or experienced? If they are separate from the body, why must they always produce changes in the body? What are changes in the "motion" of the body fluids? Are we led to the conclusion that it is by means of these changes in the body that the emotion is felt or experienced? Does Edwards recognize this when he asserts that the "animal spirits" may themselves produce emotions? If the "animal spirits" *are not* the physical sensations of emotions—but merely disturbances of the body—how can they serve to initiate particular emotions? Especially those which are saving in character? If spiritual emotions produce physical by-products, does the reverse necessarily follow—that physical by-products can produce spiritual affections? If the "animal spirits" *are* the physical sensations of the emotions, then are they not an intrinsic part of the "emotions," hence of the Will? Does Edwards recognize this when he states, "by their reaction they may make some circumstantial difference in the sensation of the mind" [4:8 and 11]? (Contrast Edwards's position on this point with that of Solomon Stoddard. See Part One.) If motions in the "animal spirits" provide the way by which emotions are experienced, are emotions, therefore, physical in orientation? Thus, can emotions exist outside the body? Thus, can there be such things as "heavenly affections" [4:11]? By his considering emotions to be "sensible," i.e., experienced through the senses, does Edwards make his interpretation invalid? Is Edwards employing the stratagem of deliberate obsfucation? Of partial revealment? Is he faced with the task of explaining something which is too complex to explain readily?

Continuing this theme further: if the emotions belong exclusively to the soul, they themselves cannot be observed by others; only bodily changes can be observed. Edwards admits that the changes wrought upon the body by nonsaving emotions are indistinguishable from those produced by saving emotions. Therefore, it is impossible to determine from one's physical state whether one is saved. If the greater part of reli-

gion consists in emotions, and if it is impossible to determine whether one is sustaining saving emotions, is it not impossible to judge whether another person is saved? How does one distinguish counterfeit emotions from the saving ones? In his "Distinguishing Marks," do any of the "certain" signs bear satisfactorily upon this point? Do these "signs" seem to flirt with "good works," or pious behavior? If so, is this not in direct conflict with the essence of Edwards's thought? If it is impossible to determine the identity of the elect, does this invalidate Edwards's change in church admission policies in 1744?

In addition to clarity and consistency, we should consider the persuasiveness of the arguments advanced by our three spokesmen. Designedly or otherwise, all of the speakers use materials and compositional elements which tend to lessen opposition and to encourage listeners to think, feel, or behave as a unit. Nevertheless, significant differences exist among the speakers—roughly identifiable with their positions on the issue of emotion in religion—both as to their rhetorical goals and as to their rhetorical methodologies. You may now wish to review Part One.

In terms of the extent to which they employ strategies to make their arguments persuasive, the three speakers can be located upon a wide scale. One end of the scale is represented by the Liberal minister, Gay, who makes scant use of persuasive strategies. For instance, he is content to state—with little apparent attempt to convince—his concept that man's spirit has an inclination toward God which is under control of the reasoning faculty (see text of 5, above note no. 11). Inasmuch as this concept is antipodal to that of Edwards—i.e., man's inclination is the Will, or man responding automatically and emotionally— one might expect Gay to attempt to make his view seem necessary and desirable. At the opposite end of the scale is Jonathan Edwards, who consistently attempts to exploit the available means of persuasion. In a mid-position, closer to the placement of Edwards than to that of Gay, is Charles Chauncy, who is obviously concerned with moving his listeners and who makes frequent use of persuasive devices [3:1].

In terms of the skill with which they use strategies to make their arguments persuasive, the three speakers occupy roughly the same comparative positions that were identified in the paragraph just above. Evidencing little skill in persuasion, Gay is basically an expository speaker who contents himself with presenting a rational argument, expecting the reasonableness of his case to sell itself to reasoning auditors. Although he is far from being an orator, Chauncy demonstrates the competent skills of a journeyman practitioner. Edwards, on the other hand, reveals himself as a master logician-rhetorician. In his "Future Punishment," he approaches almost complete polarity with his listeners, albeit by means perhaps approaching demagoguery. In his other two speeches his strategies are skillfully designed to achieve the maximum degree of polarity that is commensurate with the topic and the speaking circumstances.

Similarly, in terms of the nature of the audience which they hope to reach, and in terms of the basic persuasive thrust they use to reach that audience, the three speakers position themselves over our wide spectrum. In the case of "Natural Religion," the members of Gay's elite audience are intellectually capable of receiving his message and probably are basically receptive to his ideas. It is doubtful, perhaps, that the nature of his specific auditory influenced Gay's basic rhetorical procedures. Possibly he would have selected the same basic approach, regardless of the attitudinal predispositions or intellectual character of his listeners. Thus, if it can be said that he has a strategy of persuasion, it is merely to offer an intellectual explanation for rational consideration by those persons who are willing and able to profit therefrom. In the case of Chauncy's speech during the Harvard commencement ceremonies, he makes no concerted attempt to conciliate the opposition or to remove either logical or psychological objections to his proposals. Instead, his strategy is to storm the barricades! To summon a logical-emotional appeal that would rally the favorably predisposed, capture as many as possible of the undecided or neutral, and, if possible, put to flight those listeners who resist persuasion. Although, in comparison to Gay's argument, Chauncy's appeal seems to be directed to a broader audience, his development—like that of

Gay—would be most attractive to conservatively inclined persons, especially those of average and superior education, affluence, and social position [3:11].

In contrast to Gay and Chauncy, Edwards seems to be seeking to reach a broader base, a more general auditory. In "Future Punishment," his intent is to energize a general congregation, to engulf everyone with an emotional wave that would sweep them to the desired response. To reach the broadest possible spectrum by his commencement sermon, "Distinguishing Marks," he focuses on a combination of goals: to convince-reinforce-actuate. To effect these goals he uses a wide variety of strategies designed to disarm the opposition by making his arguments seem reasonable, necessary, and desirable; to intensify the support of those already on his side; and to arouse the convinced to overt support of the revival. In both of these speeches, however, Edwards's efforts to evoke immediate response include abrasive or shocking materials which probably placed him and the Awakening in a more vulnerable position and some of which possibly left residual opposition [2:13, 18, 19]. In his lecture, "The Nature of the Affections," which is directed to the entire church-going community of Northampton, Edwards not only attempts to make a new, complicated concept clear but also to make it seem valid and psychologically attractive.

To secure a capsulated orientation to the different approaches employed by our speakers, you may wish to review their direct clashes concerning the Church at Corinth [2:10; 3:2] and concerning censoriousness, emotional preaching, reason in religion, and irrationality [2:11; 3:5, 9, 11; 4:7; 5:9, 10]. As measured by your own reactions, as well as by your estimation of the possible response of their contemporaries, which speaker did the best job of presenting his case?

Now let us look briefly at the speakers' specific use of certain persuasive options.

Options concerning emotions. Gay abjures the use of emotional properties, thus condemning his speaking to Morphean dullness. According to his own theory, Chauncy approves the use

of emotions under the tight control of the Understanding. To what extent does he employ emotional proof in "Enthusiasm Described"? How important to the impact of his case is his use of emotions? Is his application to emotions intrinsic to his argument, or does it seem to be superimposed? Do you feel that Chauncy is directing his emotional appeal to listeners who are unified beings? Or, to compartmentalized beings, with the appeal being directed first to the Understanding and the Will, then to the Affections? How would you characterize the basic nature of his appeal? As subtle? Bald? Strident? Bellicose? Chauncy states that emotions can serve to activate the "more noble part," the "reason and judgment" [3:12]. Would you say that Chauncy himself designedly uses the emotions to accomplish this purpose? If so, does this violate the sequence of the faculties, a sequence which he substantially endorses?

In the case of Edwards, do you agree that he makes almost continuous, imaginative, and skillful application to the emotions in a variety of moods, tones, and colors? Does Edwards seem to use emotions as an appeal to the "entire" man, rather than to the compartmentalized man of traditional Puritan rhetoric? What manifestations suggest his reliance upon Locke's sensational (i.e., sensory) psychology [4:3 and 4]? If one can say that Edwards appeals basically to fear, hope, and love, to what emotions does Chauncy appeal? Why does Edwards use the contrasting emotions of fear of hell and love of God? Which appeal is stronger? Does he use the appeal to fear as a means of intensifying his appeal to love? Do you find any pattern present in the way he positions these emotional appeals? For example, does he place the appeal to fear before, or after, the appeal to love? Does he place appeals to fear in juxtaposition to those of love, or does he separate them by means of intervening commentary? Do the appeals appear as detachable patches? Or, are they filaments, unobtrusively interwoven into the fabric of the entire speech? Are they shocking? Gentle? Sad? Joyous? Why does Edwards neglect appeals to fear in "The Nature of the Affections"? How does Edwards's use of emotions to initiate the conversion process and to energize the Understanding-Will compare with Stoddard's theory and practice (see Part One)?

Options concerning ethos. According to Aristotle, the ethos "of the speaker is a cause of persuasion when the speech is so uttered as to make him worthy of belief." A speaker can scarcely avoid enhancing or diminishing the attractiveness of his case by extrinsic aspects of personal proof, such as his hearers' awareness of his reputation for character and sagacity, his physical appearance, bearing, and poise, and his apparent qualities of good will. The deliberate, direct use of ethos—that is, the designed appeal to one's own experience or judgment as a means of lending added authority or interest to one's case—received only restricted use in printed Puritan sermons. Do you find any direct attempt by Gay or Chauncy to exploit their ethos? Edwards makes a much greater use of ethos than do Gay or Chauncy. What are some of the ways that he employs personal proof? Does he make frequent use of personal pronouns, such as "I," "myself," "we," "our," and "your"? Does he identify himself with the listeners? With the revival itself? Is he indirectly using ethos when he castigates conservatives and unbelievers? Might this abrasiveness have produced a desired immediate effect, but have caused a hidden resentment that later contributed to his difficulties with his own congregation and with conservatives in general [1:9; 2:11, 13, 15, 16, 17, 19, 20, 21]?

Options concerning supportive materials. To a large extent, the effectiveness of a speaker's presentation depends upon the skill with which he develops his ideas in accord with audience anticipation, audience capability and willingness to respond, the particular needs of the occasion, the logical and psychological needs of the argument, and the personal image the speaker wishes to project. In estimating the suitability with which our speakers develop their contentions, it may be helpful to look at the types of materials and the methods of development they used.

In their selection of types of supporting materials, our speakers are basically similar. None of them include statistical data. What might be some reasons why Puritan ministers as a general rule spurned the use of statistics? Inasmuch as Puritans considered Biblical evidence to be the sole means of absolute

faculty of the Affections that the rational control of the understanding might be circumvented [5:6]. A key to Edwards's persuasion is that he exploits Locke's sensational (sensory) psychology for the purpose of translating religious truths into sensory experiences, that is, into values which have meaning to the senses. This he considers to be the means of reaching the Will of the elect and of so influencing the Will that it becomes more "inclined" to respond in accordance with the divine Will (dip into almost any section of Edwards's speeches; for examples, see 1:7, 12; 4:3). *Significance* (the promoting of involuntary attention by stressing the vital importance of an idea or by appealing to significant human wants): Although all of our speakers indicate the extreme importance of their arguments, would you agree that Edwards exceeds the others in making his ideas seem urgently significant? To what extent does Edwards exploit these human wants: the wish for change, excitement, and adventure; the desire to be secure and comfortable—both psychologically and physically; the need for satisfactory group and self status; the interest in reverence, affection, companionship, loyalty, and sex (some contemporary critics believed that revivalistic preaching stimulated the listeners sexually; after rereading Edwards's "Future Punishment," do you believe that this charge may have had merit?); the wish to have as much personal freedom as possible? *Variety* (the maintaining of interest by varying the style, mood, disposition, nature of content, kinds of support, and methods of development): Concerning the amount of variation, do you agree that Gay's speech had the least, that Chauncy's had considerably more, and that Edwards's had the most? *Humor:* Inasmuch as some Puritans used humor frequently, if perhaps not expertly, why do our speakers neglect mirth-provoking irony, witty asides, and the like?

Implication (the method of developing materials in such a way that the listeners are guided to a desired conclusion without that conclusion being explicitly stated by the speaker): Do you find any evidence that our speakers attempted to use indirection? If you do not find tangible evidence, nevertheless, do you get a feeling from Gay's lecture that he is implying more

than he feels it is safe for him to state explicitly? Why did
Puritan ministers as a genre prefer to rely upon the didactic
approach of Aristotle: first state the contention and then prove
it [4:2]?

Inference (the method in developing supportive materials
whereby the speaker draws conclusions from the data he is
presenting): Of our three speakers, do you agree that Edwards
makes the greatest use of *inductive inferences* (the projecting
of a general conclusion from one or more specific items of
support)? To what extent—if any—do Gay and Chauncy employ inductive inferences? Do you find that Edwards uses
inductive reasoning as a means of reinforcing basic premises or
Biblical truths rather than of establishing "new" truths? If so,
is this procedure necessitated by his theological approach? Does
Gay make any use of *causal inferences* (the drawing of conclusions concerning "effects" from what is known about
"causes" or concerning "causes" from what is known about "effects," etc.)? Do you agree that both Chauncy and Edwards
make repeated and effective use of causal inferences? Why do
all of our speakers base their cases upon *categorical inferences*
(the drawing of conclusions about some particular item which
is subsumed under a universal principle or covering law) [3:3,
6]? Do you agree that Edwards is marvelously adept at applying the deductive processes [1:11; 2:3, 5, 8, 14; 4:8, 10, 13]?
Do our speakers make greater explicit—or implicit—use of
alternative ("It's either this or that") and *conditional* ("If this
happens, that will follow") *inferences?* In which speech(es)
is the use of alternative and conditional inferences especially
important? Why is this so? Of our three speakers, which makes
the most frequent and effective use of *analogical inferences*
(the drawing of conclusions based upon resemblances or differences noted between two or more items) [1:1, 5, 12; 3:1,
2; 5:3, 11]?

Options concerning persuasive devices. Inasmuch as our
previous discussion of the options concerning emotions, ethos,
and supportive materials involved "persuasive devices," this
heading is a kind of "catch all" to include whatever has been

omitted. Can you identify devices used by Edwards which supplement those already pointed out in the interrogative notes: parading the bandwagon [1:14]; turning the tables [2:2, 18]; camouflaging the weakness of an argument [2:6, 9]; arguing both sides of a question [2:20]; changing the question [2:17]; appealing directly to different segments of an audience [2:2]; disguising specious reasoning as being valid [4:13]; employing the psychological gamut [2:7]? If Chauncy and Gay use similar devices, estimate their effectiveness [3:4, 9, 14, 15; 5:9].

Now that we have examined the consistency, clarity, and persuasiveness of the arguments, let us turn briefly to the question of their modernity. With the help of Part One, estimate which of the three speakers would possess the greatest appeal for the "common man." Which would make the greatest contribution to the development of the democratic spirit? To a "classless" society? To an inclination toward intercolonial unity transcending sectionalism and denominationalism? In your judgment, which speaker seems to offer man the most freedom to determine his own spiritual salvation? Which comes closest to the theology most widely taught today? To the modern conception concerning the role of the intellect and emotion in religion [3:7, 11; 5:10, 11]?

Do you agree that, whereas Gay and Chauncy seem to look at man through the lenses of scholastic psychology, Edwards approaches the modern psychologists' conception concerning the nature of man and his neuromuscular system? After studying some current treatment of theories of motivation, estimate Edwards's modernity in regard to the "arousal of drives," the "steering function of drives," the "persistence of motivated behavior," and the "energizing effect of drives." Does Edwards seem to sense the distinction which modern psychologists make between the "sensation" or the "experience" of an emotion and its "motivational effects"? In his striving for emotional reactions, does he seem to sense the "interacting components" of "physiological arousal" and "the individual's interpretation of the situation"? Does he seem to anticipate William James's assertion that bodily reactions trigger emotions, that is, we tremble and

then feel afraid, we cry and then feel sad—not the reverse order? Does Edwards anticipate modern psychology in his emphasis upon nonverbal dimensions of communication? In his attempt to gain heightened impact by moving his listeners swiftly and strikingly from the experiencing of a negative emotion to that of an affirmative emotion [2:7, 8; 3:10; 4:5]?

Do you find that any one of the speakers comes appreciably closer than the others to modern rhetorical practices in his development of arguments or in his attitudes toward himself as the speaker, toward his listeners, and toward the speaking situation? If not, can you cite specific respects in which one or another speaker—in contrast to the others—seems to be somewhat more modern [1:3; 2:1; 5:2, 3, 12]?

Strategies of Style and Composition

A requirement of the Puritan sermon was orality. It had to sound personal and immediately direct. It had to provide for instant comprehension. Nothing should be permitted to come between the listener and his contact with the word of God—not the learning of the preacher, not the abstruseness of his style and composition, not the intrusion of his personality, not the adornments of the church or the distractions of the liturgy. After you have read aloud representative excerpts from each of the speeches, do you believe the language of Gay is as "communicative" as that of Chauncy and Edwards [5:8]? Why is this so? Does Edwards maintain quite the same standard of orality in each of his speeches? What differing circumstances might have affected the degree of his orality?

A correlative requirement of the Puritan sermon was "plainness" and "painfulness." The speaker should spare himself no pain in the effort to make his speaking so plain that even the "meanest" sort could be instructed. As well as you can, measure each of the speeches against these criteria: the expression of ideas in the simplest manner consistent with accuracy of representation; the concreteness of expression, or the use of particularization and specificity instead of generalization and abstraction; the exactitude of language or the precise

choice of exactly the right word to produce the intended meaning; the appropriate use of purpose statements, definitions, and
connective and transitional words and phrases [1:3; 2:1; 3:4,
8; 4:2; 5:4, 6, 7, 12].

A third correlative requirement of the Puritan sermon was
that its language should be appropriate to the office of the
preacher, to the listeners, and to the speaking situation. Although this volume has supplied limited resources from which
you may draw, estimate the suitability of the style and composition for each of the speeches [5:1]. What evidences do
you find that the speakers are concerned about the propriety
of their utterance? For example, did each of them make determined efforts to seem appropriately objective, patient, and
charitable—thus conforming to the proper image of a Godly
servant?

To the extent that it did not interfere with clarity, sim-
plicity, and propriety, the Puritan sermon was expected to be
vigorous and impressive. Rhetoricians sometimes suggest that
in order for style to be forceful it must possess economy. How
would you define "economy" of language? Even after the prun-
ing necessitated by our space limitations, none of our speakers
are concise. Does this mean that they are wordy? That their
language lacks force? What determines whether style is redundant [1:4, 10; 2:12]? Customarily a lively style is characterized by varied sentences, with short, simple ones predominat-
ing. Do you find any significant differences among our speakers
as to the length or construction of their sentences [1:5, 8; 5:1,
5, 8]? If so, how do you account for these differences? How
do you compare our speakers in their use of vital, specific
adjectives and of "exact" nouns which evoke sense imagery in
the listeners? In their use of constructions such as similes,
metaphors, personification, antithesis, and contrast? In the
originality of their choice of language? In their adjustment of
style to fit changing rhetorical needs [1:5, 7, 8; 3:13; 5:1, 3,
5, 8]? Inasmuch as Edwards is perhaps the most sensitive
stylist among the Puritans, concentrate especial attention upon
the life and freshness of his approach [1:2, 5, 7, 8]. For instance, review his skill in guiding the listeners from the known

and experienced into the unknown and the unexperienced [1:12], his use of homey and idiomatic expressions [1:11, 12; 2:5, 7], his reliance upon specific, action-carrying verbs, and his mastery of different modes, moods, and tempos such as exhortation, dehortation, advocacy, and exposition [1:1; 2:21; 4:1].

Although Gay employs some modern rhetorical touches, do you agree that Chauncy and Edwards are more modern in their style and composition [5:2, 3]? In general, do you find that the language patterns of our speakers are very similar to those used by public speakers today?

Strategies of Disposition

Do our speakers tend to divide their speeches according to the traditional Puritan sermon format discussed in Part One: Text, Doctrine, Reasons, Application? In conformity to tradition set by the founders, do they design the Text-Doctrine-Reasons segments essentially to supply information and logical analysis for the purpose of enabling the faculty of the Understanding to render a rational judgment? Do they intend that only the Application segment should address the entire range of the faculties—Understanding, Will, and Affections? Or, do our speakers—including Gay—ignore the traditional dispositional disjunction of logic and emotions? That is, does Edwards —and Chauncy to a lesser extent—incorporate emotional proofs into his speeches at whatever places they will contribute to his argument? And, does Gay resist using emotional proofs even in the Application? Thus, so far as the logical-emotional tone is concerned, each of our speeches constitutes basically a dispositional unit?

What functions do our speakers assign to the respective sermon parts [1:4; 2:21; 4:13; 5:6]? To what extent do they use the individual parts of the sermon as sequential steps in the persuasive process, i.e., as means of "opening" the listeners to accept the persuasion which is to follow in the succeeding parts [1:4; 2:1; 3:3; 4:2; 5:4, 9]? Of the three speakers, would you agree that Edwards excels in the tightness, variety, and

general effectiveness by which he disposes his supporting arguments and materials [1:2, 11, 13; 2:3, 5, 14; 3:3, 4, 6, 8; 4:10]? Would you agree that Edwards is the only one of our speakers to structure the individual parts of the speech in such a way that the development builds to one or more peaks of attention [1:1, 17; 2:21; 4:1, 12]? Do you find any genuine variation among the speakers in their use of signposts, transitions, and internal summaries [1:3; 3:8; 5:12]?

If we agree that the dispositional characteristics of the speeches conformed to the expectations of the audiences, do you think that modern listeners would consider the speeches to be over-structured? The main heads and subheads to stand out intrusively? After consulting some current text in public speaking, do you consider that each of our speakers—in his own way—seems to represent a transitional stage between the traditional Puritan method of disposing a speech and the methods of modern speakers [1:2, 3; 2:1; 3:4, 8; 4:2; 5:2, 3, 6, 7, 12]?

Notes
Bibliography

Notes to Part One

The pagination cited here is frequently irregular for a few of the volumes containing several treatises. In such instances, to assist the reader to find the passage with minimal difficulty, the page references have been placed directly after the title of the particular treatise, indicating that the reader should first find the title and then follow the pagination to the correct location in the specific volume.

1. See Eugene E. White, "Puritan Preaching and the Authority of God," in *Preaching in American History*, ed. DeWitte Holland (Nashville, 1969), pp. 36–73.
2. As Leonard J. Trinterud points out, however, both Luther and Calvin eventually rejected the "basic patterns of the Augustian piety." "The Origins of Puritanism," *Church History*, 20 (March 1951), 40. See B. A. Gerrish, *Grace and Reason: A Study in the Theology of Luther* (Oxford, 1962).
3. Originally published in Basel, 1536, the *Institutes* has been given many later printings. For an excellent modern version, see The Library of Christian Classics edition, *Calvin: Institutes of the Christian Religion*, trans. Ford Lewis Battles and ed. John T. McNeill (Philadelphia, 1960), 2 vols.
4. Of course, in his other writings Calvin did add specificity and detail to the intellectual formulations enunciated in the *Institutes*. For example, see his *The Acts of the Apostles*, trans. John W. Fraser and W. J. G. McDonald, ed. David W. Torrance and Thomas F. Torrance (Edinburgh, 1965–66), 2 vols.; *The Epistles of Paul the Apostle to the Galatians, Ephesians, Philippians and Colossians*, trans. T. H. L. Parker, ed. David W. Torrance and Thomas F. Torrance (Edinburgh, 1965); *The Gospel According to Isaiah*, trans. Leroy Nixon (Grand Rapids, 1953); *The Gospel According to St. John, 11–21, and the First Epistle of John*, trans. T. H. L. Parker, ed. David W. Torrance and Thomas F. Torrance (Edinburgh, 1961); *The Deity of Christ and Other Sermons*, trans. Leroy Nixon (Grand Rapids, 1950).
5. Heinrich Heppe, *Reformed Dogmatics*, trans. G. T. Thompson, ed. Ernst Bizer (London, 1950).

6. See Everette H. Emerson, "Calvin and Covenant Theology," *Church History*, 25 (June 1956), 136–44; Trinterud, "The Origins of Puritanism," pp. 37–57; Jens J. Möller, "The Beginnings of Puritan Covenant Theology," *The Journal of Ecclesiastical History*, 14 (April 1963), 46–67; John Von Rohr, "Covenant and Assurance in Early English Puritanism," *Church History*, 34 (June 1965), 195–203; George M. Marsden, "Perry Miller's Rehabilitation of the Puritans: A Critique," *Church History*, 39 (March 1970), 91–105; Anthony Hoekema, "The Covenant of Grace in Calvin's Teaching," *Calvin Theological Journal*, 2 (1967); Benjamin C. Milner, Jr., *Calvin's Doctrine of the Church* (Leiden, 1970).

7. For examples of coetaneous treatments of covenant concepts, see John Preston, *Life Eternal* (London, 1634), pp. 85–89 (second set of paginations), and *The New Covenant* (London, 1634), throughout and esp. pp. 313–486; William Perkins, *The Foundation of Christian Religion*, pp. 1–8, and *A Golden Chaine*, esp. pp. 31–32, in *Workes* (London, 1616), 1; William Ames, *The Marrow of Sacred Divinity*, esp. pp. 44–48, 175–80, in *Workes* (London, 1643); Peter Bulkeley, *The Gospel-Covenant* (London, 1651); Thomas Hooker, *The Covenant of Grace Opened* (London, 1649).

8. Although the English Puritans sometimes preached imprecatory sermons (e.g., William Perkins, *A Powerful Exhortation to Repentance*, esp. pp. 411–27, in *Workes* [London, 1618], 3, pt. 2) and repeatedly emphasized the absolute values of the covenant (e.g., Preston, *The New Covenant*, pp. 37–66, and William Perkins, *A Treatise of Gods Free Grace and Mans Free Will*, pp. 720–46, in *Workes*, 1), they also came close at times to proclaiming a universal calling. For instance, Perkins almost seemed to argue that man could "will" himself to salvation, when he stated that "if any man have a willingness and a desire to obey all Gods commandments, he hath the spirit, and he who hath the spirit is in Christ, and he who is in Christ shall never see damnation" (*A Treatise Tending Unto a Declaration, Whether a Man Be in the Estate of Damnation, or in the Estate of Grace*, p. 372, in *Workes*, 1). Preston seemed almost to equate knowledge and right thinking with salvation when he wrote, "All the grace a man hath, it passes through his Understanding; and therefore, if a man would be strong in grace, let him labour to get much light, to get much truth, much knowledge in his mind." "If you be rich in knowledge, it will make you rich in grace likewise" (*The New Covenant*, pp. 451–52, 455). Also, see Preston, *The New Covenant*, pp. 38, 73–78, 93, 107, 111–12, 114–15, 133–34, 175–81, 315–40, 342–43, 345–48, 365–66, 377–78, 443–86, 503, 533, 540; Preston, *Riches of Mercy* (London, 1658), pp. 1–36, 68–120, 171–79, 212–30, 249–68, 327–47, 397–435; Preston, *The Saints Qualification* (London, 1637), pp. 510–45; Preston, *Life Eternal* (London, 1634), pt. 2, pp. 119–35; Richard Sibbes, *The Returning Backslider* (London, 1639), pp. 4, 8, 9, 60–63, 149–51, 156,

172, 205, 209, 237, 239, 355; Sibbes, *The Bruised Reede, and Smoaking Flax* (London, 1630); Sibbes, *Light from Heaven* (London, 1638), 1st treatise, pp. 23, 283; William Perkins, *A Graine of Musterd-seede,* pp. 637–44, in *Workes,* 1; Perkins, *Cases of Conscience,* pp. 19, 27, in *Workes* (London, 1617), 2; Perkins, *Epistle to the Galatians,* p. 283, in *Workes,* 2.

9. For example, see Ames, *The Marrow of Sacred Divinity,* pp. 23–31.

10. For a representative spectrum of coetaneous views concerning faculty psychology, see the following: Timothy Bright, *A Treatise of Melancholie* (London 1586); F. N. Coeffeteau, *A Table of Humane Passions* (London, 1621); John Huarte, *Examen de Ingenios* (London, 1594); Phillippe de Mornay, *The True Knowledge of a Mans Owne Selfe* (London, 1602); Edward Reynolds, *A Treatise of the Passions and Faculties of the Soule of Man* (London, 1640); Jean F. Senault, *Natural History of the Passions* (London, 1674) and *The Use of Passions* (London, 1649); William Ayloffe, *The Government of the Passions* (London, 1700); Robert Burton, *The Anatomy of Melancholy* (Oxford, 1621); William Fenner, *A Treatise of the Affections* (London, 1642); Thomas Wright, *The Passions of the Minde* (London, 1621); Sir Miles Sandys, *Prudence the First of the Foure Cardinall Virtues* (n.p., 1635); Guillaume Du Vair, *The True Way to Vertue and Happiness* (London, 1623); William Strong, *A Treatise Showing the Subordination of the Will of Man* (London, 1657); Thomas Rogers, *A Philosophicall Discourse Entituled the Anatomie of the Minde* (London, 1576); Thomas Este, *The Passions of the Spirit* (London, 1599); Thomas Hobbes, *Humane Nature* (Oxford, 1650).

11. The relationship between faculty psychology and Puritan theology is traced in Eugene E. White, "Master Holdsworth and 'A Knowledge Very Useful and Necessary,'" *The Quarterly Journal of Speech,* 53 (February 1967), 1–16. The essential relationship between the faculties and conversion was stated by Preston: "When the Understanding saith" God's promises "are true, and believes them, and when the Will . . . embraceth them, at that very instant, *salvation is come to . . . thy heart.*" Christ "hath made a covenant with thee. . . ." (*The New Covenant,* p. 412). There were differences, of course, among the Puritan theologians concerning the faculties. For example, I am following here the thinking of William Perkins that the Understanding judged both truth and goodness and that the Will accepted or rejected the decision of the Understanding. (A capsule statement of Perkins's view is given in his *A Discourse of Conscience,* p. 517, in *Workes,* 1). A somewhat different concept was suggested by Preston in his *The New Covenant,* pp. 397 and 412: the function of the Understanding was to determine the truth or falseness of a matter and the function of the Will was to decide its moral quality and then to accept or reject it. Random dipping into almost any works of the founders of the covenant theology will uncover direct or indirect

references to faculty psychology, such as the following: William Ames, *Conscience With the Power and Cases Thereof* in *Workes*, bk. 1, pp. 2–4, 15–18, bk. 3, pp. 91–94, bk. 4, p. 26; Ames, *Marrow of Sacred Divinity*, pp. 5–8, 109–14, 197–200, 221, 238–43; Perkins, *Workes*, 1, *A Golden Chaine*, pp. 20–21, *A Discourse of Conscience*, pp. 515–54, *A Graine of Musterd-seede*, pp. 637–38, and *A Treatise of Gods Free Grace*, pp. 718–46; Perkins, *Workes*, 2, *Cases of Conscience*, pp. 72, 143–48; Perkins, *Workes*, 3, pt. 2, *Epistle of Jude*, pp. 486–87; Richard Sibbes, *A Breathing After God* (London, 1639), pp. 55–56; Sibbes, *The Bruised Reede, and Smoaking Flax*, p. 103; Sibbes, *The Excellencie of the Gospell Above the Law* (London, 1639), pp. 130–42; Thomas Shepard, *The Sound Believer* (London, 1645), p. 45, et passim: Thomas Hooker, *The Soules Humiliation* (London, 1637), pp. 158–59. Also, see *Calvin: Institutes of the Christian Religion*, esp. pp. 192–96.

12. Perkins, *Epistle to the Galatians*, p. 282, in *Workes*, 2, and *A Clowd of Faithful Witnesses*, p. 9, in *Workes*, 3, pt. 2.

13. In passing it should be pointed out that the Puritans also "suspected" the intellect, though not to the same degree as the emotions. For instance, see Richard Baxter, *The Arrogancy of Reason* (London, 1655).

14. Although some of the major Puritan theologians, including Perkins and Ames upon occasion, taught that regeneration operated directly upon the Will, it is my contention that most of the covenant fathers customarily assumed that the process of regeneration required both illumination of the Understanding and infusion of the Will and that it followed the normal sequence of the faculties.

15. Perkins divided the "working and effecting of man's salvation" into two basic processes. The first of these, the "works of preparation," he considered as four separate "actions": 1. God breaks and subdues the "stubbornness of our nature" by the "outward means of salvation, especially the ministry of the word" in conjunction with "some outward or inward cross." 2. God directs "the mind of man to a consideration of the Law, and therein generally to see what is good, and what is evil." 3. God guides man through "a serious consideration of the Law" to "know his own peculiar and proper sins, whereby he offends God." 4. "When man seeth his sins," God "smites the heart with a legal fear, whereby . . . He makes him to fear punishment and hell, and to despair of salvation, in regard of anything in himself." These first four stages contained "no fruits of grace" and were within the power of the reprobate. The second basic process, however, involved the "effects of grace," and its six "actions" were limited to the elect. 5. God stirs "the mind to a serious consideration of the promise of salvation." 6. God kindles "in the heart some seeds or sparks of faith, that is, a will and desire to believe." At this "same instant" God also "justifies the sinner, and withal begins the work of

sanctification." 7. As soon as man receives faith, his being is disturbed by "combat" between, on the one hand, "doubting, despair, and distrust," and, on the other hand, faith, which manifests itself "by fervent, constant, and earnest invocation for pardon." 8. God then "quiets and settles the Conscience" and man experiences a "persuasion of mercy." 9. Man's heart is then stirred "to evangelical sorrow," to a "grief for sin, because it is sin, and because God is offended." 10. "Lastly, God giveth a man grace to endeavor to obey his commandments by a new obedience." Perkins, *Cases of Conscience,* pp. 12–21, esp. p. 13. Also, see his *A Golden Chaine,* pp. 77–81, and *Two Treatises,* pp. 455–74, in *Workes,* 1.

16. Ames, *Conscience With the Power and Cases Thereof,* bk. 2, pp. 8–12.
17. White, "Master Holdsworth and 'A Knowledge Very Useful and Necessary.'"
18. See *Oxford University Statutes,* trans. G. R. M. Ward, 1 (London, 1845); *Statua Antigua Universitatis Oxoniensis,* ed. Strickland Gibson (Oxford, 1931); *Collection of Statutes for the University and the Colleges of Cambridge,* ed. James Heywood (London, 1840); *Early Cambridge University and College Statutes,* ed. James Heywood (London, 1855); *Documents Relating to the University and Colleges of Cambridge* (London, 1852), 3 vols.
19. Especially rich repositories of such materials are housed at the British Museum, Cambridge University Library, the Bodleian Library of Oxford University, and at the scores of college libraries and archival collections associated with Cambridge and Oxford.
20. Between 1550 and 1650, more than a thousand separate printings were issued of the individual treatises of Ramus (1515–72) and of his collaborator Omer Talon (ca. 1510–62). Their most important works were *Dialecticae Libri Duo,* which was given about 250 editions, and *Rhetoricae Libri Duo.* See Father Walter J. Ong's *Ramus: Method, and the Decay of Dialogue* and *Ramus and Talon Inventory,* published conjointly by the Harvard University Press, 1958.
21. See William Perkins, *A Direction for the Governement of the Tongue,* pp. 440–52, and *A Warning Against the Idolatry of the Last Times,* pp. 707–11, in *Workes,* 1, *Cases of Conscience,* pp. 70–72, *Epistle to the Galatians,* pp. 222, 294–95, 380–81, and *The Arte of Prophecying,* pp. 645–73, in *Workes,* 2, *A Treatise of the Duties and Dignities of the Ministerie,* pp. 429–39, 455–56, in *Workes,* 3, pt. 2; Ames, *Conscience with the Power and Cases Thereof,* bk. 4, pp. 25–26, 71–81, and *The Marrow of Sacred Divinity,* pp. 154–62, 238–43; Preston, "A Pattern of Wholesome Words," pp. 271–326, in *Riches of Mercy.*
22. As stated by William Ames, "The duty of an ordinary preacher is to propound the Will of God out of the Word, unto the edification of the hearers. 1 *Tim.* 1:5. The end of preaching is love out of a pure heart, and a good conscience, and faith unfainted." *The Marrow of Sacred Divinity,* p. 155.

23. *The Rhetoric of Aristotle,* trans. Lane Cooper (New York, 1932). In his *Rhetorical Criticism* (New York, 1965), pp. 91–131, Edwin Black argued that to Aristotle rhetoric was "a faculty that realized its end in the act of judgment."

24. For example, on occasion Preston went so far as to suggest that "the end of preaching is to beget knowledge in the people." "A Pattern of Wholesome Words," p. 303.

25. With probably some slight exaggeration Perry Miller stated that "Puritan piety was formulated in logic and encased in dialectic; it was vindicated by demonstration and united to knowledge." *The New England Mind: The Seventeenth Century* (Cambridge, Mass., 1954), p. 112.

26. *Aristotle: The Organon, The Categories, On Interpretation,* trans. Harold P. Cooke, *Prior Analytics,* trans. Hugh Tredennick (Cambridge, Mass., 1960); *Aristotle: Posterior Analytics,* trans. Hugh Tredennick, *Topica,* trans. E. S. Forster (Cambridge, Mass., 1960); *The Rhetoric of Aristotle,* pp. 11–12.

27. Especially see Miller, *The New England Mind: The Seventeenth Century* and his *Errand into the Wilderness* (Cambridge, Mass., 1964).

28. Wilbur S. Howell, *Logic and Rhetoric in England, 1500–1700* (New York, 1961). Keith L. Sprunger continues the now traditional interpretation of Miller and Howell in his "Ames, Ramus, and the Method of Puritan Theology," *The Harvard Theological Review,* 59 (April 1966), 133–51, and "Technometria: A Prologue to Puritan Theology," *Journal of the History of Ideas,* 29 (January–March 1968), 115–22. I am now preparing a volume for the press which suggests new interpretations of the role of Ramus in the education of the Puritan preachers.

29. Both Cicero, who defined the "supreme orator" as "one whose speech instructs, delights and moves the minds of his audience" (*De Optimo Genere Oratorum,* in *Cicero: De Inventione, De Optimo Genere Oratorum, Topica,* trans. H. M. Hubbell [Cambridge, Mass., 1949], pp. 357 and 367), and Quintilian, who defined rhetoric as "the art of speaking well" (*The Institutio Oratoria of Quintilian,* trans. H. E. Butler [Cambridge, Mass., 1958], 1, 299–300, 315, 319), developed intricate systems of rhetoric whose basic thrust was to effect persuasion. References to Quintilian and Cicero in this section are drawn from the works cited above in this note or from the following works of Cicero's: *Cicero: De Oratore,* bks. 1 and 2, trans. E. W. Sutton and H. Rackham (Cambridge, Mass., 1959); *Cicero: De Oratore,* bk. 3, *De Fato, Paradoxa Stoicorum, De Partitione Oratoria,* trans. H. Rackham (Cambridge, Mass., 1960); *Cicero: Brutus,* trans. G. L. Hendrickson, *Orator,* trans. H. M. Hubbell (Cambridge, Mass., 1952).

30. Gerard Vossius, *Rhetorices Contractae, sive Partitionum Oratoriarum* (Oxford, 1631), pp. 3–4.

31. This bifurcation had been anticipated by Cicero who wrote (*Brutus,*

p. 83) "that of the two chief qualities which the orator must possess, accurate argument looking to proof and impressive appeal to the emotions of the listener, the orator who inflames the court accomplishes far more than the one who merely instructs it. . . ." Perkins merely recognized what had long been taught by classical and neoclassical rhetoricians when he wrote: "We are to observe the properties of the ministrie of the word. The first, that it must be plain, perspicuous, and evident, as if the doctrine were pictured, and painted out before the eyes of men. . . . The second propertie of the ministry of the word, is, that it must be powerful and lively in operation, & as it were crucifying Christ within us, and causing us to feel the virtue of his passion. The word preached must pierce into the heart, like a two-edged sword. . . . Know, therefore, that the effectual and powerful preaching of the word stands in three things. The first is true and proper interpretation of the Scripture, and that by itself: for Scripture is both the glosse and the text. The second is savory and wholesome doctrine, gathered out of the Scriptures truly expounded. The third is the Application of the said doctrine, either to the information of the judgment or to the reformation of the life." *Epistle to the Galatians*, p. 222. Also, see Robert Middlekauff, "Piety and Intellect in Puritanism," *The William and Mary Quarterly*, 3rd series, 22 (July 1965), 457–70.

32. In his final conceptualization in the *Dialecticae*, Ramus considered that his "method" had absorbed the traditional parts of the oration. I have used the following edition which is known to have been used by Harvard College students: *P. Rami Regii Professoris Dialecticae Libri Duo* (Lutetiae, 1574).

33. All references in this section to Aristotle's theories of public speaking are drawn from his *Rhetoric*.

34. Everett H. Emerson, "John Udall and the Puritan Sermon," *The Quarterly Journal of Speech*, 44 (October 1958), 282–84.

35. In this section all quotations from Perkins are taken from his *The Arte of Prophecying*.

36. Frequently Puritan ministers followed Perkins in incorporating the Reasons segment with the Doctrine. In such cases the disposition conformed especially closely to the Ramist principle of bifurcated divisions: the Text thus divided itself into two members—the "part" of explanation and the "part" of application.

37. Henry Dunster MS., Massachusetts Historical Society.

38. As Ames stated, "regularly and ordinarily the principal work of the sermon, if it be not catechetical, is in the Use and Application." *Conscience with the Power and Cases Thereof*, 4th bk., pp. 77–78.

39. See note no. 14 above.

40. As suggested by Perkins, "Any point of doctrine . . . is simply of itself to be believed and doth demonstrate." Thus the emphasis during the Text and Doctrine-Reasons segments of the sermon was upon demonstrating Scriptural truths to the Understanding. With the Under-

standing thus convinced, the Will would accept this rational decision without the necessity of its being subjected to emotional coercion.

41. See note no. 36 above.
42. For example, upon occasion Perkins suggested—very much as Solomon Stoddard and Jonathan Edwards were later to do—that the route to spiritual understanding passed through the Affections and the Will to the Understanding. *Exposition of Christ's Sermon in the Mount,* pp. 169–74, in *Workes,* 3, pt. 1.
43. Thomas Hooker, *A Survey of the Summe of Church-Discipline* pt. 2 (London, 1648), pp. 19–20.
44. See note no. 8 above.
45. See Cotton's *A Sermon Preached . . . at Salem, 1636. To Which Is Prefixed a Retraction of His Former Opinion Concerning Baptism* (Boston, 1713). Also, see Everett H. Emerson, *John Cotton* (New York, 1965), pp. 86–90.
46. Compare the interpretations of David Kobrin ("The Expansion of the Visible Church in New England: 1629–1650," Church History, 36 [June 1967], 189–209) with those of Edmund S. Morgan (*Visible Saints* [New York, 1963], pp. 123–24, and *The Puritan Family* [Boston, 1956], pp. 90–104).
47. I have discussed these changes in greater depth in "Puritan Preaching and the Authority of God."
48. See Darrett B. Rutman, *Winthrop's Boston: Portrait of a Puritan Town, 1630–1649* (Chapel Hill, N.C., 1965), esp. pp. vii–ix, 274–79.
49. For representative sermons suggesting the sequential relationship of sin-reformation-forgiveness-prosperity, see the following: Thomas Shepard, *Eye-Salve* (Cambridge, Mass., 1673); Urian Oakes, *New England Pleaded With* (Cambridge, Mass., 1673); Cotton Mather, *A Midnight Cry* (Boston, 1962); Solomon Stoddard, *The Danger of Speedy Degeneracy* (Boston, 1705); Increase Mather, *Ichabod . . . A Discourse Shewing . . . that the Glory of the Lord Is Departing from New England* (Boston, 1702). Although throughout I have qualified the traditional interpretation stemming from Perry Miller, I do not approach the revisionism of Gerald J. Goodwin's "The Myth of 'Arminian-Calvinism' in Eighteenth-Century New England," *The New England Quarterly,* 41 (June 1968), 213–37.
50. Consult the indexes of *Records of the Governor and Company of the Massachusetts Bay in New England,* ed. Nathaniel Shurtleff (Boston, 1853–54), 5 vols.
51. In 1679, a Reforming Synod proclaimed that the social covenant was in danger, catalogued the sins of the people, and urged emergency efforts toward reformation. *The Necessity of Reformation. . . . What Are the Evils that Have Provoked the Lord to Bring His Judgments on New England? . . . What Is to Be Done . . . ?* (Boston, 1679).
52. For the Reverend Michael Wigglesworth's records concerning several testimonies given in his church by candidates seeking membership,

see Edmund S. Morgan's edited version of Wigglesworth's "Diary" in *Transactions* of the Colonial Society of Massachusetts, 35 (Boston, 1951), 426–44.

53. Of the large mass of materials concerning the early New England way, the following items are among the more helpful: Morgan, *Visible Saints*, pp. 64–152; Thomas Shepard, *New Englands Lamentations* (London, 1645); Richard Mather, *An Apologie of the Churches in New-England* (London, 1643) and *Church-Government and Church-Covenant Discussed* (London, 1643); John Cotton, *The Bloudy Tenet Washed* (London, 1647), *The Way of the Churches of Christ in New-England* (London, 1645), *The Way of Congregational Churches Cleared* (London, 1648), *A Treatise of the Covenant of Grace, as It Is Dispensed to the Elect Seed*, 3rd ed. (London, 1671); Hooker, *A Survey of the Summe of Church-Discipline*, esp. pt. 1, 60–67, and pt. 3; Francis Cornwell, *A Conference Mr. John Cotton Held at Boston with the Elders of New England* (London, 1646); Thomas Lechford, *Plain Dealing or News from New England*, introduction and notes by J. Hammond Trumbull (Boston, 1867), esp. pp. 18–36; John Clark, *Ill Newes from New-England* (London, 1652); *Good News from New-England* (London, 1648).

54. Increase Mather, *Concerning the Subject of Baptisme* (Cambridge, Mass., 1675); Thomas Shepard, *The Church Membership of Children, and Their Right to Baptisme* (Cambridge, Mass., 1663); John Davenport, *Another Essay for Investigation of the Truth* (Cambridge, Mass., 1663); Hooker, *A Survey of the Summe of Church-Discipline*, pt. 3, pp. 8–32; John Cotton, *The Grounds and Ends of the Baptisme of the Children of the Faithful* (London, 1647); Morgan, *Visible Saints*, pp. 113–38.

55. In 1648 a synod had attempted to temporize by stating that the church was composed of "proved saints" and "the children of such who are holy." *A Platform of Church Discipline* (Cambridge, Mass., 1649). For the report of the synod of 1662, see *Propositions Concerning the Subject of Baptism and Consociation of Churches* (Cambridge, Mass., 1662).

56. Robert G. Pope, *The Half-Way Covenant: Church Membership in Puritan New England* (Princeton, N.J., 1969).

57. Perry Miller, *The New England Mind: From Colony to Province* (Cambridge, Mass., 1953), p. 114.

58. For example, see Bulkeley, *The Gospel-Covenant*, pt. 2, pp. 151–66.

59. See Samuel Willard, *Covenant-Keeping* (Boston, 1682) and *The Barren Fig Trees Doom* (Boston, 1691); Increase Mather, *The Greatest Sinners Exhorted* (Boston, 1686); Cotton Mather, *A Midnight Cry*; Solomon Stoddard, *The Duty of Gospel-Ministers* (Boston, 1718) and *The Presence of Christ* (Boston, 1718).

60. Michael Wigglesworth MS. workbooks, New England Historic Genealogical Society.

61. For an introduction to Mather, see Barrett Wendell, *Cotton Mather:*

The Puritan Priest (New York, 1963), also the *Diary of Cotton Mather* (New York, n.d.), 2 vols.

62. See Eugene E. White, "Cotton Mather's *Manuductio ad Ministerium,*" *The Quarterly Journal of Speech,* 49 (October 1963), 308–19.

63. Three editions of the *Manuductio,* varying slightly among themselves, but all possessing the same title page, were published in Boston, probably within a few days of February 3, 1726. Later editions include the London printings of 1781, 1789, and 1800, as well as the 1938 reproduction by the Facsimilie Text Society of New York City. All the quotations in this section are drawn from one of the 1726 editions.

64. An evidence of the popularity of the *Manuductio* is that for a number of years it was presented to outstanding Harvard College students as part of the Hopkins Prize for scholarship. Consult the index of Clifford K. Shipton's *Sibley's Harvard Graduates,* 8 (Boston, 1951), and 9 (Boston, 1956).

65. Miller stated that the *Manuductio,* along with the *Magnalia, Bonifacius,* and *The Christian Philosopher,* "justifies" Mather's "place in American literature." *The New England Mind: From Colony to Province,* p. 417.

66. Insights concerning Mather's indictment of formal logic may be acquired by examining his *Reasonable Religion* (Boston, 1700), *Reason Satisfied* (Boston, 1712), *A Man of Reason* (Boston, 1718), and *The Christian Philosopher* (London, 1721).

67. Eugene E. White, "Solomon Stoddard's Theories of Persuasion," *Speech Monographs,* 29 (November 1962); Thomas A. Schafer, "Solomon Stoddard and the Theology of the Revival," in *A Miscellany of American Christianity: Essays in Honor of H. Shelton Smith,* ed. S. C. Henry (Durham, N.C., 1963), pp. 328–61; Perry Miller, "Solomon Stoddard, 1643–1729," *Harvard Theological Review,* 34 (October 1941), 277–320, and " 'Preparation for Salvation,' in Seventeenth-Century New England," *Journal of the History of Ideas,* 4 (June 1943), 253–86; William Williams, *The Death of a Prophet Lamented* (Boston, 1729).

68. Compare Stoddard's *A Guide to Christ* (Boston, 1714) with Cotton Mather's *Manuductio ad Ministerium* and Increase Mather's *A Discourse Proving that the Christian Religion Is the Only True Religion* (Boston, 1702). An essential theological difference between Stoddard and the Mathers concerned Stoddard's attitude toward admission to the Lord's Supper. For the attitude of the Mathers on this topic, see Eugene E. White's Foreword to Cotton Mather's *A Companion for Communicants* (forthcoming); Increase Mather's *The Order of the Gospel* (Boston, 1700), *A Dissertation, Wherein the Strange Doctrine Lately Published in a Sermon . . . Is Examined and Confuted* (Boston, 1708), *Ichabod,* and his Preface to Cotton Mather's *Ecclesiastes* (Boston, 1697). For Stoddard's defense of his policies, see his *An Appeal to the Learned* (Boston, 1709), *The Inexcusableness of Neglecting the*

Worship of God (Boston, 1708), and his *The Doctrine of Instituted Churches* (London, 1700).

69. James P. Walsh, "Solomon Stoddard's Open Communion: A Reexamination," *The New England Quarterly*, 43 (March 1970), 97–114. Morgan suggests that Stoddardism was not a general panacea. Ministers who emulated Stoddard had difficulty in persuading regular communicants to become full church members. Edmund S. Morgan, "New England Puritanism: Another Approach," *The William and Mary Quarterly*, 3rd series, 18 (April 1961), 236–42.

70. Stoddard, *An Examination of the Power of the Fraternity*, appended to *The Presence of Christ with the Ministers of the Gospel* (Boston, 1718); Williston Walker, *The Creeds and Platforms of Congregationalism* (New York, 1893), pp. 495–507.

71. Stoddard disseminated his theories by means of sermons, lectures—for many years he gave the annual lecture in Boston following the Harvard commencement—and the publication of more than a score of tracts which stretched about 2,000 pages. In *The New England Mind: From Colony to Province*, on page 282, Miller stated that Stoddard's "last works—*Three Sermons Lately Preach'd at Boston*, 1717; *A Treatise Concerning Conversion*, 1719; *The Defects of Preachers Reproved*, 1724—are as searching investigations of the religious psychology as any published in New England between the analyses of Hooker or Sheppard and the *Religious Affections* of his grandson (much in the latter being, in fact, indebted to them)." On pages 232–33 of the same work, Miller offered this judgment concerning Stoddard's *The Safety of Appearing at the Day of Judgment*, 1724: "It was widely read and admired . . . and it was to be a powerful influence in the Great Awakening. . . . Stoddard's book is one of the ten or dozen key works of the period and . . . is the only speculative treatise since the founders and before Edwards that makes any constructive contribution to New England theology."

72. See especially Stoddard's *A Guide to Christ; A Treatise Concerning . . . Conversion* (Boston, 1719); *The Safety of Appearing at the Day of Judgment; The Defects of Preachers Reproved* (New London, 1724); *Three Sermons Lately Preach'd at Boston* (Boston, 1717); *The Way for a People to Live Long in the Land that God Hath Given Them* (Boston, 1703); *An Appeal to the Learned; The Efficacy of the Fear of Hell to Restrain Men from Sin* (Boston, 1713). The quotations from Stoddard in this section have been drawn from the above-cited works.

73. In this analysis of Stoddard's conceptualization of the role of emotion and reason in the receiving of saving grace, I correct what I believe to be errors in interpretation by Conrad Cherry (*The Theology of Jonathan Edwards: A Reappraisal* [Garden City, N.Y., 1966], pp. 34–35) and Thomas Schafer ("Solomon Stoddard and the Theology of the Revival," esp. p. 348, n. 88).

74. Among the more useful works on Edwards are the following: Cherry, *The Theology of Jonathan Edwards: A Reappraisal;* Douglas J. Elwood, *The Philosophical Theology of Jonathan Edwards* (New York, 1960); Ola E. Winslow, *Jonathan Edwards, 1703–1758* (New York, 1961); Perry Miller, *Jonathan Edwards* (New York, 1949); Miller, "Jonathan Edwards and the Great Awakening," "The Rhetoric of Sensation," and "From Edwards to Emerson," in *Errand into the Wilderness* (Cambridge, Mass., 1964); Miller, "Jonathan Edwards on the Sense of the Heart," *Harvard Theological Review,* 41 (April 1948), 123–29; Robert C. Whittemore, "Jonathan Edwards and the Theology of the Sixth Way," *Church History,* 35 (March 1966), 60–75; Gerhard T. Alexis, "Jonathan Edwards and the Theocratic Ideal," *Church History,* 35 (September 1966), 328–43; John H. Gerstner, *Steps to Salvation: The Evangelistic Message of Jonathan Edwards* (Philadelphia, 1960); Thomas Schafer, "Jonathan Edwards and Justification by Faith," *Church History,* 20 (December 1951), 55–67; Arthur E. Murphy. "Jonathan Edwards on Free Will and Moral Agency," *Philosophical Review,* 68 (April 1959), 181–202.
75. Jonathan Edwards, *A Faithful Narrative of the Surprising Work of God in the Conversion of Many Hundred Souls in Northampton,* 3rd ed. (Boston, 1738), pp. 3–4.
76. Edwards's notebooks, which contain more than 3,000 pages, are chiefly housed in the Yale Collection, Yale University Library.
77. My interpretation of Edwards's conception of the role of emotion-reason in religion is drawn from his works, such as the following: *"The Mind" of Jonathan Edwards: A Reconstructed Text,* ed. Leon Howard (Berkeley, 1963); *Jonathan Edwards: Freedom of the Will,* ed. Paul Ramsey (New Haven, 1957); *Jonathan Edwards: Religious Affections,* ed. John E. Smith (New Haven, 1959); *The Nature of True Virtue,* Foreword by William K. Frankena (Ann Arbor, 1960); *Images or Shadows of Divine Things,* ed. Perry Miller (New Haven, 1948); *Concerning the End for which God Created the World . . .* (Boston, 1765); *Discourses on Various Important Subjects* (Boston, 1738); *A Divine and Supernatural Light* (Boston, 1734); *A Faithful Narrative; God Glorified in the Work of Redemption* (Boston, 1731); *A History of the Work of Redemption* (Edinburgh, 1774); *Some Thoughts Concerning the Present Revival of Religion in New-England* (Boston, 1742); *Works,* ed. Sereno E. Dwight (New York, 1829, 1830), 10 vols.; *The Philosophy of Jonathan Edwards from His Private Notebooks,* ed. Harvey G. Townsend (Eugene, Ore., 1955).
78. Smith, ed., *Jonathan Edwards: Religious Affections,* p. 96.
79. Ibid., p. 285.
80. Ibid., p. 200.
81. For supplementary readings concerning the Great Awakening and George Whitefield, see works such as the following: Alan Heimert, *Religion and the American Mind: From the Great Awakening to the*

Revolution (Cambridge, Mass., 1966); C. C. Goen, *Revivalism and Separatism in New England, 1740–1800* (New Haven, Conn., 1962); Edwin Scott Gaustad, *The Great Awakening in New England* (1957; reprint ed., New York, 1968); Eugene E. White, "Decline of the Great Awakening in New England: 1741 to 1746," *The New England Quarterly*, 24 (March 1951), 35–52, "George Whitefield and the Paper War in New England," *The Quarterly Journal of Speech*, 39 (February 1953), 61–68, "The Preaching of George Whitefield during the Great Awakening in America," *Speech Monographs*, 15 (1948), 33–43, "The Protasis of the Great Awakening in New England," *Speech Monographs*, 21 (March 1954), 10–20; Joseph Tracy, *The Great Awakening* (New York, 1969); Stuart C. Henry, *George Whitefield: Wayfaring Witness* (New York, 1957); C. Harold King, "George Whitefield: God's Commoner," *The Quarterly Journal of Speech*, 29 (February 1943), 32–36; Luke Tyerman, *The Life of the Rev. George Whitefield* (London, 1890), 2 vols.; William H. Kenney, 3rd, "George Whitefield, Dissenter Priest of the Great Awakening, 1739–1741," *William and Mary Quarterly*, 3rd series, 26 (January 1969), 75–93; David Lovejoy, *Religious Enthusiasms and the Great Awakening* (Englewood Cliffs, N.J., 1969). Perhaps the best way of following Whitefield's life and career through the Great Awakening is to consult installments of his accounts and journals: *A Brief and General Account of the First Part of the Life of the Reverend Mr. George Whitefield, from His Birth, to His Entring into Holy Orders* (Boston, 1740); *A Further Account of God's Dealings with the Rev. Mr. George Whitefield from the Time of His Ordination to His Embarking for Georgia* (Philadelphia, 1746); *A Journal of a Voyage from London to Savannah in Georgia*, 5th ed. (London, 1739); *A Continuation of the Reverend Mr. Whitefield's Journal, from His Arrival at Savannah, to His Return to London*, 2nd ed. (London, 1739); *A Continuation . . . During the Time He was Detained in England by the Embargo*, 3rd ed. (London, 1739); *A Continuation . . . from His Embarking after the Embargo, to His Arrival at Savannah in Georgia* (London, 1740); *A Continuation . . . from a Few Days after His Return to Georgia to His Arrival at Falmouth, on the 11th of March, 1741* (London, 1741).

82. Clinton Rossiter, *The First American Revolution* (New York, 1956), 95–96.

83. *Boston Evening-Post*, October 29, 1744.

84. *Boston Evening-Post*, August 18, 1746; [Charles Chauncy?], *The Late Religious Commotions in New-England Considered* (Boston, 1743), p. 6; *The State of Religion in New-England, Since the Reverend Mr. George Whitefield's Arrival There* (Glasgow, 1742), p. 4; Benjamin Colman, *Souls Flying to Jesus Christ* (Boston, 1740).

85. For Whitefield's discussion of his New England tour, see his *A Continuation of the Reverend Mr. Whitefield's Journal, from a few Days*

after His Return to Georgia to His Arrival at Falmouth (London, 1741).
Hereafter referred to as *Journal*.

86. Timothy Cutler, letter dated September 24, 1743, in the manuscript collections of the Boston Public Library.

87. *Boston Evening-Post*, October 29, 1744.

88. Probably not until Daniel Webster's Bunker Hill Address in 1825 would an audience so large gather to hear a speaker. Whitefield believed that nearly 30,000 persons were in the audience: *Journal*, p. 41. The estimate of approximately 23,000 appears in the *Boston Weekly News-Letter*, October 16, 1740, and in the appendix of the anti-Whitefield pamphlet, *The Wiles of Popery* (Charlestown, 1740), p. 11. In 1740 Boston possessed only 17,000 inhabitants, according to Carl Bridenbaugh, *Cities in the Wilderness* (New York, 1960), p. 303.

89. Edwards, *Works*, 1, 160–61.

90. Following his seven-week tour of New England, Whitefield itinerated to New York City and to Philadelphia and embarked for Charleston. He sailed for England on January 24, 1741.

91. MS. "The Spiritual Travels of Nathan Cole," Connecticut Historical Society. For reprintings see Henry, *George Whitefield: Wayfaring Witness*, pp. 68–70; George L. Walker, *Some Aspects of the Religious Life of New England* (New York, 1897), pp. 89–91; Richard L. Bushman, ed., *The Great Awakening* (New York, 1970), pp. 67–71.

92. Whitefield's sermon "Abraham's Offering Up His Son Isaac" appears in several early collections of his sermons, as *Nine Sermons* (Boston, 1743). For a modern printing, see Robert T. Oliver and Eugene E. White, eds., *Selected Speeches from American History* (Boston, 1966).

93. Cutler MS.

94. Frequently reprinted, this sermon was first issued shortly after its delivery: *Sinners in the Hands of an Angry God. A Sermon Preached at Enfield, July 8th, 1741. At a Time of Great Awakenings; and Attended with Remarkable Impressions on Many of the Hearers* (Boston, 1741).

95. See *Boston Weekly Post-Boy*, August 10, September 28, and October 5, 1741; *Boston Evening-Post*, August 2, 1742; Charles Chauncy, *Seasonable Thoughts on the State of Religion in New-England* (Boston, 1743), pp. 98, 99, 103–8 ff.

96. For instance, see *Boston Weekly Post-Boy*, September 28, 1741; *Boston Weekly News-Letter*, December 8, 1743; Isaac Stiles, *A Prospect of the City of Jerusalem* (New London, 1742); *The State of Religion in New England, Since the Reverend Mr. George Whitefield's Arrival There*, pp. 8–9.

97. Charles J. Hoadly, ed., *Public Records of the Colony of Connecticut*, 8 (Hartford, 1874), 456.

98. *Boston Weekly News-Letter*, July 22, 1742; *Boston Evening-Post*, July 26, 1742; *Pennsylvania Gazette*, August 12, 1742. For public letters attacking or defending the "apology," see *Pennsylvania Gazette*, September 2 and December 7 (Postscript, dated December 8), 1742; *Bos-*

ton Weekly News-Letter, September 23 and October 28, 1742; *Boston Evening-Post,* November 1 and November 8, 1742.

99. *Pennsylvania Gazette,* July 1, 1742; *Boston Evening-Post,* June 7, 1742; *Boston Weekly News-Letter,* July 1, 1742.

100. *Boston Weekly News-Letter,* August 26, 1742; *Boston Evening-Post,* September 6, 1742.

101. *Boston Evening-Post,* July 5, 1742; *Boston Weekly Post-Boy,* July 5, 1742; *Boston Weekly News-Letter,* August 26, 1742.

102. *Boston Evening-Post,* April 11, 1743; Chauncy, *Seasonable Thoughts,* pp. 220–23.

103. *The Testimony of the Pastors of the Churches in the Province of the Massachusetts-Bay in New-England, at Their Annual Convention in Boston, May 25, 1743* (Boston, 1743).

104. *The Testimony and Advice of an Assembly of Pastors of Churches in New-England, at a Meeting in Boston July 7, 1743* (Boston, 1743), pp. 7, 9.

105. *Boston Evening-Post,* August 13, 1744; Thomas Prince, Jr., ed., *The Christian History,* September 22, 1744. See *The Reverend Mr. James Davenport's Confession and Retractions* (Boston, 1744).

106. For example, see *The Testimony of an Association or Club of Laymen, Conven'd at Boston Respecting the Present Times* (Boston, 1745).

107. See *Invitations to the Reverend Mr. Whitefield, from the Eastern Consociation of the County of Fairfield* (Boston, 1745); *The Testimony of a Number of Ministers Conven'd at Tauton* (Boston, 1745).

108. See *A Letter from Two Neighbouring Associations of Ministers in the Country, to the Associated Ministers of Boston and Charlestown* (Boston, 1745); *The Declaration of the Association of the County of New-Haven in Connecticut* (Boston, 1745); Nathaniel Eells, *A Letter to the Second Church and Congregation in Scituate* (Boston, 1745). Also, see *The Sentiments and Resolution of an Association of Ministers* (*Convened at Weymouth, Jan. 15th, 1744,5*) (Boston, 1745); *Some Reasons Given by the Western Association Upon Merrimack River, Why They Disapprove of the Reverend Mr. George Whitefield's Preaching* (Boston, 1745).

109. Upon Whitefield's arrival in New England in September 1740, he had preached and recorded in his *Journal* that Harvard was little superior in piety and Godliness to the English universities which were "mere halls of paganism." Although he had very little opportunity for on-the-site assessment, at the conclusion of his visit he condemned Harvard and Yale in sweeping terms: "Their light is become darkness . . . I *pray God those foundations may be purified. . . .*" Shortly after the evangelist's return, Harvard issued a testimonial against him: *The Testimony of the President, Professors, Tutors, and Hebrew Instructor of Harvard College in Cambridge, Against the Reverend Mr. George Whitefield, and His Conduct* (Boston, 1744). In his defense, Whitefield published *A Letter to the Rev. the President, and Professors, Tu-*

tors, and Hebrew Instructor, of Harvard-College . . . In Answer to a Testimony Publish'd by Them Against the Reverend Mr. George Whitefield, and His Conduct (Boston, 1745). In response, Harvard's president, Edward Holyoke, and its professor of divinity, Edward Wigglesworth, issued *A Letter to the Reverend Mr. George Whitefield, by Way of Reply. . . .* (Boston, 1745).

110. *The Declaration of the Rectors and Tutors of Yale-College in New-Haven Against the Reverend Mr. George Whitefield, His Principles and Designs* (Boston, 1745).

111. Also, see *Boston Evening-Post,* March 25, 1745; J. F., *A Letter to the Reverend Mr. Thomas Foxcroft* (Boston, 1745).

112. Alice M. Baldwin, *The New England Clergy and the American Revolution* (Durham, N.C., 1928), p. 80.

113. Heimert, *Religion and the American Mind: From the Great Awakening to the Revolution,* esp. pp. 12, 21, 43.

114. Carl J. Friedrich and Robert G. McCloskey, *From the Declaration of Independence to the Constitution* (Indianapolis, 1954), pp. lii–liii.

115. Heimert, *Religion and the American Mind: From the Great Awakening to the Revolution,* p. 46.

Bibliography

In preparing Part One I have chiefly relied upon the interpretations gained through long-term investigations in this general area, including the close study of most of the textbooks in logic, rhetoric, and psychology used during this period at the English universities and at Harvard—a task of translation that has given me a Benjamin Franklin appearance well before due time, the examination of many hundreds of manuscripts—most of them written in a perversely crabbed hand and some in "delightfully" unorthodox Latin or short-hand, the significant Puritan theological works, and huge numbers of sermons and other imprints of all relevant kinds published in England and America. Too, I have drawn upon my special experience in the history and development of rhetorical theory.

To make the notes accompanying Part One as helpful as possible, I designed them to provide serviceable starting points for those who wish to pursue particular lines of thought more fully. Also, I assigned to notes some details which, though significant, might tend to burden the text and slow the essential development of thought.

Because of the extensive character of the notes to Part One, I have limited the following bibliography to a listing of secondary sources which offer unusual rewards to the interested reader and which provide extensions or modifications of the themes contained in this study.

Akers, Charles W. *Called Unto Liberty: A Life of Jonathan Mayhew, 1720–1766.* Cambridge, Mass., 1964.

Baldwin, Alice M. *The New England Clergy and the American Revolution.* New York, 1958.

Battis, Emery. *Saints and Sectaries: Anne Hutchinson and the Antinomian Controversy in the Massachusetts Bay Colony.* Chapel Hill, N.C., 1962.

Birdsall, Richard D. "The Second Great Awakening and the New

England Social Order," *Church History*, 39, September 1970, 345–64.

Bridenbaugh, Carl. *Cities in the Wilderness: The First Century of Urban Life in America 1625–1742*. New York, 1960.

————. *Mitre and Sceptre: Transatlantic Faiths, Ideas, Personalities, and Politics, 1689–1775*. New York, 1962.

Brumm, Ursula. *American Thought and Religious Typology*. New Brunswick, N.J., 1970.

Cherry, Conrad. *The Theology of Jonathan Edwards: A Reappraisal*. Garden City, N.Y., 1966.

Emerson, Everett H. *English Puritanism from John Hooper to John Milton*. Durham, N.C., 1968.

Gaustad, Edwin. *The Great Awakening in New England*. New York, 1957; rpt., 1968.

Gerrish, B. A. *Grace and Reason: A Study in the Theology of Luther*. Oxford, 1962.

Haller, William. *The Rise of Puritanism*. New York, 1938; rpt., 1957.

Haroutunian, Joseph. *Piety versus Moralism: The Passing of the New England Theology*. New York, 1932; rpt., 1964.

Heimert, Alan. *Religion and the American Mind from the Great Awakening to the Revolution*. Cambridge, Mass., 1966.

Henry, Stuart C. *George Whitefield: Wayfaring Witness*. New York, 1957.

Hill, Christopher. *Puritanism and Revolution*. New York, 1958.

————. *Society and Puritanism in Pre-Revolutionary England*. New York, 1964.

Hofstadter, Richard. *Anti-Intellectualism in American Life*. New York, 1966.

Knappen, M. M. *Tudor Puritanism: A Chapter in the History of Idealism*. Chicago, 1939; rpt., 1965.

McGiffert, Michael. "American Puritan Studies in the 1960's," *The William and Mary Quarterly*, 3rd series, 27, no. 1, January 1970, 36–67.

Meade, Sidney E. "The Rise of the Evangelical Conception of the Ministry in America (1607–1850)." *The Ministry in Historical Perspectives*. Ed. H. Richard Niebuhr and Daniel D. Williams. New York, 1956.

Middlekauff, Robert. *The Mathers: Three Generations of Puritan Intellectuals, 1596–1728*. New York, 1971.

Miller, Perry. *Errand Into the Wilderness*. Cambridge, Mass., 1956; rpt., 1964.

———. *Jonathan Edwards*. New York, 1949; rpt., 1963.

———. *The New England Mind: From Colony to Province*. Cambridge, Mass., 1953.

———. *The New England Mind: The Seventeenth Century*. Cambridge, Mass., 1939; rpt., 1954.

———. *Orthodoxy in Massachusetts 1630–1650*. Cambridge, Mass., 1933; rpt., 1959.

Milner, Jr., Benjamin C. *Calvin's Doctrine of the Church*. Leiden, 1970.

Morgan, Irvonwy. *The Godly Preachers of the Elizabeth Church*, London, 1965.

Niebuhr, H. Richard. *The Kingdom of God in America*. New York, 1935; rpt., 1959.

Pettit, Norman. *The Heart Prepared: Grace and Conversion in Puritan Spiritual Life*. New Haven, Conn., 1966.

Rutman, Darrett B. *Winthrop's Boston: Portrait of a Puritan Town, 1630–1649*. Chapel Hill, N.C., 1965.

Seaver, Paul S. *The Puritan Lectureships*. Stanford, Calif., 1970.

Tucker, Louis L. *Puritan Protagonist: President Thomas Clap of Yale College*. Chapel Hill, N.C., 1962.

Wendel, François. *Calvin: The Origins and Development of His Religious Thought*. Trans. Philip Mairet. New York, 1963.

Wright, Conrad. *The Beginnings of Unitarianism in America*. Boston, 1955; rpt., 1966.

Ziff, Larzer. *The Career of John Cotton: Puritanism and the American Experience*. Princeton, N.J., 1962.

Date Due

Printed in P. E. I. by ISLAND OFFSET